Science NG
Student Guide

5

At Stride, Inc. (NYSE: LRN) – formerly K12 Inc. – we are reimagining lifelong learning as a rich, deeply personal experience that prepares learners for tomorrow. Since its inception, Stride has been committed to removing barriers that impact academic equity and to providing high-quality education for anyone—particularly those in underserved communities. The company has transformed the teaching and learning experience for millions of people by providing innovative, high-quality, tech-enabled education solutions, curriculum, and programs directly to students, schools, the military, and enterprises in primary, secondary, and post-secondary settings. Stride is a premier provider of K–12 education for students, schools, and districts, including career learning services through middle and high school curriculum. Providing a solution to the widening skills gap in the workplace and student loan crisis, Stride equips students with real world skills for in-demand jobs with career learning. For adult learners, Stride delivers professional skills training in healthcare and technology, as well as staffing and talent development for Fortune 500 companies. Stride has delivered millions of courses over the past decade and serves learners in all 50 states and more than 100 countries. The company is a proud sponsor of the Future of School, a nonprofit organization dedicated to closing the gap between the pace of technology and the pace of change in education. More information can be found at stridelearning.com, K12.com, destinationsacademy.com, galvanize.com, techelevator.com, and medcerts.com.

ISBN: 978-1-60153-598-6

Printed by Bradford & Bigelow, Newburyport, MA, USA, May 2021.

Table of Contents

Unit 1: Water Resources
Lesson 1: Freshwater 1
Lesson 2: Water Uses and Treatment...13
Lesson 3: Water Pollution...20
Lesson 4: What's a Watershed?..32
Lesson 5: Topographic Maps: Tools for Environmental Studies.......36
Lesson 6: Wetlands and Watersheds...44
Lesson 7: Water Resources: Unit Review and Assessment............49

Unit 2: The World's Oceans
Lesson 1: Ocean Water...53
Lesson 2: Ocean Currents...64
Lesson 3: Ocean Waves...68
Lesson 4: Ocean Tides...72
Lesson 5: Life at the Edge of the Ocean...81
Lesson 6: Ocean Floor...85
Lesson 7: Life Zones of the Ocean...89
Lesson 8: Ocean Resources...94
Lesson 9: The World's Ocean: Unit Review and Assessment........96

Unit 3: Earth's Atmosphere
Lesson 1: The Atmosphere 101
Lesson 2: Why the Wind Blows.. 112
Lesson 3: Humidity, Dew, and Frost.. 117
Lesson 4: Clouds and Precipitation.. 123
Lesson 5: Severe Weather 129
Lesson 6: Fronts and Forecasts... 131
Lesson 7: Climate 140
Lesson 8: Climates and Change 145
Lesson 9: Earth's Atmosphere: Unit Review and Assessment 153

Unit 4: The Solar System and Beyond
Lesson 1: The Solar System: Planets and Orbits............................ 157
Lesson 2: The Sun... 175
Lesson 3: The Inner Planets... 180
Lesson 4: The Outer Planets.. 186
Lesson 5: Stars of the Night Sky 193
Lesson 6: Constellations: Star Patterns 194
Lesson 7: Galaxies.. 201
Lesson 8: Gravity and Motion at the Earth's System 205
Lesson 9: The Solar System and Beyond: Unit Review and Assessment 209

Unit 5: Chemistry

Lesson 1: Atoms and Elements.. 211
Lesson 2: The Periodic Table of Elements............................ 216
Lesson 3: Compounds and Molecules 223
Lesson 4: Chemical Reactions 227
Lesson 5: Acids and Bases 234
Lesson 6: Identification of Compounds 240
Lesson 7: Molecules of Life 244
Lesson 8: Reaction Rates 250
Lesson 9: Chemistry: Unit Review and Assessment 258

Unit 6: Cells and Cell Processes

Lesson 1: The Cell Theory... 263
Lesson 2: Cell Organelles... 267
Lesson 3: Diffusion, Osmosis, and Active Transport 277
Lesson 4: Photosynthesis and Respiration 286
Lesson 5: Cells and Cell Processes: Unit Review and Assessment......................... 296

Unit 7: Taxonomy of Plants and Animals

Lesson 1: Naming and Classifying Life 301
Lesson 2: The Tools of Taxonomy... 304
Lesson 3: Phylogenetic Trees and the Kingdom of Life ... 308
Lesson 4: Kingdom Archaebacteria....................................... 312
Lesson 5: Kingdom Eubacteria... 314
Lesson 6: Kingdom Protista... 318
Lesson 7: Kingdom Fungi 325
Lesson 8: Kingdom Planta 331
Lesson 9: Kingdom Animalia 336
Lesson 10: Taxonomy of Plants and Animals: Unit Review and Assessment 337

Unit 8: Animal Physiology

Lesson 1: The Miracle of Life.. 341
Lesson 2: The Nervous and Endocrine Systems 344
Lesson 3: The Respiratory System 348
Lesson 4: The Circulatory System.. 352
Lesson 5: The Digestive System 354
Lesson 6: The Excretory System 358
Lesson 7: The Immune System and the Reproductive System 362
Lesson 8: Animal Physiology: Unit Review and Assessment 366

Unit 9: Ecosystems: Interdependence of Life

Lesson 1: Ecosystems and the Environment......................... 369
Lesson 2: Producers, Consumers, and Decomposers 372
Lesson 3: Food Webs: Energy Flow in an Ecosystem.......... 376
Lesson 4: Cycles in Ecosystems 383
Lesson 5: Changing Environmental Conditions.................... 389
Lesson 6: Ecosystems: Interdependence of Life: Unit Review and Assessment... 396

Student Guide
Freshwater

Water is one of our most valuable resources. We need it to sustain our bodies. We use it to water our crops, produce our electricity, and get our housework done. Yet only one percent of all the water on Earth is available freshwater. Protecting this resource from misuse and pollution is a concern for all people on Earth.

Water is one cool liquid. You can't survive without water. It keeps you clean, it hydrates your body, and it is necessary for plants to grow—plants that you may eat for food! Find out exactly where your water comes from and why it is important to keep water resources clean.

Lesson Objectives

- Explore concepts to be addressed during the year in Science 5.
- Explain the parts of the water cycle: evaporation, condensation, precipitation, runoff, collection, and seepage.
- Explain that an aquifer stores groundwater.
- Identify and describe water resources.
- Describe ways the geosphere, biosphere, hydrosphere, and/or atmosphere interact.
- Describe ways the geosphere, biosphere, hydrosphere, and/or atmosphere interact in Michigan or the Great Lakes basin.
- Describe or graph the amounts or percentages of water and freshwater in various reservoirs to provide evidence about the distribution of water on Earth.
- Describe or graph the amounts or percentages of water and freshwater in the Great Lakes to provide evidence about the distribution of water on Earth.

PREPARE

Approximate lesson time is 60 minutes.

Advance Preparation

- It's important that you read the Course Introduction for Science 5 before your student begins the course. You can find the course introduction at the beginning of the Freshwater lesson.
- If you don't already have it, you will need a 2-liter plastic bottle, a long eyedropper, and nylon stockings for this lesson.
  It's important that you read the course introduction for Science 5 before starting this lesson.

Materials

For the Student

    Water Graphs Assignment
    Water Graphs Assignment Key
    Make a Model Aquifer
    clay - 1/2 stick, any color
    sand - coarse sand - 240 mL
    stockings, nylon
    twist tie
    bottle, plastic - 2-liter
    eyedropper - long
    food coloring - red, green, or blue
    gravel - pea gravel - 240 mL
    pencil
    soil - 1 cup
    water - 480 mL

Keywords and Pronunciations

aquifer (A-kwuh-fuhr) **:** An underground geological formation that contains large amounts of water. Water can be pumped from an aquifer by drilling a well.

permeability (puhr-mee-uh-BIH-luh-tee) **:** The measure of how easily water can travel through soil or rock. Water travels more easily through sand than clay because sand has a higher permeability.

permeable rock: Rock that water can flow through. Sandstone is a type of permeable rock.

porosity (puh-RAH-suh-tee) **:** The measure of the space between particles in rock or soil; the porosity of soil allows it to soak up rainwater.

reservoir: A place where water is collected and stored

saturated: Thoroughly soaked. We left the sponge out in the backyard, and when we came back after the rain, the sponge was saturated.

sinkhole: A depression in the ground caused when water dissolves underlying materials of the Earth's surface. If water dissolves a layer of limestone, the layer will weaken and collapse, forming a sinkhole.

water table: The top of the water in the saturated part of the rocky earth. A long, dry spell with no rain will cause the water table to drop.

LEARN

Activity 1: Science 5 *(Online)*

Activity 2: Understanding Water *(Online)*

Knowing where we get our water and how we use it helps us make decisions about how to protect it. We need to make wise decisions about water use, because we cannot live without clean, fresh water.

Activity 3: Water World *(Online)*

Water is needed for life and that is what makes Earth so unique. Water exists on Earth in a lot of different ways. Whether in the ground, in the oceans, or in lakes and rivers water can be found all over the planet.

Activity 4: Groundwater *(Online)*

An *aquifer* is a formation of rocks and soil that stores water in the spaces within it. Water seeps into an aquifer through soil or rock, then people may draw the water from a well. Keeping aquifers free of pollutants maintains safe water for people to use.

ASSESS

Lesson Assessment: Freshwater *(Offline)*

You will complete an offline assessment covering the main objectives of this lesson. Your learning coach will score this assessment.

Name _____   Date _____

Assignment

Water Graphs

For this assignment, you will use the data given to determine percentages and create graphs based on water facts. Remember for this activity that 96.5 percent of the world's water supply is salt water and about 3.5 percent is fresh water.

1. 3.5 percent of Earth's water is fresh water. That equates to about 11.4 million trillion gallons of fresh water! Using your computer or paper and pencil, find the percentage of each supply of fresh water on Earth in the data table. Remember, to find the percentage, divide the water supply value (lakes, rivers, and swamps, for example) by the total freshwater supply value, which is 11.4 million trillion gallons.

Answer:

Freshwater Supply	Total Amount	Percentage of Fresh Water
Lakes, Rivers and Swamps	.228 million trillion gallons	
Groundwater	3.42 million trillion gallons	
Icecaps and Glaciers	7.752 million trillion gallons	

2. Now that you have your percentages from question 1, use a computer program or paper and pencil to create a graph to represent the fresh water supply on Earth.

Answer:

3. Based on your graph for number 2, where is fresh water more likely to be found?

_____

_____

4. The Earth contains about 326 million trillion tons of water. If 96.5 percent is salt water and 3.5 percent is fresh water, how many million trillion gallons of salt water and fresh water are there?

_____

_____

5. Create a graph or chart to show the percentage of fresh water and salt water on Earth.

Answer:

6. Take a look at your graph from number 4. Describe the relationship between the two different kinds of water on Earth. Is one larger than the other? What does that mean about the drinkable water supply on Earth?

_____

_____

_____

_____

7. On Earth, the Great Lakes make up 21 percent of the freshwater on the surface. What percentage of surface water exists in other swamps, rivers, and lakes? Draw a pie chart to represent your answer.

Answer:

8. There is a total of 332,500,000 cubic miles of water on Earth. There is 2,551,100 cubic miles of fresh water on Earth. The Great Lakes contain 5,439 cubic miles of fresh water. Describe how much of the total water and total fresh water on Earth is contained in the Great Lakes. You may use a graph to aid in your explanation.

_____

_____

_____

_____

Assignment Key
Water Graphs

For this assignment, you will use the data given to determine percentages and create graphs based on water facts. Remember for this activity that 96.5 percent of the world's water supply is salt water and about 3.5 percent is fresh water.

1. 3.5 percent of Earth's water is fresh water. That equates to about 11.4 million trillion gallons of fresh water! Using your computer or paper and pencil, find the percentage of each supply of fresh water on Earth in the data table. Remember, to find the percentage, divide the water supply value (lakes, rivers, and swamps, for example) by the total freshwater supply value, which is 11.4 million trillion gallons.

Fresh Water Supply	Total Amount	Percentage of Fresh Water
Lakes, Rivers and Swamps	.228 million trillion gallons	2%
Groundwater	3.42 million trillion gallons	30%
Icecaps and Glaciers	7.752 million trillion gallons	68%

2. Now that you have your percentages from question 1, use a computer program or paper and pencil to create a graph to represent the freshwater supply on Earth.

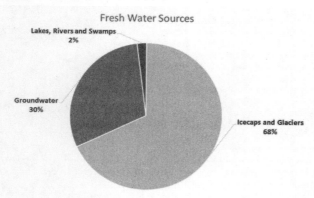

3. Based on your graph for number 2, where is fresh water more likely to be found?

   Answer: Most freshwater is found in icecaps and glaciers.

4. The Earth contains about 326 million trillion tons of water. If 96.5 percent is salt water and 3.5 percent is fresh water, how many million trillion gallons of saltwater and fresh water are there?

   Answer: There are about 314.6 million trillion gallons of salt water and there are about 11.4 million trillion gallons of fresh water on Earth.

5. Create a graph or chart to show the percentage of fresh water and salt water on Earth.

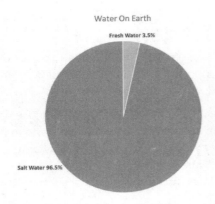

Water On Earth

Fresh Water 3.5%

Salt Water 96.5%

6. Take a look at your graph from number 4. Describe the relationship between the two different kinds of water on Earth. Is one larger than the other? What does that mean about the drinkable water supply on Earth?

   Answer: There is a lot less fresh water on Earth than salt water. The drinkable water supply on Earth is very small relative to the total amount of water on Earth.

7. On Earth, the Great Lakes make up 21 percent of the surface water. What percentage of surface water exists in other swamps, rivers, and lakes? Draw a pie chart to represent your answer.

   Answer: 79 percent of surface water is in other lakes, rivers and swamps.

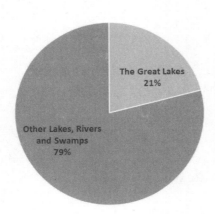

Fresh Surface Water

The Great Lakes
21%

Other Lakes, Rivers
and Swamps
79%

8. There are 332,500,000 cubic miles of water on Earth. There is 2,551,100 cubic miles of fresh water on Earth. The Great Lakes contain 5,439 cubic miles of fresh water. Describe how much of the total water and total fresh water on Earth is contained in the Great Lakes. You may use a graph to aid in your explanation.

   Answer: Answers will vary but should be describe that there is a tiny fraction of water (less than 2 one-thousandths of one percent) in the Great Lakes as compared to the total amount of water on Earth. A pie chart would not even show a sliver to represent water from the Great Lakes in a graph of Great Lakes water to total water on Earth. When compared to total fresh water, the Great Lakes makes up a tiny fraction (0.2%) of the total water. A graph would not show a sliver to represent water from the Great Lakes in a graph of Great Lakes water to total fresh water.

Name _____   Date _____

Freshwater

Make a Model Aquifer

A formation of rocks and soil that stores enough water for a well is called an aquifer. The aquifer is composed of layers of rock and soil with different permeability.

Permeability

Permeability describes how easily water will move through the material. The higher the permeability, the faster the water will move through the material. That's pretty simple – but it's important to remember that permeability describes the material, not the whole layer. So, if you say "this sand is very permeable" that means that water can travel through the sand quickly. But if sand is hundreds of meters thick, it may still take a long time for the water to travel through the layer.

Water is drawn from an aquifer through a well. Wells are holes drilled into and through the layers of rocks and soil. Water that seeps into the ground, either from rainfall or another source, recharges an aquifer by providing it with more water. Should the area near the aquifer become polluted, the water that seeps into the aquifer will become polluted, too.

In this activity, you will build a small model aquifer to see how aquifers hold water and how pollution affects the water that is drawn from an aquifer.

Procedure and Observations

1. Make the Aquifer.

    (a) With help from an adult, make a container by cutting off the top half off a clear two-liter bottle.

    (b) Fill the bottle with about 3 cm of coarse sand.

    (c) Make a layer of clay above the sand about 1cm thick. Make the layer thinner if you do not have enough clay, but make sure the clay goes all the way to the sides.

    (d) Add about 3 cm of pea gravel to the top of the clay.

    (e) Add a about 3 cm of top soil above the pea gravel

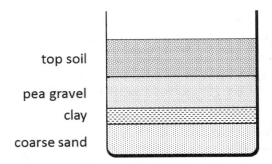

2. Look at the layers. Predict the permeability of each material. Remember, the more permeable, the easier water will travel through the layer. Write your prediction.

    _____

    _____

    _____

    _____

3. Carefully pour a little bit of water onto the surface. Observe how fast the water moves through each layer. Record your observations and compare your observations to your prediction.

    _____

    _____

    _____

    _____

4. Wrap a piece of nylon around the end of a pencil. Secure it at the top with the twist tie. Make a well by drilling a hole down through the layers with the pencil. Drill until you reach the layer of coarse sand.

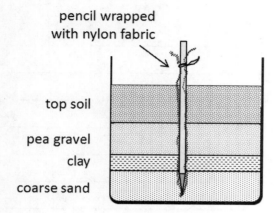

pencil wrapped with nylon fabric

top soil

pea gravel

clay

coarse sand

5. Untie the twist tie and slip the pencil out, leaving the nylon in the hole.

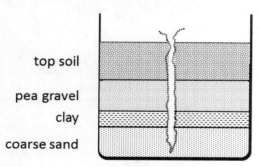

top soil

pea gravel

clay

coarse sand

6. Put the eyedropper into the well and see if you can draw water. What happened?

_____

_____

_____

_____

7. Next you will add pollution to the aquifer. Add a large amount of food coloring to the areas outside the well. Continue drawing water from the well with the eyedropper. What happened after you added the "pollution" to the water? How could you tell?

_____

_____

_____

_____

_____

_____

_____

9. What types of things in your home might contaminate drinking water if poured on the ground?

_____

_____

_____

_____

Student Guide

Water Uses and Treatment

We need water for the basic functions of our lives. Yet freshwater is limited, and we use it in many ways you may not recognize. Water irrigates land, cools hot machines, and even generates power. Because water has so many uses, we need to conserve it, not waste it.

Lesson Objectives

- Describe three or more ways in which water is used, such as for domestic, public, commercial, and irrigation purposes.
- Explain why it is important to conserve water.
- Name three or more ways to conserve water, such as keeping showers short, turning off water while brushing teeth, and fixing leaking pipes.
- Identify the typical steps water-treatment plants go through to purify drinking water.
- Identify the various sources of water, its uses, and different ways to conserve it.

PREPARE

Approximate lesson time is 60 minutes.

Advance Preparation

- Refer to page 2 of The Water Treatment Plant printout to collect the materials and prepare some parts of the experiment in advance.
- You will need 4 2-liter plastic bottles, 30 mL of alum, and 125 mL of activated charcoal (activated carbon). You can purchase activated charcoal at most pet stores. If you don't find activated charcoal as labeled, buy a couple of large filter bags for fish tank filters and cut them open to get the activated charcoal. You can purchase alum at a pharmacy or chemist supply.
- Before you begin the lesson, prepare the dirty water by adding about 600 mL of soil or mud to 4 L of water. Cut one 2-liter bottle in half, cut the bottom from another bottle, and cut the top from a third bottle. You may also wish to construct the filter for the project in advance.

Materials

For the Student

The Water Treatment Plant
activated charcoal - 125 mL
alum - 30 mL
bleach - 15 mL
coffee filter (2)
rubber band
sand - 150 mL coarse
sand - 200 mL fine

bottle, plastic - 2 liter (4)
graduated cylinder
gravel - (About 600 mL) enough to fill the rest of the bottle, coarse
gravel - 200 mL pea
safety goggles
soil - 600 mL (1 gallon)
water

Keywords and Pronunciations

aeration (air-AY-shun)**:** The process of purifying water by exposing it to moving air. Air is pumped into water during aeration.

coagulation (koh-a-gyuh-LAY-shun)**:** The process of purifying water by adding alum and other chemicals that cause clumping of some impurities. Alum causes the coagulation of dirt in water.

conservation: Protection of a resource by using it wisely and not wasting it. Conservation of water is very important, since water supplies are not unlimited.

consumptive water: Water that is used and lost to the local environment via pollution or evaporation, or by being incorporated into plants or animals.

disinfection: Adding a small amount of chlorine or other disinfectant to kill any germs. Chlorine disinfects wastewater.

filtration: Forcing water through material such as sand, charcoal, or gravel to remove impurities. During filtration, water is cleaned of particles that may be too small to see.

non-consumptive water: Water that is not consumed or used up. Water that is used, then returned to the environment, is considered non-consumptive.

sedimentation: The settling of solid material to the bottom of a liquid. Sedimentation separates large particles of dirt from water.

water treatment: The industrial process that purifies water. Before water is ready for drinking, it must go through water treatment.

LEARN

Activity 1: Finding and Using Water (Online)

Activity 2: Making Water Safe to Drink (Offline)

Some people have access to fresh, clean water from natural springs or wells, but most people use water from public systems. That water goes through a treatment process. In this activity, you'll see how water-treatment plants make water safe. Then, in the next activity, you'll be able to apply these steps to treat water yourself.

Activity 3: Treat Your Water Well *(Offline)*

Follow the instructions to treat dirty water in a water-treatment plant. You'll find these on page 2 of The Water Treatment Plant activity sheet. Refer to page 1 as you do each step. If you look carefully, you'll be able to observe each of the five stages of water treatment.

The water that you treat during the activity is NOT safe to drink. Do not drink it or sniff it.

Safety

Wear safety goggles during the disinfection stage of the water-treatment activity. The water that you treat during the activity is NOT safe to drink. Do not drink it or sniff it.

ASSESS

Lesson Assessment: Water Uses and Treatment *(Offline)*

You will complete an offline assessment covering the main objectives of this lesson. Your learning coach will score this assessment.

LEARN

Activity 4: Optional: Are You a Water Waster? *(Offline)*

Find out how well your family is conserving water. Take a poll of all the members of your family. Ask them the following questions and then summarize the results.

Record the answers as ALWAYS, SOMETIMES, or NEVER. You may add a few questions of your own based on what you learned in today's lesson.

1. Do you turn off the water while you brush your teeth?
2. Do you leave the hose dripping?
3. Do any faucets in your home leak?
4. Do you or your family clean up after your pet's waste?
5. Does anyone who does laundry run the washing machine with just a few items in it?
6. Do you use a small amount of detergent to wash your car?
7. Do you or a family member pour any unused chemicals down the drain?
8. Do you pick up litter when you see it?
9. Do you litter when you are near water, such as at the beach, a lake, or a stream?
10. Do you avoid pouring fertilizer on the lawn before a rainstorm?
11. _____
12. _____

When you have finished, tell your family the results of your poll. Provide them with helpful hints on conserving water.

Name _____ Date _____

Water Uses and Treatment
The Water Treatment Plant

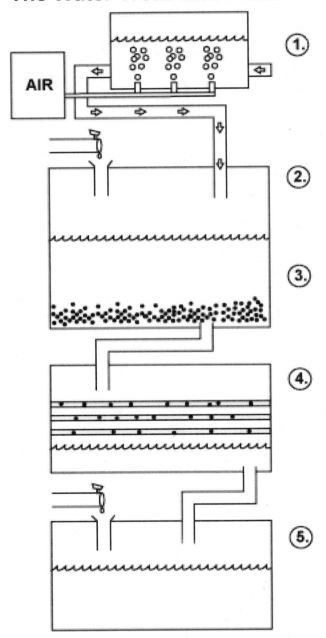

1. Aeration: Water is first mixed with air to get rid of any other gases that might be mixed with it. Imagine a big mixer whipping the water around.

2. Coagulation: To *coagulate* means to thicken. During this process, alum and other chemicals are added to the water to form small, sticky particles called *floc*. Floc attracts dirt particles in the water.

3. Sedimentation: The particles formed during coagulation are too heavy to float and settle to the bottom of the water.

4. Filtration: Water is filtered by pouring it through layers of materials that trap things that did not settle to the bottom. Some of these materials that are trapped by a filter are too small to see!

5. Disinfection: This removes any germs, such as bacteria or microorganisms, that may be in the water. A small amount of chlorine is added to do this.

Treat Your Water Well

Now that you have studied how water is made safe in a water treatment plant, you can make a model of how this process works. As you create your model, use the picture of the water treatment plant and process to help you answer the questions.

Observe the dirty water you have. Does it look like water you'd like to drink?

Begin Treatment

1. Pour about 1.6 liters of dirty water into the uncut 2-liter bottle. Put the cap on the bottle and shake the bottle for 30 seconds. What stage of water treatment are you demonstrating?

2. Pour the water into the 2-liter bottle with the top cut off.

3. Add 2 tablespoons (about 30 mL) of alum. Stir the mixture slowly for 5 minutes. What process are you demonstrating now?

4. Let the water stand undisturbed for 20 minutes. Check the water every 5 minutes and describe what you see. What process is happening now?

Make a Filter

5. To make the filter, use the bottle with the bottom cut off. Turn the bottle upside down.

6. Place the coffee filters over the mouth of the bottle and secure them with a rubber band. This will plug the bottom of the filter. If water does not filter through, try reducing the amount of coffee filters to 1.

7. Use the graduated cylinder to estimate all volumes. Be sure to rinse and dry the graduated cylinder between measurements. Pour 200 mL of fine sand over the plug in the bottle. Evenly add a layer of 125 ml of activated charcoal over the fine sand. Next add 150 ml of coarse sand, and then 200 ml of pea gravel. Fill the rest of the bottle with coarse gravel.

Filter the Water

8. Carefully hold the filter system over a sink or container large enough to collect 2 liters of water. Clean the filter by pouring 2 liters of clean tap water through it.

9. To collect the filtered water, hold the bottle over the 2-liter bottle cut in half. Do not rest the filter in the bottle half; it could get stuck.

10. Pour about 200 mL of the dirty water through the filter. Be careful not to disturb the sediment. What step are you doing now?

11. Once about 100 mL of the water has been collected from the filter, add 15 mL of chlorine-based bleach to the water. What step of water treatment is this?

Compare

Compare the amount of water you treated to the amount you started with. Is it the same amount? Some water is lost during treatment.

Compare the treated water to the dirty water.

1. How has treatment changed the water? Does the water look different?

    _____

    _____

    _____

    _____

Student Guide
Water Pollution

Keeping water clean should be at the top of the list of ways to take care of the Earth. Protecting our precious water supply means knowing how it can be damaged, what kinds of pollution are most harmful to it, and what we can do to stop pollution. Armed with the knowledge of how pollution happens, we all can contribute to keep our water safe. Part of keeping water clean is addressing the problems that oil spills produce. The design process is a useful tool to use to solve water pollution problems.

Lesson Objectives

- Compare *point-source* and *nonpoint-source* pollution.
- Describe how both natural processes and human activities affect water quality.
- Name ways in which nonpoint-source water pollution can be reduced.
- Define a simple design problem describing a need or a want that includes specified criteria for success and constraints on materials, time, or cost.
- Generate or compare multiple possible solutions to a problem based on how well each is likely to meet the criteria and constraints of the problem.
- Plan and carry out fair tests in which variables are controlled and failure points are considered to identify aspects of a model or prototype that can be improved.

PREPARE

Approximate lesson time is 60 minutes.

Advance Preparation

Place a large, clear bowl or aquarium in a location where you can view it from all sides, then fill it with water.

Materials

For the Student

> food - waste or trash
> sand - 1/4 cup
> shoebox, clear plastic
> twig - several
> bowl - large clear
> food coloring
> paper - shredded (or twigs)
> paper towels
> pebble - 1/4 cup
> soil - 1/4 cup
> water
> Cleaning Up an Oil Spill
> cotton ball (5)
> drinking straw
> feather

rock
vegetable oil
baking dish - or shallow container
soap - liquid detergent
spoon
Oil Spill Design a Solution Rubric
Oil Spill Design a Solution Graded Assignment

Keywords and Pronunciations

aquifer (A-kwuh-fuhr) **:** An underground geological formation that contains large amounts of water. Water can be pumped from an aquifer by drilling a well.

nonpoint-source pollution: Pollution that enters a water body from a wide area rather than a specific point. When oil and grease from cars collects on streets and washes into surface water during storms, it becomes nonpoint-source pollution.

point-source pollution: Pollution that enters water from a single source, such as a drainage pipe. Point-source pollution can occur when an oil tanker spills oil directly into the sea.

runoff: Water that flows off land into streams and other waterways. During a rainstorm, fertilizer from a field may be carried into a stream as runoff, causing nonpoint-source pollution.

LEARN

Activity 1: Water Pollution (Online)

You might think twice the next time you try to pour something down the drain. Protecting water resources means keeping them clean. Find out how water becomes polluted and how you can help reduce pollution.

Activity 2: Nonpoint-Source Pollution (Online)

You have probably seen a storm drain on a neighborhood or city street. Storm drains control flooding by channeling rainwater away from streets. Many people think storm drains lead to a water-treatment plant. They don't! Storm drains lead to streams, rivers, bays, and even the ocean.

Motor oil, trash, dirt, and even chemicals collect on sidewalks and streets and are washed into storm drains. Some people pour chemicals or sweep trash into storm drains, not realizing the drains lead to bodies of water. Many communities label storm drains to prevent people from dumping pollution into the drains. These labels might say "No Dumping, Leads to River" to make people aware of where pollution in the drain will end up. In this activity, you will gain a good sense of how easily pollution can enter water.

- Observe the water in the large, clear bowl of water you filled yesterday.
- Cut a hole in the bottom or side of the shoebox and place the box on top of the container of water. The hole in the box represents a storm drain.
- Which of the materials in front of you might be pollutants? How could each one get into the storm drain?
- Place your pollutants into the shoebox. Wash the pollutants out through the drain and into the water using the watering can to represent rain.
- Examine the water. How has it changed?

Answer these questions on paper, and then place the page in your Science Notebook:

1. What types of pollution are natural?

2. What types of pollution were caused by people? Did those people intend to damage the water?

3. What ideas do you have for stopping these pollutants from entering storm drains?

Activity 4: Cleaning Up an Oil Spill (*Online and Offline*)

Follow the instructions on the Cleaning Up an Oil Spill activity sheet to see what happens to wildlife after an oil spill. Find out the best way to clean up the spill.

Learn about the problems that generate from oils spills. You will be introduced to a few current solutions to solve these problems. You will recognize the opportunity to use the design process to come up more solutions.

Activity 5: Oil Spill Design a Solution (*Online and Offline*)

You will be reminded of the steps in the design process. Here you will come up with an oil spill solution using materials in and around the home. Use each step of the design process to complete the Oil Spill Design a Solution Assignment.

ASSESS

Lesson Assessment: Water Pollution (*Offline*)

You will complete an offline assessment covering the main objectives of this lesson. Your learning coach will score this assessment.

Name _____   Date _____

Water Pollution

Cleaning Up an Oil Spill

Oil spills occur when oil enters the ocean. Oil may come from oil refineries or tanker accidents. Oil may also seep naturally into the environment or be carried by runoff. Oil spills are rare, but they do a great deal of damage to the environment.

There are many ways to clean up an oil spill, but none can clean all the oil. Oil spill clean-up is affected by the type of oil, the source, water currents, and weather, which may make the water surface smooth or choppy.

If you had to clean up an oil spill, what might you try? First, see what happens when oil enters the water.

1. Fill the pan halfway with water. Add five drops of blue food coloring and stir.

2. Pour a small amount of cooking oil into the water. Record your results below.

3. Wait five minutes. Record any changes.

4. Stir the water gently. Record any changes.

5. Stir the water harder to break up the oil. Place the rock, stick, and feather into the water. Gently stir the water. After five minutes remove the items and feel each one. Record how the oil affects them.

Results

1. What happened to the cooking oil when you poured it into the water?

_____

_____

2. What changes had happened after five minutes?

_____

_____

3. What changes happened after you stirred the water?

_____

_____

4. How did the oil affect the items?

_____

_____

Part 2

Now you will try to clean up the spill. *Clean up* means either removing the oil or breaking it up chemically using liquid detergent. Time is important in cleaning an oil spill. The more an oil spreads, the more damage it can do and the harder it is to clean up.

Try to clean up the spill using the cotton, paper towel, and liquid detergent. Use the liquid detergent last. If necessary, add more oil to the water after each attempt. Blow into the straw to create waves. Try to clean up the oil spill again. Record your results in the chart.

Material	Calm or rough water	Estimate of how much oil was removed or cleaned	Comments (did not clean or remove oil, created dirty, oily water, etc.)

1. Which items removed the oil?

_____

_____

2. Some oil spills are cleaned by *absorption*, which means the oil is soaked up into certain materials. Which materials soaked up the oil? What did the liquid detergent do to the oil? When would using detergent be a safe way to clean up the oil?

_____

_____

_____

_____

Conclusion

1. What effects might an oil spill have on organisms living in the water?

_____

_____

2. Why is it important for people to clean up oil spills?

_____

_____

_____

_____

Rubric
Oil Spill Design a Solution (30 points)

Criterion/Prompt	Exemplary	Proficient	Emerging	Not Evident	Comments
	High-scoring students will do the following:	Middle-scoring students will do the following:	Low-scoring students will do the following:		
1. Define the problem. Focus on one problem and make a statement that is clear and to the point.	• Student provides a detailed statement about the problem that demonstrates understanding. **Award 3 points.**	• Student provides a statement about the problem. **Award 2 points.**	• Student makes a statement about the problem that does not demonstrate understanding. **Award 1 point.**	• Student makes an incorrect statement about the problem or no statement at all. **Award 0 points.**	
Score/Points Possible: #/3 pts.					
2. Define solution criteria. Criteria is articulated that will determine the success or failure of a design or solution.	• Student clearly articulates 3 or more points or goals for a design solution to meet that will determine the success or failure of the design. **Award 3 points.**	• Student articulates 2 goals for a design solution to determine success or failure of a design. **Award 2 points.**	• Student gives 1 goals for a design solution to determine success or failure of a design. **Award 1 point.**	• Student does not give goals for a design solution to determine success or failure of a design. **Award 0 points.**	
Score/Points Possible: #/3 pts.					

Criterion/Prompt	Exemplary High-scoring students will do the following:	Proficient Middle-scoring students will do the following:	Emerging Low-scoring students will do the following:	Not Evident	Comments
3. Describe constraints for the design. Describe possible design constraints that could prove to be a problem in the design and solution. **Score/Points Possible: #/3 pts.**	Student clearly articulates 3 or more constraints for the design and solution. **Award 3 points.**	Student clearly articulates 2 constraints for the design and solution. **Award 2 points.**	Student gives 1 constraint for the design and solution. **Award 1 point.**	Student does not give constraints for the design and solution. **Award 0 points.**	
4. Describe 2-3 possible solutions. Describe 2 or 3 possible solutions based on research. **Score/Points Possible: #/3 pts.**	Student fully describes 2 or 3 possible solutions to solve the problem based on research. **Award 3 points.**	Student partially describes 2 possible solutions to solve the problem based on research. **Award 2 points.**	Student gives 1 possible solution to solve the problem based on research. **Award 1 point.**	Student does not give possible solutions based on research. **Award 0 points.**	
5. Analyze possible solutions. Describe ways each possible solution may or may not work to solve the problem. **Score/Points Possible: #/4 pts.**	Student fully describes the problems of each possible solution. **Award 4 points.**	Student partially describes the problems of each possible solution. **Award between 2 and 3 points.**	Student describes the problems of 1 possible solution. **Award 1 point.**	Student does not describe the problems with any solution. **Award between 0 points.**	

Criterion/Prompt	Exemplary	Proficient	Emerging	Not Evident	Comments
	High-scoring students will do the following:	Middle-scoring students will do the following:	Low-scoring students will do the following:		
6. Build your design. Describe your design and the materials you used to create it.	Student thoroughly describes the design and all materials used to build it.	Student describes the design and all materials used to build it.	Student weakly describes the design and some materials used to build it.	Student does not describe the design and all materials used to build it.	
Score/Points Possible: #/4 pts.	**Award 4 points.**	**Award between 2 and 3 points.**	**Award 1 point.**	**Award 0 points**	
7. Test your solution. Describe the steps of the test.	Student clearly describes the all steps of the test.	Student clearly describes most of the steps of the test.	Student does not describe each step of the test.	Student does not describe the steps of the test.	
Score/Points Possible: #/4 pts.	**Award 4 points.**	**Award between 3 and 2 points.**	**Award 1 point.**	**Award 0 points.**	
8. Analyze the results. Thoughtfully analyze the results of the test and design to describe whether the design was a success or failure.	Student does all of the following: • analyzes the results of the test • analyzes the design • describes whether it was a success or failure	Student does 2 of the following: • analyzes the results of the test • analyzes the design • describes whether it was a success or failure	Student does 1 of the following: • analyzes the results of the test • analyzes the design • describes whether it was a success or failure	Student does not give the results of the test and design to describe whether the design was a success or failure (or a combination of the two).	
Score/Points Possible: #/3 pts.	**Award 3 points.**	**Award 2 points.**	**Award 1 point.**	**Award between 1 and 0 points.**	

Criterion/Prompt	Exemplary	Proficient	Emerging	Not Evident	Comments
	High-scoring students will do the following:	Middle-scoring students will do the following:	Low-scoring students will do the following:		
8. Suggest improvements. Describe 2 or 3 improvements based on the results that would increase the success of a future design.	Student clearly articulates 2 or 3 improvements based on the results that would increase the success of a future design.	Student articulates 1 improvement based on the results that would increase the success of a future design OR Student articulates 2 or 3 improvements not based on the results.	Student gives 1 improvement based on the results that would increase the success of a future design.	Student does not give improvements based on results that would increase the success of a future design.	
Score/Points Possible: #/3 pts.	**Award 3 points.**	**Award 2 points.**	**Award 1 point.**	**Award 0 points.**	

Student Name:

Total score: _____ of 30 points

Name _____ Date _____

Graded Assignment
Oil Spill Design a Solution

Total score: _____ of 30 points

This assignment will require you to use the design process in order to create a solution to oil spill problems.

(Score for Question 1: ___ of 3 points)

1. **Define the problem.** This step is to make sure that you focus on one specific problem. When you define a problem, you come up with a statement about what the problem is. Keep the statement clear and to the point.

Answer:

(Score for Question 2: ___ of 3 points)

2. **Define criteria for the solution.** This means that you figure out the different parts of a solution that fix the problem. Whatever the solution is, it needs to meet certain goals.

Answer:

(Score for Question 3: ___ of 3 points)

3. **Describe some constraints for the design.** Constraints are limitations to a design. Time and money are typical constraints. This step is to try and figure out and work around problems and be prepared. It would be great to have unlimited resources, but that rarely happens in real life. As a student, one of your constraints would be that you are only using household items.

Answer:

(Score for Question 4: ___ of 3 points)

4. **Describe 2-3 possible solutions.** Briefly write out 2 or 3 plans that will solve the problem.

Answer:

(Score for Question 5: ___ of 4 points)

5. **Analyze the possible solutions to determine which solution will work best.** Look at each solution as if it is new to you. Try and think of a reason why each solution might not work and record your thoughts. Then choose the strongest option.

   A. What is your possible solution or solutions? Make a list and do some research to answer this question.

   B. Will this solution likely solve the problem? After finding a solution revisit the problem. Does it solve all or part of the problem? If not, move on.

   C. Is this solution realistic? Do you have the resources and time to try this out? Do you have parent/guardian permission?

Answer:

(Score for Question 6: ___ of 4 points)

6. **Build your design.** Think about the solution you decided on from step 5. Now, think about the items you have around your house that can be used to make your design. Create your design and describe the materials and final design.

Answer:

(Score for Question 7: ___ of 3 points)

7. **Test your solution (on a small scale).** It is time to test your design. How much oil was removed?

Answer:

(Score for Question 7: ___ of 4 points)

8. **Analyze the results of the test.** Look at the results from you test. Was your device successful? What did you learn from the test? What problems or failure points came up?

Answer:

(Score for Question 8: ___ of 3 points)

9. **Suggest improvements based on the analysis.** Think about the problems or failure points that came up during your analysis. Write down suggestions to improve the device based on the analysis.

Answer:

Student Guide

What's a Watershed?

Everyone lives in a watershed. Find out about the watershed in which you live, and learn about other watersheds around the world.

Lesson Objectives

- Identify and describe the parts of a watershed.
- Describe how both natural processes and human activities affect water quality in watersheds.

PREPARE

Approximate lesson time is 60 minutes.

Materials

For the Student
    Compare Watersheds

Keywords and Pronunciations

basin: The large area where all waters gather into larger streams and rivers. The basin is the largest part of the watershed.

boundary: The boundary of the watershed is the outer edge of the divide, basin, and collection area. The boundary divides one watershed from a neighboring watershed.

collection area: A lake or ocean where the water ends up. The Atlantic Ocean is a collection area for watersheds in North America.

divide: The high point of land that divides one watershed from another. The divide is like the peak of a roof off which water flows.

watershed: The specific area of land off which water drains. Also called a drainage system. We know that Kansas is in the Mississippi River watershed because all of the precipitation that falls there flows into the Mississippi River.

LEARN

Activity 1: What's a Watershed? *(Online)*

When it rains, where does all the water go? The area of land off which water drains is called a *watershed*. Find out about the parts of a watershed.

Activity 2: Locate Your Watershed *(Online)*

Every city on the planet is part of a watershed, from a coastal city to a dry desert town. Find out about the watershed in which you live and compare it to another watershed in a different part of the world.

ASSESS

Lesson Assessment: What's a Watershed? *(Offline)*

You will complete an offline assessment covering the main objectives of this lesson. Your learning coach will score this assessment.

Name _____ Date _____

What's a Watershed?
Compare Watersheds

In this activity, you will locate the watershed in which you live and compare it to another watershed in another part of the world.

Part A

Locate your watershed by following these directions:

1. Search online for a world map showing geological features and major water bodies. (There are many great websites of world maps online that allow clicking to zoom in and view more detail of particular regions.)

2. Locate the continent and area where you live on the map.

3. Find the major river closest to your home. For example, suppose you live in Texas, and see that you are near the Brazos River.

4. Using your search engine, type in the name of the river and "watershed" to find a list of websites for information on your watershed. For example, if you are near the Brazos River, then in the search engine you would type, "Brazos River watershed".

5. Look through the list of websites produced by your search and select several reliable websites to read through to gather information on your watershed. (Websites with a .gov, .edu, or .org extension will usually provide the most reliable information.) If you locate a map of your watershed, print it out. Record important data that you can find about your watershed in the chart. You may not be able to find all of the types of data listed in the chart for your watershed. You may find other interesting data not listed on the chart and can add the additional information.

Part B

Locate another watershed by following these directions:

1. Search online for a world map showing geological features and major water bodies. (There are many great websites of world maps online that allow clicking to zoom in and view more detail of particular regions.)

2. Choose an area in another part of the world.

3. Find the major river closest to the area you chose. (Choosing a larger or well-known river will make it easier to find good data online.)

4. Using your search engine, type in the name of the river and "watershed" to find a list of websites for information on this watershed.

5. Look through the list of websites produced by your search, and select several reliable websites to read through to gather information on this watershed. (Websites with a .gov, .edu, or .org extension will usually provide the most reliable information.) If you locate a map of this watershed, print it out. Record important data that you can find about your watershed in the chart. You may not be able to find all of the types of data listed in the chart for this watershed. You may find other interesting data not listed on the chart and can add the additional information.

Watershed characteristics	Name of Your Watershed:_____	Name of Other Watershed Selected: _____
Continent where watershed is located		
Major cities within the watershed		
Examples of some species in this watershed		
Approximate size (area) of the watershed		
Shape of the watershed		
Percentage of land use, i.e., developed, wetlands, forested, agricultural, etc.		
Approximate human population in the watershed		
Water quality/Threats to water quality		
Other interesting facts		

1. What are some similarities that you found between your watershed and the other watershed that you chose?

_____

_____

_____

_____

2. What are some differences that you found between your watershed and the other watershed that you chose?

_____

_____

_____

_____

Student Guide

Topographic Maps: Tools for Environmental Studies

Reading a topographic map is one of the best ways for someone to understand "the lay of the land." Learn to read the symbols on a topographic map and interpret contour lines. Then create your own topographic profile.

Lesson Objectives

- Explain how people use topographic maps to help them study watersheds.
- Explain how reading a contour map can help people find ways to keep the environment healthy.
- Identify contour lines and use them to determine elevation.
- Interpret symbols on a topographic map.
- Interpret a topographic map to identify the boundaries of a watershed.

PREPARE

Approximate lesson time is 60 minutes.

Materials

For the Student

Reading Valley Topographic Map
pencil - assorted colored (5)
Creating a Topographic Profile
Profile Guide
ruler, standard
paper

Keywords and Pronunciations

scale: the ratio of objects on a map to objects in real life. The scale on our road map is 1 inch to 25 miles.

aerial photograph: A photo taken from the sky, looking down on an area. The aerial photograph of our neighborhood showed the tops of houses, the tops of trees, and the entire lake.

cartographer (kahr-TAH-gruh-fuhr): A map maker. A cartographer places details of land and sea features on a flat map.

contour lines: A closed-loop line that represents a specific elevation on a topographic map. Each contour line represents an elevation difference of 100 feet.

elevation: The height of one object above another. The elevation of Mt. Everest is almost 30,000 feet (almost 9,000 meters) above sea level, whereas the elevation of Mt. Baldy in California is about 10,000 feet (3,000 meters) above sea level.

topographic (tah-puh-GRA-fihk)

topographic map (tah-puh-GRA-fihk): A map that shows the physical features of the land, such as the rise and fall. A topographic map identifies features such as rivers, buildings, hiking trails, hills, and homes in a watershed.

LEARN

Activity 1: Discover Topographic Maps *(Online)*

Understanding the characteristics of land is important to understanding water resources. Reading topographic maps is one of the best ways to do this.

Activity 2: Read a Topographic Map *(Offline)*

People use maps to study water resources. A topographic map shows where watersheds begin and end and include rivers, creeks, and the rise and fall of the land.

Activity 3: Making a Profile from a Topographic Map *(Offline)*

Topographic maps show a view from above the land. Make a profile from a topographic map to see how the land might look at your eye level.

ASSESS

Lesson Assessment: Topographic Maps: Tools for Environmental Studies *(Offline)*

You will complete an offline assessment covering the main objectives of this lesson. Your learning coach will score this assessment.

Name _____   Date _____

Topographic Maps: Tools for Environmental Studies
Reading Valley Topographic Map

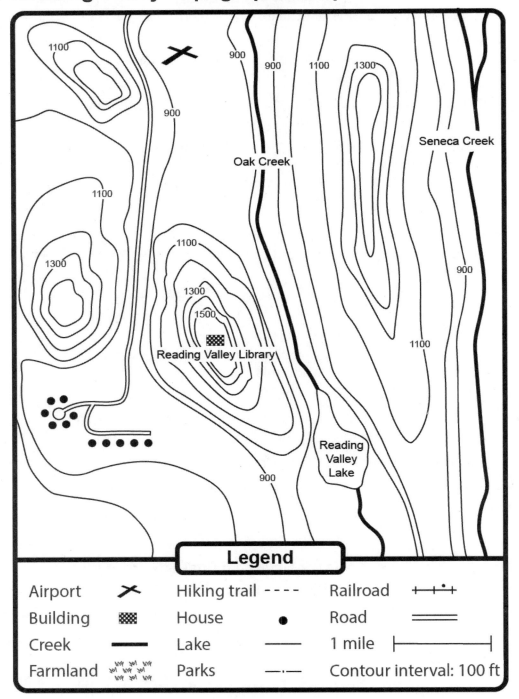

Legend

Airport	✕	Hiking trail	- - - -	Railroad	┼┼·┼	
Building	▨	House	●	Road	═══	
Creek	——	Lake	——	1 mile	├───────┤	
Farmland	ᵥᵥ ᵥᵥ ᵥᵥ	Parks	—·—	Contour interval: 100 ft		

If keeping your watershed healthy is important to you, you will want to know how to read a topographic map. With a little practice, you can become a skilled map-reader.

This topographic map shows the area around the Reading Valley Library. Use the contour lines to read elevations on the map. Each line represents a 100-foot change in elevation. The library is at an elevation of 1500 feet and is marked with a patterned box.

1. On a standard topographic map, streams are shown in blue and contour lines are shown in brown. Trace the streams, creeks, and lakes with a blue colored pencil. Trace the contour lines in brown.

2. Find the Oak Creek and Seneca Creek. They are basins in this watershed. The Oak Creek drainage basin includes the land from which runoff flows into Reading Valley Lake.

3. Find the elevations for the following:

    (a) Seneca Creek _____

    (b) Oak Creek _____

    (c) Reading Valley Lake _____

4. Why do you think that creeks, rivers, and lakes would be found at the lowest elevations on a topographic map?

    _____

    _____

    _____

5. The Reading Valley Library is built on the top of a hill. Which basin does the water that falls on the library eventually drain into?

    _____

6. On the map, draw a hiking trail. Hikers may want to have water available. Will people have to drive to the trail, or will most people be able to walk?

    _____

7. Find the airport. Do you think this is the best place to build an airport? How might a topographic map be used to build things such as these?

_____

_____

_____

8. There are plans to build a hotel for travelers flying into the airport near the library. How might the construction of a hotel affect the water in Reading Valley Lake? Is building a hotel in this location good for the health of the watershed? Give reasons for your answer.

_____

_____

_____

_____

_____

9. Add some features to your map that will affect the water quality in the basins. These may include farmland, homes, roads, railroad, businesses, or parks. Use the key for the symbols.

10. Choose two features you added and explain why you added them where you did. Tell how they might affect water quality.

_____

_____

_____

_____

_____

_____

Name _____ Date _____

Topographic Maps: Tools for Environmental Studies
Creating a Topographic Profile

Imagine that when you look at a topographic map, you are looking at land from an airplane. How might Reading Valley look from eye-level? By making a topographic profile, then a model watershed, you can get an idea of how the elevations in Reading Valley might look. Use the Reading Valley Topographic Map for this activity.

1. On a standard topographic map, streams are shown in blue and contour lines are shown in brown. Trace the streams, creeks, and lakes with a blue colored pencil. Trace the contour lines in brown.

2. Draw a straight line. Label the start of your line A1 and the end B1. Draw a second line, parallel to the first, and label it A2 – B2.

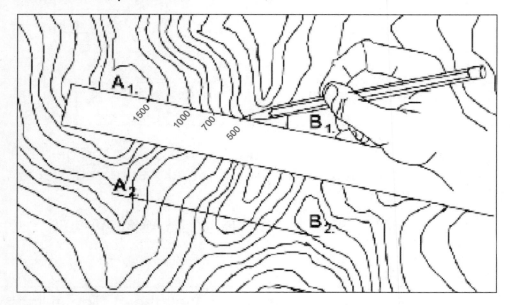

3. Lay a strip of paper along the first line. Label this strip A1 - B1.

4. Mark where streams, creeks, lakes, or highways cross the strip. Label them.

5. Mark where each contour line crosses the strip.

6. Below each mark, write the elevation point.

    Tips:

    Remember, contour lines that are small and close together represent a hill. Elevation decreases toward a stream, lake, or creek. To figure out the elevation of each contour line, you will need to lift the paper strip at times and count lines.

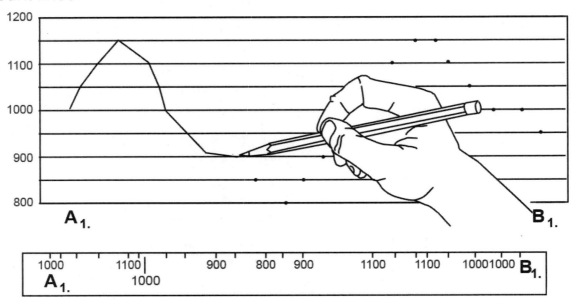

7. Place the strip at the bottom of one profile guide. Draw a dot on the guide at the elevations of the marks you made. Use a ruler to make sure your dot is directly above the mark on the paper strip.

8. Connect the points to get a profile view. Below the guide, label streams, creeks, lakes, highways, etc.

9. Repeat for the other profile line.

When you are finished, you will see two profiles of your watershed. These lines represent what Reading Valley might look like if you were a visitor there, standing on the ground.

Name _____ Date _____

Topographic Maps: Tools for Environmental Studies
Profile Guide

Student Guide
Wetlands and Watersheds

A *wetland* is an area of land that is wet for all or most of the year. Wetlands are important to the health of a watershed. Polluting a model watershed illustrates the partnership between wetlands and watersheds.

Wetlands and watersheds represent the hydrosphere. All four spheres of the Earth interact together. What happens in the hydrosphere can have an impact on the biosphere, geosphere, and atmosphere, as well.

Lesson Objectives

- Describe reasons why wetlands are important to the overall health of a watershed.
- Describe different types of wetlands.
- Explain how wetlands can improve water quality.
- Explain how wetlands form.
- Describe ways the geosphere, biosphere, hydrosphere, and/or atmosphere interact.
- Describe ways the geosphere, biosphere, hydrosphere, and/or atmosphere interact in Michigan and the Great Lakes basin.

PREPARE

Approximate time is 60 minutes.

Advance Preparation

For this lesson you will need the model of the watershed made in the previous lesson. If you left it in a warm, dry place, it should now be hard and dry.

Materials

For the Student

A Wetland in Your Watershed
Reading Valley Topographic Map
aluminum foil
baking pan
flour
glue
household item - sponge
household item - watering can
food coloring
masking tape
pebbles
plastic wrap
poster board
rocks

salt
scissors
soil
vegetable oil
water

Keywords and Pronunciations

carnivorous (kahr-NIH-vuh-ruhs)

pocosin (puh-KOH-suhn)

wetland: Land covered with water for all or part of the year. A marsh is a wetland that contains reeds or sawgrass.

LEARN

Activity 1: What Is a Wetland? *(Online)*
Instructions

What do you think a wetland is? You probably already know it's an area of land that is wet for all or most of the year. Wetlands are important to the health of a watershed. Find out about the partnership between wetlands and watersheds by polluting your model watershed.

Wetlands provide homes for plants and animals, they clean water that drains into the watershed, and they provide areas for people to study nature, bird watch, fish, or canoe. Amazingly, people once thought paving over wetlands did not damage the environment.

Activity 2: Four Spheres of Earth *(Online)*
Instructions

Read through the activity that explains the four spheres of the Earth. You will be introduced to the hydrosphere, geosphere, atmosphere, and biosphere. This will help you prepare for the next activity.

Activity 3: Model of Spheres *(Online)*

You will be given the task to make or use a model that represents your area to identify each of the four spheres of the Earth. For example if you live in Michigan you would make a model of the Great Lakes River Basin. Review the rubric to help you successfully meet expectations for and explain how each of the spheres interact with one another.

Activity 4: Wetlands Protect Wetlands *(Online and Offline)*
Instructions

Wetlands protect watersheds by cleaning organic matter from water flowing through creeks and streams. Investigate how a wetland would protect your watershed model.

Activity 5: America's Wetlands *(Online)*
Instructions

You can find wetlands all over the world. View areas of wetlands in the United States by using an interactive mapping tool.

Name _____   Date _____

Wetlands and Watersheds
Reading Valley Topographic Map

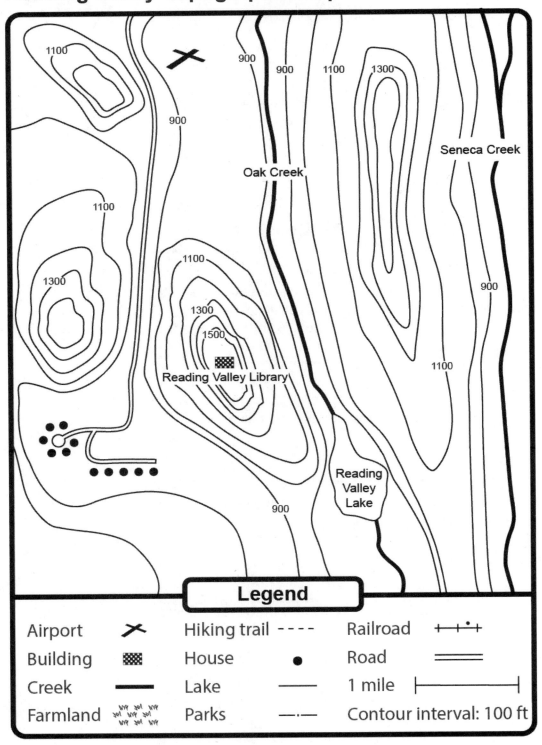

Name _____ Date _____

Wetlands and Watersheds
A Wetland in Your Watershed

Keeping a watershed healthy involves keeping it free of pollution. By understanding your watershed's drainage patterns, you can predict which areas pollutants will damage. Wetlands help protect watersheds by filtering out materials that may pollute streams, rivers, ponds, and lakes.

Materials

sponge

watering can

food coloring

plastic wrap

soil

water

Procedure

1. Lay a large sheet of plastic wrap over your watershed model.

2. Carefully cover the model by starting in the center and working outward. Secure the corners with pennies as needed.

3. Place your topographic map and model next to each other, facing the same direction.

4. Make it rain in Reading Valley by using a watering can with water tinted blue with food coloring.

Notice how the water runs off the land and in what direction. Does it collect in lakes and rivers as shown on your map?

Next see how pollution will affect your watershed.

Pollution

1. Add a drop of red food coloring at the start of one of the streams or lakes. Make it rain again. Can you see how rainwater carries pollution through the watershed?

2. Imagine that the hotel were to be built on the hill near the Reading Valley Library. Construction would loosen a lot of soil. Add a small pile of soil to this hill and make it rain again.

Notice how the soil runs off the land and into the creeks and streams. This is soil erosion caused by runoff.

Now, add your wetland.

Add a Wetland

1. Place a piece of sponge at the base of the hill, on the shore of the creek. This is one place where water can collect and form a wetland. The sponge represents a wetland.

2. Add a small amount of soil at the construction site and another drop of food coloring at the start of the stream leading to the creek.

3. Make it rain again.

Does more or less water flow into your collection areas now that you've added a wetland? Wetlands "soak up" a lot of excess water. Destroying wetlands has led to flooding in some areas.

What happens to the pollution added to your watershed? Does the wetland protect the creek from pollution? How might this affect the wetland?

Many organisms live in a wetland environment. It's important that wetlands as well as watersheds are kept healthy and free from damaging pollution.

Student Guide
Water Resources: Unit Review and Assessment

Have you become an expert on water resources? Find out if you can earn a water conservationist's badge.

Lesson Objectives

- Identify and describe the parts of a watershed.
- Interpret a topographic map to identify the boundaries of a watershed.
- Describe how both natural processes and human activities affect water quality in watersheds.
- Differentiate between *point-source pollution* and *nonpoint-source pollution* and identify some ways by which they can both be reduced.
- Identify the typical steps water-treatment plants go through to purify drinking water.
- Identify the various sources of water, its uses, and different ways to conserve it.

PREPARE

Approximate lesson time is 60 minutes.

Materials

For the Student

    Question Review Table

Keywords and Pronunciations

aeration (air-AY-shun)**:** The process of purifying water by exposing it to moving air. Air is pumped into water during aeration.

aquifer (A-kwuh-fuhr)**:** An underground geological formation that contains large amounts of water. Water can be pumped from an aquifer by drilling a well.

coagulation (koh-a-gyuh-LAY-shun)**:** The process of purifying water by adding alum and other chemicals that cause clumping of some impurities. Alum causes the coagulation of dirt in water.

dendritic (den-DRIH-tik)

nonpoint-source pollution: Pollution that enters water from a wide area rather than a specific point. Oil and grease from streets are washed into surface water and cause nonpoint-source pollution.

permeability (puhr-mee-uh-BIH-luh-tee)**:** The measure of how easily water can travel through soil or rock. Water travels more easily through sand than clay because sand has a higher permeability.

point-source pollution: A single source, such as a drainage pipe, that allows pollutants to enter directly into the water. Point-source pollution occurs when an oil tanker spills oil directly into the sea.

porosity (puh-RAH-suh-tee): the measure of the space between particles in rock or soil; the porosity of soil allows it to soak up rainwater

sedimentation: The settling of solid material to the bottom of a liquid. Sedimentation separates large particles of dirt from water.

topographic map (tah-puh-GRA-fihk): A map that shows the physical features of the Earth such as the rise andfall of the land. A topographic map identifies features such as rivers, buildings, hiking trails, hills, and homes in a watershed.

watershed: The specific area of land off which water drains. Also called a drainage system. We know that Kansas is in the Mississippi River watershed because all the precipitation that lands there flows into the Mississippi River.

wetland: Land covered with water for all or part of the year. A marsh is a wetland that contains reeds or sawgrass.

LEARN

Activity 1: Be A Conservationist! *(Online)*

Do you have what it takes to be a conservationist? This review will help you decide. If you qualify, you'll have the chance to find a place where water is in danger, then decide how you can solve the problem.

ASSESS

Unit Assessment: Water Resources: Unit Assessment *(Offline)*

You will complete an offline assessment covering the main objectives of this unit. Your learning coach will score this assessment.

LEARN

Activity 2: Unit Assessment Review Table *(Online)*

If you earned a score of **less than 80%** on the Unit Assessment, complete the activity.

If you earned a score of **80% or greater**, you may skip this activity.

Let's prepare to retake the Unit Assessment:

- Print the Question Review Table.
- Identify the questions that you answered incorrectly.
- Complete the appropriate review activities listed in the table.

Note: This Unit Assessment Review Tables Learning Coach Video will guide you through the process of using the Unit Assessment Review Tables. You may skip this video if you've already viewed it in another unit or course. As always, check in with your student's teacher if you have any questions.

Name _____   Date _____

Water Resources: Unit Review and Assessment
Question Review Table

Before you retake the Unit Assessment, use the table to figure out which activities you should review.

Circle the numbers of the questions that you missed on the Unit Assessment. Review the activities that correspond with these questions.

Question	Lesson	Review Activity
1,2	What's a Watershed?	Explore: What's a Watershed? Locate Your Watershed
3	Topographic Maps: Tools for Environmental Studies	Explore: Discover Topographic Maps
4	Topographic Maps: Tools for Environmental Studies	Explore: Discover Topographic Maps Read a Topographic Map
5	Water Uses and Treatment	Making Water Safe to Drink Treat Your Water Well
6	Water Uses and Treatment	Explore: Finding and Using Water
7	Water Pollution	Explore: Water Pollution Nonpoint-Source Pollution Cleaning Up an Oil Spill Your Water
8	Water Pollution	Your Water
9	Water Pollution	Explore: Water Pollution Cleaning Up an Oil Spill Your Water
10,11	Water Uses and Treatment	Are You a Water Waster?

Student Guide

Ocean Water

We live on a very watery planet, yet we don't really know that much about our vast oceans. Discover how ocean water differs in salinity and in temperature. Find out how you can use these two characteristics to determine the difference between water at the surface of the ocean and water from the depths.

Lesson Objectives

- State that the Earth's four oceans are connected, allowing ocean water to circulate globally.
- Define *salinity* as the amount of salt and other dissolved minerals in ocean water.
- Describe how the density of ocean water modifies with changes in salinity and temperature.
- State that approximately three quarters of the Earth's surface is covered by water.

PREPARE

Approximate lesson time is 60 minutes.

Materials

For the Student

> Salty Layers
> cup, plastic - 8 oz. (3)
> salt - 135 mL - 9 tablespoons
> eyedropper
> food coloring - (red, green, yellow) (3)
> graduated cylinder
> spoon
> water
> Hydrostation
> Hydrostation Grid
> Temperature and Density Experiments
> cup, plastic (2)
> thermometer, Celsius/Fahrenheit (2)
> bowl - clear plastic with lid
> food coloring
> ice cubes

Optional

> household item - hose or faucet
> household item - small fan

Keywords and Pronunciations

density: How tightly the matter of an object is packed together. The density of rock is higher than the density of foam rubber.

remote sensing: The technique of using satellite-based instruments to measure temperature and other properties of the Earth's surface. Using remote sensing, scientists can check the temperature of places that are uninhabited by humans.

salinity (suh-LIH-nuh-tee): the degree of saltiness of a salt solution, especially applied to ocean water

LEARN

Activity 1: Ocean Water *(Online)*

Three-quarters of the Earth is covered with water, yet scientists know much more about the land we live on than they do about the world's oceans. Knowing about ocean water and currents is a first step in understanding our watery planet, Earth.

Activity 2: Ocean Layers *(Offline)*

Find out how salinity affects ocean water.

Activity 3: Water Warmth *(Offline)*

Besides salinity, in what other ways are deep water and surface water different? Study the data from an ocean platform called a *hydrostation* to see how water temperature changes in the ocean.

ASSESS

Lesson Assessment: Ocean Water *(Offline)*

You will complete an offline assessment covering the main objectives of this lesson. Your learning coach will score this assessment.

LEARN

Activity 4: Optional: Temperature and Density Experiments *(Offline)*

This activity is OPTIONAL. It's provided for enrichment or extra practice, but not required for completion of this lesson. You may skip this activity.

Observe the interaction of cold and warm water by showing how water in lakes turns over, and how deep-water masses form in oceans.

Activity 5: Optional: ZlugQuest Measurement *(Online)*

Name _____   Date _____

Ocean Water
Salty Layers

It is easy to think of layers when describing a cake, or a pile of blankets, or even the layers of the Earth. It is not so easy to think of layers of water. It all just seems to flow together. Do layers of water exist? If they do, how would you be able to tell them apart?

Ocean water is salty. You would expect water that is very salty to be found in deeper water. It makes sense to think that water at the bottom of the ocean would be saltier than water at the surface. Do you think the ocean has different salinity at different depths? Which layer is saltiest?

Materials

salt - 9 tablespoons (135 mL)

food coloring (red, green, and yellow)

3 bottles

graduated cylinder

eye dropper

4 plastic cups

spoon

water

Hypothesis

Write a hypothesis telling whether or not you think the ocean has different salinity at different depths.

_____

_____

Procedure:

Part 1

1. Fill each cup with 100 mL of water.

2. Add 90 mL of salt to one cup. Mix well.

3. Add 45 mL of salt to a second cup. Mix well.

4. Do not add salt to the third cup.

5. If these amounts don't work, try using 45 mL instead of 90 mL, and 10 mL instead of 45, or try other variations

6. Add different colors of food coloring to each cup. Mix until the colors are strong. Rinse the spoon between mixing.

7. Use the eyedropper to add the saltiest water to the cylinder to a height of 20 mL.

8. Rinse the eye dropper. Gently add the medium salty water to the cylinder to 40 mL. Place the dropper against the side of the cylinder and squeeze out the water against the cylinder's sides.

9. Rinse the eye dropper. As before, gently add the water without salt to the cylinder to 60 mL.

10. Let the cylinder sit for a while. Complete Part One of your observations.

Part 2

1. Re-do the experiment but this time do not add any salt to the water.

2. Complete Part Two of your observations.

Scientist Notes

Remember that in an investigation, scientists test how one thing will affect something else. This one thing is called a "variable." That comes from the word "vary" or change. To test a variable, you change it in some way to see if there are any effects. A variable may or may not have an effect on something in your experiment. Only one variable at a time can be tested!

Read your procedure carefully and observe your experiment. You are testing the effect of one variable on the density of water. Which variable are you testing? Circle it below.

    A. amount of salt

    B. water temperature

    C. water quality

You also know that in experiments, you can't avoid small differences or errors, even if you are very careful. Scientists use replication to make sure their experiment results really are true results. To replicate this experiment, you will have to perform it twice.

Observations

Part One

1. Observe the cylinder of water. Can you see any layers?

2. Do the three types of water stay separated, even if just a bit?

3. Draw the appearance of the water in the cylinder.

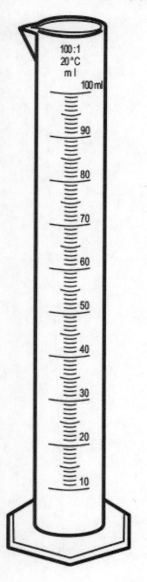

Part Two

1. Observe the cylinder of water. Can you see any layers?

2. Do the three types of water stay separated, even if just a bit?

3. Draw the appearance of the water in the cylinder.

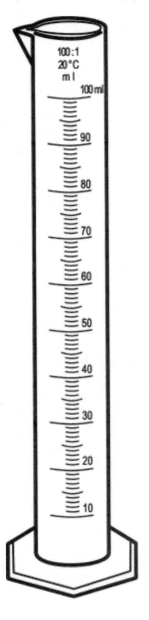

Conclusion

Reread your hypothesis.

1. Based on this experiment, do you think that water in the ocean could have different layers of differing salinity? Tell about this with examples from the experiment.

   _____

   _____

   _____

2. Do you think you could identify ocean layers by testing the amount of salt in the water?

   _____

   _____

   _____

Name _____ Date _____

Ocean Water

Hydrostation

Ocean water varies in salinity and temperature. Surface water is usually warmer than deeper water because the sun strikes the surface directly.

At an ocean platform called a *hydrostation*, scientists would study properties of water such as salinity, density, and temperature. The next page shows data gathered from a hydrostation near an island in a warm climate. You will graph the data to compare the temperature of the water at different depths.

On your graph paper, label the vertical axis Ocean Depth in Meters. Starting with 0 at the TOP of the graph, label each line by 200, all the way to 4000 at the BOTTOM.

Label the horizontal axis *Temperature in Degrees Celsius*. Label each line 25 to 0 starting with the first line on the left.

Graph the data by making a dot for each temperature at each depth. When you are finished, connect the dots to make a line graph.

What does the data from this hydrostation show about water temperature?

_____

_____

In the previous activity, you identified layers based on salinity. Can you identify any water layers based on temperature?

Studying water temperature and salinity helps tell the difference between layers. Warmer water indicates the surface layer. Colder water is a clue that you are working with deep water.

Temperature in Degrees Celsius	Ocean Depth in Meters
25.0	3.0
25.0	12.0
25.0	32.0
22.6	52.0
19.7	71.0
19.5	89.0
19.0	113.0
18.9	128.0
18.8	150.0
17.7	401.3
15.0	603.7
11.0	806.9
7.6	896.0
5.6	1100.0
4.7	1301.6
4.0	1599.0
3.6	2000.0
3.0	2401.0
2.4	2998.8
2.3	3800.0
2.0	3999.0

Name _____   Date _____

Ocean Water
Hydrostation Grid

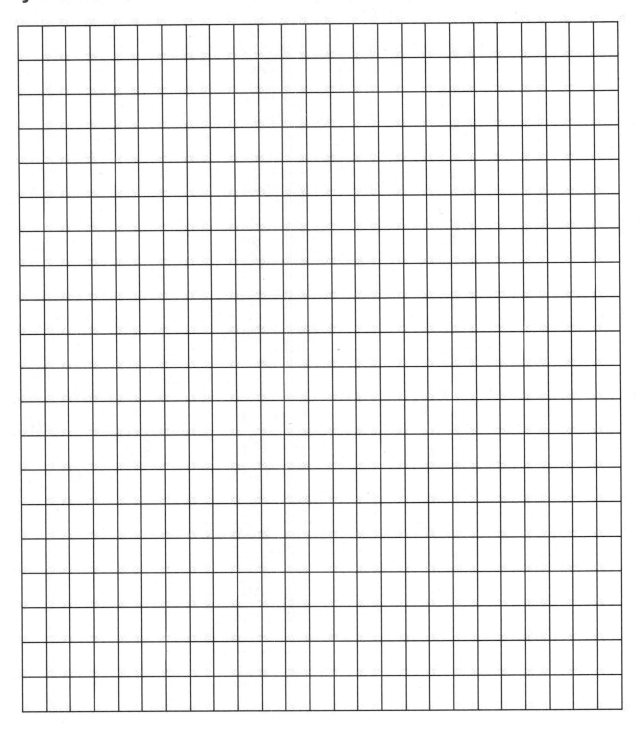

Name _____   Date _____

Ocean Water

Temperature and Density Experiments

Water forms layers based on salinity and temperature. Less dense water rests on top of denser water. Water becomes denser as it gets colder, but once it reaches 4°C something interesting happens. Between 4°C and 0°C water becomes less dense. Ice is less dense than water (remember, ice cubes float!)

During cold winters, ponds and lakes can freeze. In the spring, the ice melts. As the ice warms up, it becomes denser and begins to sink. The nutrients at the bottom of the water begin to rise. This is called turnover. The same thing happens in the fall as the warm surface water cools.

1. Obtain two water samples, one at room temperature and one warm (but not boiling).

2. Put a few drops of different food coloring in each sample.

3. Measure the temperature of each sample.

4. Pour the coldest sample into the bowl first, then the warm sample, to create layers. The warm water on top represents water heated by the sun.

5. Add ice to the the bowl.

6. Observe as the ice melts.

You should see that as the ice melts, the colder water will move to the bottom. The water at the bottom will begin to circulate and move toward the top. Measure the temperature of the water at the top, middle, and bottom. Watch throughout the day as the ice continues to melt.

Some other things to try:

*   Use a small fan to test the effects of wind on the circulation of water.
*   Use a hose or faucet and add water to simulate a stream. How does this affect water circulation?

Student Guide

Ocean Currents

Ocean water does not sit still; it moves. Moving ocean water creates ocean *currents*. Learn about the two major types of ocean currents, then mix warm and cold water to get an "ocean view" of how these currents form.

Lesson Objectives

- State that surface currents are caused by prevailing winds on the ocean's surface.
- Describe the movements of deep-water currents in the ocean.
- Explain how the Gulf Stream helps moderate the climate of Western Europe.
- State that deep-water currents are caused by differences in the salinity, temperature, and density of water.

PREPARE

Approximate lesson time is 60 minutes.

Materials

For the Student

> Deep-Water and Surface Currents
> drinking glass
> drinking straw
> salt
> baking dish - clear, deep
> food coloring
> graduated cylinder - 100 mL
> spoon
> water

Keywords and Pronunciations

current: A river-like flow of water in the ocean. Ocean water does not sit still, it flows in currents.

deep-water current: The movement of water below the surface caused by differences in salinity, temperature, and density. Deep-water currents occur when water rises and pushes away large amounts of warmer water.

riptide: A shoreline current running parallel to the shore. If swimmers are not careful, a strong riptide can carry them away.

shoreline current: The movement of water near the shore. Shoreline currents occur where water meets land.

surface current: Moving water at the top layer of the ocean. Wind causes most surface currents.

LEARN

Activity 1: Two Types of Currents *(Online)*

The ocean has two major types of currents. *Surface currents* move water in the upper layers of the ocean. *Deep water currents* cause movements of water deep in the seas.

Activity 2: Causes of Currents *(Offline)*

Mix cold and warm water to see how deep-water currents flow. Then create wind to observe surface currents.

ASSESS

Lesson Assessment: Ocean Currents *(Offline)*

You will complete an offline assessment covering the main objectives of this lesson. Your learning coach will score this assessment.

Name _____ Date _____

Ocean Currents

Deep-Water and Surface Currents

There are two types of ocean currents you have learned: **deep-water currents** and **surface currents**.

The movement of **deep-water currents** depends on how salty the water is, its temperature, and its density.

Surface currents are mainly caused by wind, which is a result of the rotation of the Earth.

This activity will demonstrate both types of currents.

Deep Water Currents

1. Measure 97 mL of very cold water in the graduated cylinder.
2. Add salt to the water in the cylinder until the water line reaches 100 mL.
3. Pour the mixture into a glass.

Observe the salty water. Compare it to freshwater. Notice that it is denser than freshwater because it is so salty. Add blue food coloring to the glass of salty water and set it aside.

4. Measure 60 mL of salt into the graduated cylinder.
5. Pour 2 L of very warm water into a clear baking dish.
6. Add the salt and stir until the salt is dissolved.
7. Let the water sit until it is still. While you wait, read and answer the questions below.

Think about how deep-water currents form in the ocean. Cold, salty water near the North Pole is very dense. It sinks, and then flows toward the equator where it is heated. Then it rises, because it is less dense, and flows back toward the North Pole as more cold water moves in.

Next you will add the cold water to the warm water. What do you expect to happen? Will the cold water sink, just as it does in the ocean?

_____
_____
_____

If your water is still, slowly pour the cold salt water into one end of the pan. Observe what happens to the cold, dense water. You should see the cold salt water sink and move across the bottom of the pan, creating a current.

Surface Currents

1. Blow gently through a straw across the surface of the pan of water.
2. Observe the ripples that occur from your "wind." These are surface currents.

Student Guide
Ocean Waves

Not only are ocean waves beautiful, but they can also tell us a lot about the flow of energy. Many things affect the movement and size of ocean waves. Some waves can rise more than 75 feet high, while other waves are gentle and welcoming.

Lesson Objectives
- Explain how changing the frequency of a wave affects its wavelength.
- Explain the factors that influence the size of an ocean wave and describe a wave's motion.
- Identify and describe the different parts of a wave (wave height, wavelength, crest, and trough).

PREPARE

Approximate lesson time is 60 minutes.

Materials
For the Student

> Making Waves
> ruler, standard
> tray, styrofoam
> baking dish - clear
> lamp
> scissors, round-end safety
> water
> bowl - small, with lid

Keywords and Pronunciations

crest: the high point of a wave

frequency: The length of a cycle of a complete wave. High-frequency waves have shorter wavelengths than low frequency waves.

ocean wave: The way that energy of motion moves from one place in the ocean to another through the water. The ocean waves carried the energy in the form of motion from Africa to Cuba.

rogue wave: A wave that is more than 75 feet high. Because a rogue wave is so huge, it can do a lot of damage to property when it hits the shore.

trough (trawf): the low point of a wave

tsunami (tsou-NAH-mee): A huge wave caused by an underwater earthquake or volcano. A tsunami is a terrifying sight, and for good reason—it can kill.

wave: A way in which the energy of motion moves through a substance. The wave of water crashed onto the rocks with a mighty roar of sound energy.

wave height: the vertical distance between a trough and a crest

wavelength: The distance between two crests or two troughs. The wavelengths between crests can vary greatly, depending on location and weather.

LEARN

Activity 1: The Ocean Wave *(Online)*

Ocean waves can have a powerful effect on people. Artists draw them, poets write about them, and sailors study them. Scientists work to understand ocean waves and the energy they hold.

Activity 2: Making Waves *(Online)*

Ocean waves can be long and slow or short and quick. Investigate the changes in wave height and wavelength between slow and quick waves.

ASSESS

Lesson Assessment: Ocean Waves *(Offline)*

You will complete an offline assessment covering the main objectives of this lesson. Your learning coach will score this assessment.

LEARN

Activity 3: Wave Refraction *(Offline)*

When ocean water becomes shallow or meets an obstacle such as land, waves begin to move at different speeds. The difference in speed makes the wave appear curved, with the slower parts dragging behind. This effect is called *refraction*, which means *bending*.

Follow these steps to cause refraction in waves:

1. Fill a clear baking dish with a shallow layer of water.

2. Fill the small bowl with water to give it weight and place it in the dish so it rests on the bottom. Place it in the center of the baking dish.

3. From one end of the baking dish, push the plastic lid gently forward to make a wave.

Observe the shape of the wave. How does the shape of the wave change when it hits the bowl? In what way does this represent what happens when an ocean wave hits an obstacle near land?

Wave refraction plays a part in shaping shores. Refracted waves erode land at the shore. The parts of the shore exposed to the bent, slower part of the wave do not erode as quickly as the land at the sides.

Activity 4: Optional: ZlugQuest Measurement *(Online)*

Name _____   Date _____

Ocean Waves
Making Waves

Question:

How are a wave's frequency, wavelength, and speed related?

Hypothesis:

Changing the frequency of a wave will change its wavelength. Fill in the blanks with the word *longer* or *shorter* to complete the hypothesis below.

High frequency waves will cause _____ wavelengths. Low frequency waves will cause _____ wavelengths.

Procedure

1. Cut the tray into 4 strips.

2. Line the sides of the clear baking dish with the strips, creating a border. The border will reduce reflections from the sides of the dish.

3. Place the dish on top of a piece of white paper. Set an overhead lamp over the dish.

4. Fill the dish with about 3 cm of water.

Notice the light and dark lines in the ripples you make. The light lines are focused on the bottom of the pan by wave crests. The wave troughs produce the dark lines. You can get an idea of wavelength by watching these dark lines. The distance between two dark lines is one wavelength.

5. Tap the surface of the water with the end of your pencil to produce ripples.

6. Let the water become still. Tap the surface of the water again, slowly. How does wavelength compare to when you tapped the surface of the water before?

7. Float a small piece of paper on top of the water. Tap the surface of the water. Does the paper move?

Observations and Analysis

1. In step 4, how did you increase the frequency of the waves? Do high frequency waves have longer or shorter wavelengths? _____

2. In step 5, how did you decrease the frequency of the waves? Do low frequency waves have longer or shorter wavelengths? _____

3. Waves represent a flow of motion or energy until this energy breaks up. Where did the energy break up in the waves you made?

   _____

   _____

Conclusion

1. How does wavelength change with an increase in frequency? With a decrease in frequency?

   _____

   _____

2. Was your hypothesis correct? _____

3. What other ideas do you have for testing wavelength and frequency?

   _____

   _____

   _____

   _____

   _____

   _____

Student Guide

Ocean Tides

Tides come in and go out, and have been doing so for billions of years. But what causes tides? Find out how the sun, moon, and Earth are related in the movement of tides. Explore adaptations of organisms that live in tidal waters.

Lesson Objectives

- Identify the relative positions of the Earth, sun, and moon during spring and neap tides.
- Describe the characteristics of an intertidal zone and how organisms have adapted to live there.
- Explain how the gravitational pull of the sun and moon causes daily high and low tides.

PREPARE

Approximate lesson time is 60 minutes.

Materials

For the Student

> Tides Go In, Tides Go Out
> Drying Out
> cup, plastic - 8 oz. (2)
> household item - crayon
> salt - 1 tablespoon
> bags, zipper-close (3)
> paper towels (4)
> water

Keywords and Pronunciations

high tide: The highest rise of tidal water during a day. At high tide, the water came halfway up the cliff.

intertidal zone: The area between the highest high tide and the lowest low tide. Many ocean animals live in the intertidal zone.

low tide: The lowest level of tidal water during a day. At low tide, we could pick up shells on the beach that had once been underwater.

neap tide: tides with a smaller than normal range of highs and lows, during a neap tide, the gravity of the sun and moon work against each other

spring tide: Tides with a greater than normal range of highs and lows. The spring tide made the water level rise nearly to the floor of the boathouse.

tide: The rise and fall of the surface level of the ocean or a lake. The tide came in and washed away my beach blanket.

LEARN

Activity 1: The Rise and Fall of the Tides *(Online)*

Have you ever wondered what causes ocean tides? Gravity is the answer. The plants and animals that live along the shore have adapted to the ebb and flow of the tides.

Activity 2: Earth, Sun, Moon...and Tides? *(Offline)*

Neap tides and spring tides occur as a result of the position of the sun and moon. The moon's position changes every day as it orbits the Earth. Study tides and relate them to the position of the moon in its orbit.

Activity 3: Does Drying Out Mean Dying Out? *(Online)*

Show some of the behaviors and adaptations that help rocky intertidal organisms keep from drying out during the low tide.

ASSESS

Lesson Assessment: Ocean Tides *(Offline)*

You will complete an offline assessment covering the main objectives of this lesson. Your learning coach will score this assessment.

Name _____   Date _____

Ocean Tides

Tides Go In, Tides Go Out

Study the calendar of high and low tides. The data was collected during the month of May 2002.

Week 01

Wed 01	Thurs 02	Fri 03	Sat 04
Low	Low 0.05 m 12:03 A	Low 0.07 m 12:57 A	Low 0.09 m 01:55 A
High 0.48 m 05:13 A	High 0.52 m 06:06 A	High 0.49 m 07:06 A	High 0.46 m 08:12 A
Low 0.01 m 12:09 P	Low 0.03 m 01:01 P	Low 0.04 m 01:54 P	Low 0.06 m 02:46 P
High 0.47 m 06:08 P	High 0.45 m 07:08 P	High 0.44 m 08:11 P	High 0.45 m 09:12 P

Week 02

Sun 05	Mon 06	Tues 07	Wed 08	Thurs 09	Fri 10	Sat 11
Low 0.10 m 02:55 A	Low 0.10 m 03:55 A	Low 0.09 m 04:51 A	Low 0.08 m 05:45 A	High 0.53 m 12:25 A	High 0.55 m 01:00 A	High 0.56 m 01:31 A
High 0.45 m 09:19 A	High 0.46 m 10:20A	High 0.46 m 11:14 A	High 0.48 m 12:03 P	Low 0.08 m 06:34 A	Low 0.07 m 07:20 A	Low 0.07 m 08:04 A
Low 0.06 m 03:37 P	Low 0.07 m 04:26 P	Low 0.07 m 05:12 P	Low 0.07 m 05:55 P	High 0.49 m 12:47 P	High 0.49 m 01:28 P	High 0.50 m 02:05 P
High 0.46 m 10:08 P	High 0.48 m 10:59 P	High 0.50 m 11:44 P	High	Low 0.08 m 06:35 P	Low 0.09 m 07:14 P	Low 0.10 m 07:52 P

Week 03

Sun 12	Mon 13	Tues 14	Wed 15	Thurs 16	Fri 17	Sat 18
High 0.58 m 02:00 A	High 0.59 m 02:31 A	High 0.60 m 03:05 A	High 0.61 m 03:44 A	High 0.60 m 04:28 A	High 0.58 m 05:17 A	Low 0.12 m 12:18 A
Low 0.08 m 08:47 A	Low 0.08 m 09:30 A	Low 0.08 m 10:12 A	Low 0.10 m 10:55 A	Low 0.10 m 11:40 A	Low 0.10 m 12:27 P	High 0.56 m 06:11 A
High 0.50 m 02:39 P	High 0.50 m 03:13 P	High 0.49 m 03:48 P	High 0.49 m 04:28 P	High 0.49 m 05:13 P	High 0.49 m 06:04 P	Low 0.10 m 01:17 P
Low 0.10 m 08:30 P	Low 0.11 m 09:08 P	Low 0.12 m 09:49 P	Low 0.12 m 10:33 P	Low 0.13 m 11:22 P	Low	High 0.49 m 07:01 P

Week 04

Sun 19	Mon 20	Tues 21	Wed 22	Thurs 23	Fri 24	Sat 25
Low 0.12 m 01:21 A	Low 0.11 m 02:29 A	Low 0.09 m 03:37 A	Low 0.06 m 04:43 A	Low 0.03 m 05:45 A	High 0.60 m 12:01 A	High 0.63 m 12:51 A
High 0.54 m 07:12 A	High 0.52 m 08:20 A	High 0.51 m 09:31 A	High 0.51 m 10:38 A	High 0.51 m 11:39 A	Low 0.01 m 06:43 A	Low 0.01 m 07:38 A
Low 0.09 m 02:11 P	Low 0.08 m 03:06 P	Low 0.06 m 04:03 P	Low 0.04 m 04:58 P	Low 0.02 m 05:52 P	High 0.52 m 12:35 P	High 0.52 m 01:28 P
High 0.50 m 08:04 P	High 0.52 m 09:08 P	High 0.55 m 10:10 P	High 0.57 m 11:08 P	High	Low 0.01 m 06:44 P	Low 0.01 m 07:35 P

Week 05

Sun 26	Mon 27	Tues 28	Wed 29	Thurs 30	Fri 31
High 0.62 m 01:40 A	High 0.63 m 02:27 A	High 0.62 m 03:14 A	High 0.57 m 04:01 A	High 0.54 m 04:49 A	High 0.52 m 05:40 A
Low 0.00 m 08:31 A	Low 0.00 m 09:21 A	Low 0.01 m 10:10 A	Low −0.00 m 10:57 A	Low 0.01 m 11:44 A	Low 0.03 m 12:30 P
High 0.51 m 02:19 P	High 0.50 m 03:09 P	High 0.49 m 04:00 P	High 0.48 m 04:51 P	High 0.46 m 05:44 P	High 0.46 m 06:39 P
Low 0.01 m 08:24 P	Low 0.02 m 09:12 P	Low 0.03 m 10:00 P	Low 0.05 m 10:49 P	Low 0.07 m 11:38 P	Low

1. Notice how a high tide occurs about every 12 hours. Low tides occur about 6 hours after high tides. Write each high and low tide and their corresponding times for May 22.

   (a) High tide _____

   (b) Low tide _____

2. Calculate the difference between the morning high and low tides for each day. Write the differences into the correct days on the calendar.

3. On what two days were the differences between morning high tide and low tide the greatest? What kind of tides are these?

   _____

   _____

4. On what two days were the differences between morning high and low tide the least? What kind of tides are these?

_____

_____

5. Draw a diagram to show the position of the sun and moon during spring tides and during neap tides.

Spring

Neap

6. The moon takes about one month to complete its orbit around the Earth. Explain how this relates to the fact that there are two spring tides and two neap tides per month.

_____

_____

_____

Name _____ Date _____

Ocean Tides
Drying Out

1. Mix the salt into one cup of water. Fill the other cup with freshwater.

2. Tear each paper towel into four pieces. Label each one with a number from one to sixteen.

3. Fold, crush, or wad up the pieces into different sizes and shapes. Leave some unfolded as well. Dip the first eight into saltwater and the rest into freshwater. Place some in the plastic bag, and leave the others in a sunny spot or in the shade. Try many different combinations with your 16 paper pieces. Try to determine the best shape and location to keep your "organism" from drying out.

4. Which organisms will dry the fastest? Which will dry the slowest?

_____

_____

5. Make a chart to record your results. Going down the left side of your data sheet, list what you did to the paper towel. Across the top, make two columns—your guess and what really happens.

6. Leave your pieces for 1 hour, 6 hours, and 1 day. Compare their dryness.

_____

_____

_____

7. If you are familiar with the shapes of animals at the seashore, compare them to the shapes of your paper towels. Are any of your pieces similar to the way a tide pool animal is shaped?

_____

_____

_____

Student Guide

Life at the Edge of the Ocean

Purple sea urchins, Sally lightfoot crabs, barnacles, and sea stars make their home at the edge of the sea. Find out what life would be like if you lived there, too!

Lesson Objectives

- Define an *estuary* as a bay or inlet where fresh river water mixes with ocean water.
- Describe environmental impacts in estuaries.
- Describe life on sandy beaches.
- Explain why salt marshes and mangroves are some of the most biologically productive areas on Earth.
- Describe life on rocky shores near the sea.

PREPARE

Approximate lesson time is 60 minutes.

Materials

For the Student

Marshes, Flats, Dunes, and Forests

Keywords and Pronunciations

chiton (KIY-tuhn)

estuary (EHS-choo-wair-ee)**:** The region where a river flows into the sea, and freshwater and saltwater mix. In an estuary, fresh river water mixes with salty water from the ocean.

mangrove: A type of tree that is adapted for life in brackish water and that has strong roots and knees. The roots of a mangrove tree can help keep a coastline from eroding.

tide pool: A small pool of water left in the rocks when the tide goes out. Animals such as sea urchins, sea stars, and barnacles live in tide pools.

LEARN

Activity 1: Life Where Saltwater Meets Land *(Online)*

Learn about the many different environments that exist at the edge of the ocean. Meet the organisms that live there.

Activity 2: An Estuary Habitat *(Offline)*

Decide which animals and plants belong in the numerous habitats that exist at the coast

ASSESS

Lesson Assessment: Life at the Edge of the Ocean *(Offline)*

You will complete an offline assessment covering the main objectives of this lesson. Your learning coach will score this assessment.

Name _____   Date _____

Life at the Edge of the Ocean
Marshes, Flats, Dunes, and Forests

Estuaries are found where rivers meet the sea, forming a unique ecosystem between ocean and land. An estuarine environment contains habitats that vary in salinity, presence or absence of water, type of soil, availability of food or shelter, temperature, currents, and availability of light. These are limiting factors for the organisms that live in these habitats.

Study the descriptions of estuarine habitats in the chart below. Then use the information in this chart to complete the charts on the plants and animals that live in them.

Estuarine Habitat	Description
Mangrove Forest	High salinity water Salty sediment Affected by high tides
Dunes	Little available water Loose, shifting sand Some salinity due to salt spray High temperatures and plenty of light
Salt Marsh	Brackish water Salty soil Affected by tides Large temperature and salinity changes Little available oxygen
Mud Flat	High salinity water Muddy and sandy bottom Little protective cover Largely affected by tides Large temperature and salinity changes

Animals	Food	Water	Soil/Shelter	Habitat
flounder	fish/crustaceans	salty	mud/sand	
pelican	fish/crustaceans		salty	salt marsh

Animals	Food	Water	Soil/Shelter	Habitat
ghost crab	coquina clams	fresh/salty		dunes
gull	fish/invertebrates	fresh/salty	loose sand	
oyster	detritus*/plankton			mud flats
blue crab	detritus/plankton/oysters	salty	mud/sand	
King prawn	detritus	salty	salty sediment	
fiddler crab	detritus	salty	burrow into burrow into sand and mud	
sea star	snails/mussels	salty		mud flat
yellowfin bream	fish/crabs	salty		mangrove forest
rail	aquatic plants		mud/sand	

Plants	Salinity	Light	Moisture	Soil/Substrate	Habitat
glasswort	brackish	high	moderate/high	salty	
sea oats	salty	high	minimal	sand	
salt marsh cordgrass	brackish	high	high	salty	
mangrove tree	salty	moderate	high	salty sediment	
black needle rush	salty	moderate/high	high	sand/mud	

*Detritus is decaying plant matter.

Using the charts that you have already completed, list the plants and animals found in each of the estuarine habitats below.

Habitat	Animals	Plants
Mangrove forest		
Dunes		
Salt marsh		
Mud flat		

1. List the limiting factors for animals to survive in an estuarine habitat.

_____

_____

2. List the limiting factors for plants to survive in an estuarine habitat.

_____

_____

3. How are sand dunes different from mudflats?

_____

_____

_____

_____

_____

_____

_____

_____

Student Guide
Ocean Floor

Underneath the vast expanse of ocean water is the ocean floor. The ocean floor is nothing like the sandy beach you sometimes see at the edge of the sea. It has huge mountain ranges and underwater volcanoes, deep trenches and endless flat stretches. These are just a few examples of the fantastic formations you'll see on the ocean floor.

Lesson Objectives

- Identify and describe the major features of the ocean floor (for example, the continental shelf, continental slope, continental rise, abyssal plains, trenches, ridges, seamounts, and reefs).

PREPARE

Approximate lesson time is 60 minutes.

Advance Preparation

- Mix salt, flour, vegetable oil, and 240 mL (1 cup) water to make salt dough. Adding flour will make the dough soft. Adding salt will make the dough more granulated. Add water as needed, but do not make the dough too moist. Wrap the dough in plastic and then store it in the refrigerator. Let the dough sit overnight. The dough will be used to make the model of the ocean floor in the Ocean Floor Topography activity.

Materials

For the Student

Ocean Floor Topography
flour - 480 mL (2 cups)
marker
salt - 480 mL (2 cups)
shoebox, clear plastic - small
vegetable oil - 30 mL (2 tablespoons)
food coloring - blue
plastic wrap
ruler, metric
tape - masking
water

Keywords and Pronunciations

abyssal (uh-BIH-suhl)

abyssal plain: A vast deep-sea plain that lies beyond the continental shelf. The abyssal plain seems flat, dark, and lifeless, but it is actually full of life.

atoll (A-tahl): A circular island or group of islands formed around the rim of a submerged volcano.

bathymetric (ba-thih-MEH-trihk)

bathymetry (buh-THIH-muh-tree): The study of the formations of the ocean floor. Using bathymetry, you can plot a course though the ocean. A bathymetric map shows the rise and fall of the ocean floor.

continental rise: An accumulation of sediment at the foot of the continental slope. The continental rise is usually a place of much gravel and silt near the bottom of the sea.

continental shelf: The shallow part of the ocean floor, which lies at the edge of the continents. The continental shelf begins at the edge of the land and extends to the continental slope.

continental slope: The edge of the continental shelf that drops deeply down to the ocean floor. The continental slope connects the continental shelf to the bottom of the ocean.

guyot (GEE-oh): An underwater mountain whose top has been worn flat by the motion of ocean water. You can recognize a guyot by its flat top.

mid-ocean ridge: A range of mountains under the sea. The Mid-Atlantic Ridge is a mid-ocean ridge that runs the entire length of the Atlantic Ocean.

oceanic (oh-shee-A-nihk)

oceanographer (oh-shuh-NAH-gruh-fuhr)

reef: A ridge in the ocean made of coral, rock, or sand. The Great Barrier Reef in Australia is home to a variety of living things.

sonar (SOH-nahr): A device that helps find underwater objects by reflecting short bursts of sounds. A research vessel uses sonar to detect the topography of the ocean floor.

topography (tuh-PAH-gruh-fee)

LEARN

Activity 1: The Land Under the Sea *(Online)*

Activity 2: Ocean Floor Topography *(Online)*

If you took away all that ocean water, you'd be surprised to find that the ocean floor looks a lot like what you see on dry land. In other words, the topography is similar. Learn more by building a model of steep seamounts, old volcanoes, mountainous ridges, deep slopes, and more.

Safety

As always, you may wish to preview any websites before your student views them.

ASSESS

Lesson Assessment: Ocean Floor *(Online)*

You will complete an online assessment covering the main objectives of this lesson. Your assessment will be scored by the computer.

Name _____   Date _____

Ocean Floor

Ocean Floor Topography

Here's a word to impress your friends: BATHYMETRY. *Bathymetry* is the study of the topography of the ocean floor. A person using bathymetry would measure the heights and depths of the mountains, volcanoes, ridges, and canyons lying on the ocean floor.

Below is some *bathymetric* data taken from an area of the ocean that runs from Nova Scotia, Canada, to Cape Hatteras, North Carolina, USA. You'll make a model of the ocean floor in this part of the world that will be *to scale*. That means that although your model will be very small, if it were enlarged, the features in your model would be similar in size to those same features in this part of the ocean.

The container for your model is about 10 cm deep. You may want to mark your box every 1 cm from top to bottom. Read the chart carefully to figure out how deep to make the ocean floor features in your container.

Ocean Floor Feature	Actual Depth	Shoebox Depth
Continental shelf	200 m	Shallow slope: 5 cm from the top, covering about ¼ of your box
Continental slope	200 m – 4000 m	Steep slope ending 8 cm from the top. (Don't forget the continental rise!)
Abyssal plain	4000 – 5000 m	Flat: 8 – 10 cm from the top

Things to consider:

- The abyssal plain is covered with a layer of ooze from the remains of marine organisms.
- A guyot in your model would reach to about 2 cm from the top.
- An ocean trench is formed when oceanic crust moves beneath a continental plate or another oceanic plate.

1. Start your model with the short side of the box representing the coast.

2. Create the base of your ocean floor using the chart.

3. Add features to your ocean floor such as flat-topped guyots, hollowed-out atolls, or a mid-ocean range.

4. Let your model dry for about an hour.

5. Cover your model gently with plastic wrap.

6. Make very light blue water with water and just a few drops of blue food coloring.

7. Fill your model, making sure that the right landforms are underwater!

8. Hide your model, and then teach a partner about features of the ocean floor. Share your model, then have your partner identify the features you put in it. If your partner can identify all of them, you can give your partner a little prize.

Think about it:

Which varies more, the depth of the continental rise or the width of the continental shelf?

Student Guide

Life Zones of the Ocean

Imagine sinking down slowly to the bottom of the ocean. The temperature and density of the water change as you go down. The light gets dimmer, too, and you begin to see changes in the organisms at different depths. Explore these ocean zones and some of the things that live there, including fish that glow in the dark and worms that hang out around a very unusual ocean feature—the hydrothermal vent.

Lesson Objectives

- Identify the different zones within the ocean and describe the organisms that live there.
- Describe the characteristics of a hydrothermal vent.
- Recognize that many varieties of organisms live in a vent community.

PREPARE

Approximate lesson time is 60 minutes.

Materials

For the Student

Make a Hydrothermal Vent
bottle, plastic - small
bowl - large glass
food coloring
string
water - cold
water - hot

Optional

household item - dust, sand, mud, algae
household item - raisins, rice, leaves
household item - toothpick
salt - 36 grams
sponge
balance
glass, drinking
glue
paper towels
peanut butter
water - 1 Liter

Keywords and Pronunciations

abyssal (uh-BIH-suhl)

Archaebacteria (ahr-kee-bak-TIHR-ee-uh)

bioluminescent (biy-oh-loo-muh-NEH-snt)

diatom (DIY-uh-tahm)

hydrothermal vent: Deep-sea hot springs along ocean ridges. The deep-sea vessel Alvin took pictures of the smoky hydrothermal vent.

nekton: Organisms that swim freely in the ocean, including bony fish, sharks, rays, squid, octopuses, dolphins, porpoises, and whales. In the waters of Cape Cod, mackerel are the most common nektons.

neritic (nuh-RIH-tihk)

oceanic (oh-shee-A-nihk)

photosynthesis (foh-toh-SINT-thuh-suhs): The process by which plant cells convert light energy from the sun into chemical energy. During photosynthesis, plants use the sun´s energy to make glucose out of carbon dioxide and water, releasing oxygen. Photosynthesis means "putting together with light."

phytoplankton (fiy-toh-PLANGK-tuhn): Plant-like plankton that use photosynthesis to make their own food. Diatoms and other algae are common phytoplanktons.

plankton: Organisms that are usually microscopic and float in water and cannot move by themselves. The upper reaches of the neritic zone are loaded with plankton.

zooplankton (zoh-uh-PLANGK-tuhn): Animal-like plankton that eat other organisms. Many zooplankton are protists—one-celled organisms that eat phytoplankton and other zooplankton.

LEARN

Activity 1: Life in the Sea *(Online)*

Visit several zones of the ocean and learn about the fascinating creatures that live there. Discover strange "smoking chimneys" deep in the ocean.

Activity 2: Around a Hydrothermal Vent *(Online)*

Great, tall towers of hot water and black smoke are spewing around all over the ocean bottom. Does this seem strange? Discover what causes hydrothermal vents. Review the unique kinds of marine life found around these vents.

ASSESS

Lesson Assessment: Life Zones of the Ocean *(Offline)*

You will complete an offline assessment covering the main objectives of this lesson. Your learning coach will score this assessment.

LEARN

Activity 3: Optional: Marine Snow *(Offline)*

Settled in the deepest parts of the ocean floor are particles that have drifted down from the ocean above. These particles are called marine snow. Organic matter and particles such as uneaten phytoplankton and bacteria stick together. Sometimes they stick together on their own. Other times they're held together by sticky substances, such as mucus, that are present on the matter themselves.

Marine snow takes on many shapes and sizes and falls through the ocean at an average rate of 50 to 100 meters (164 to 328 feet) a day. Marine snow may look like round pellets, webs of plankton, or spiraling bits of matter as it comes to rest on the ocean floor. The speed at which it falls depends on its shape and density.

Investigate the speeds of falling marine snow by making "snowflakes" similar to those in the ocean.

Procedure:

1. Make sea water in a large glass. Do this by mixing 1 liter of water and 36 grams of salt.

2. Choose five of the items from the list and drop them into the water. Watch how they fall. Do they sink or float?

3. Try sticking some of the other items together. Will they stick naturally? Will you need glue to attach them? If so, use the glue.

4. Drop your marine snowflake into the sea water. Do all the objects sink? Do they separate in water? Try different materials to make marine snowflakes.

The density of water plays a role in how fast marine snow sinks through the ocean. Additionally, bacteria and zooplankton eat the snow, and some is broken up into particles too light to sink. Did you notice this in any of your "snowflakes"?

Choices for Marine Snow Items

Dust

Sand

Mud

Algae

Raisins

Rice

Nuts

Leaves

Paper towels

Sponge

Toothpick

Peanut butter

Safety

This lesson involves eating or working with food. Check with your doctor, if necessary, to find out whether your student will have any allergic reaction to the food.

Name _____   Date _____

Life Zones of the Ocean
Make a Hydrothermal Vent

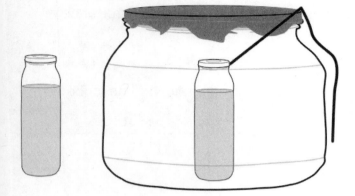

Procedure

1. Fill the large container with very cold water.

2. Tie one end of the string around the neck of the small bottle.

3. Fill the small bottle with hot water and add a few drops of food coloring. Do not put a top on the bottle.

4. Carefully lower the small bottle into the glass container keeping the bottle upright. Let it rest on the bottom.

Questions

1. What happened after you lowered the bottle into the glass? How did this affect the cold water in the container?

    _____

    _____

2. Black smokers are a type of hydrothermal vent. What causes the black, solid tube and smoke to rise from these vents?

    _____

    _____

3. Why are organisms that live near underwater vents so unique and interesting to scientists?

    _____

    _____

Student Guide
Ocean Resources

When talking about ocean treasures, many people dream of gold and jewels in a sunken pirate ship. But the ocean provides far more valuable gifts than these. Discover the importance of ocean resources such as fish, fuels, and minerals.

Lesson Objectives

- Identify some ocean resources, such as fisheries, oil, and minerals, and describe how they are harvested.

PREPARE

Approximate lesson time is 60 minutes.

Advance Preparation

- Your student will conduct research about ocean resources such as fisheries, oil, and minerals and then describe how they are harvested. You may wish to provide resources ahead of time or plan a trip to the library for your student to complete the research.

Materials

For the Student

Ocean Treasures

Keywords and Pronunciations

aquaculture: The controlled raising of living things in water to provide food. Growing algae for food has long been a kind of aquaculture in Japan.

mariculture: The aquaculture of sea creatures. Mussels and oysters are often raised using mariculture practices.

resource: A natural supply of something that people can use. Manganese nodules on the ocean floor are one of the sea's many natural resources.

LEARN

Activity 1: The Bounty of the Sea *(Online)*

The sea provides us with an amazing amount of resources. If we use them wisely, we can benefit from them for a long time. If not, we may lose these resources forever.

Activity 2: Ocean Treasures *(Offline)*

The gifts of the sea vary among the oceans on Earth. Research and compare the resources provided by the Atlantic, Pacific, Indian, and Arctic Oceans.

ASSESS

Lesson Assessment: Ocean Resources *(Offline)*

You will complete an offline assessment covering the main objectives of this lesson. Your learning coach will score this assessment.

94

Name _____   Date _____

Ocean Resources

Ocean Treasures

As you have read, valuable ocean resources are in danger of being limited or even used up. This might be hard to imagine, given that most of the Earth is covered with oceans!

Use the chart below to find out and compare what resources are available in Earth's four oceans. For each category in the first three columns, list at least three ocean resources found in that ocean. In the last column, describe how one of the resources is harvested. Then, write a one-paragraph summary for each ocean describing the valuable resources it provides for us.

You may use any resources you have available to complete your research. These may include books, encyclopedias, or online encyclopedias. Perhaps you know an oceanographer or marine fisher who can give you a first-hand look at working with ocean resources. Copy this table into your notebook, then fill in the information. Search the websites listed in the lesson resource section to complete the table.

Ocean	Fish resources	Mineral resources	Fuel resources	Resource / How Harvested
Atlantic Ocean				
Pacific Ocean				
Arctic Ocean				
Indian Ocean				

Student Guide

The World's Oceans: Unit Review and Assessment

Review and test what you've learned about ocean water, ocean life, ocean resources, and conservation.

Lesson Objectives

- Define *salinity*, and explain how density changes with salinity and temperature.
- Describe characteristics of ocean habitats and explain how various organisms are adapted to living in them.
- Describe major features of the ocean floor, such as abyssal plains, trenches, ridges, seamounts, and reefs.
- Describe the movements of both the ocean's surface currents and its deep-water currents.
- Explain how ocean waves form, identify their properties—such as wave height, wavelength, crest, and trough—and describe their motion.
- Explain how the gravitational pull of the sun and moon causes daily high and low tides.
- Explain that the continental margin extends into the ocean and has three regions: the continental shelf, the continental slope, and the continental rise.
- Explain that the monthly cycle of spring tides and neap tides occurs because the Earth, sun, and moon change their relative positions.
- Explain that water covers approximately three quarters of the Earth's surface and that all the oceans are connected, allowing their water to circulate.
- Identify some ocean resources, such as fish, oil, and minerals, and describe how they are harvested.

PREPARE

Approximate lesson time is 60 minutes.

Materials

For the Student

> Unit Review, Part 2
> Question Review Table

LEARN

Activity 1: The World's Ocean's Unit Review *(Online)*

The world's oceans provide a wealth of information, beauty, and resources for our lives. Review what you've learned about the fascinating environment beyond the beach.

Print the Unit Review, Part 2 worksheet, then select the arrow to begin the Unit Review online.

ASSESS

Unit Assessment: The World's Oceans (*Offline*)

You will complete an offline assessment covering the main objectives of this unit. Your learning coach will score this assessment.

LEARN

Activity 2: Optional: Unit Assessment Review Table (*Online*)

If you earned a score of **less than 80%** on the Unit Assessment, complete the activity.

If you earned a score of **80% or greater**, you may skip this activity.

Let's prepare to retake the Unit Assessment:

- Print the Question Review Table.
- Identify the questions that you answered incorrectly.
- Complete the appropriate review activities listed in the table.

Note: This Unit Assessment Review TablesLearning Coach Video will guide you through the process of using the Unit Assessment Review Tables. You may skip this video if you've already viewed it in another unit or course. As always, check in with your student's teacher if you have any questions.

Name _____ Date _____

The World's Oceans: Unit Review and Assessment
Unit Review, Part 2

1. Review the organisms and environment at the edge of the sea from the lesson Life at the Edge of the Ocean. Write a five-sentence postcard to a friend or family member describing this environment. Choose to write about a tide pool, estuary, or mangrove forest. Draw a picture on your postcard to match what you write.

2. Review the lesson Ocean Resources. Find out how each resource listed below is retrieved from the ocean, and describe some ways we are trying to conserve these resources.

Resource	Example	How Retrieved	Conservation
Food			
Minerals			

Name _____   Date _____

The World's Oceans: Unit Review and Assessment

Question Review Table

Before you retake the Unit Assessment, use the table to figure out which activities you should review.

Circle the numbers of the questions that you missed on the Unit Assessment. Review the activities that correspond with these questions.

Question	Lesson	Review Activity
1, 2	3: Ocean Waves	Explore: The Ocean Wave Making Waves
3, 4, 5, 6	6: Ocean Floor	Explore: The Land Under the Sea Ocean Floor Topography
7, 8, 9	1: Ocean Water	Explore: Ocean Water Ocean Layers Temperature and Density Experiments
10, 11	1: Ocean Water	Explore: Ocean Water
12, 13	2: Ocean Currents	Explore: Two Types of Currents Causes of Currents
14	4: Ocean Tides	Explore: The Rise and Fall of the Tides Earth, Sun, Moon…and Tides?
15	4: Ocean Tides	Explore: The Rise and Fall of the Tides Earth, Sun, Moon…and Tides?
16	5: Life at the Edge of the Ocean	Explore: Life Where Saltwater Meets Land An Estuary Habitat
17	5: Life at the Edge of the Ocean	Explore: Life Where Saltwater Meets Land

Question	Lesson	Review Activity
18, 19	7: Life Zones of the Ocean	Explore: Life in the Sea
20	8: Ocean Research	Explore: Into the Deep
		Research Tool Review
		Your Ocean Toolbox
21, 22, 23	9: Ocean Resources	Explore: The Bounty of the Sea
		Ocean Treasures

Student Guide
The Atmosphere

- Interpret weather maps to forecast the weather.
- Distinguish between *weather* and *climate* and describe some factors that influence climate (such as latitude, altitude, and ocean currents).
- Describe possible causes of climate changes (such as El Nino and the Greenhouse Effect) and their potential effects on climate.
- Describe some properties of the atmosphere, such as its composition, temperature, and pressure
- Identify the five layers of the atmosphere: troposphere, stratosphere, mesosphere, thermosphere, and exosphere.
- Explain that the uneven heating of the Earth's surface transfers heat through convection currents in the atmosphere.
- Define *humidity* as the amount of water vapor in the air and the *dew point* as the temperature at which the air cannot hold any more water vapor.
- Explain how clouds form and identify common weather patterns associated with different types of clouds.
- Identify types of precipitation (rain, snow, sleet, hail) and explain how each is formed.
- Identify sources of air pollution.
- Identify the three main types of storms and describe the air movements that produce them.
- Identify the four types of fronts (cold, warm, stationary, and occluded) and describe how air masses interact.

Breathe in the air around you and smell how sweet it is. Step out into the warm sun and look up at the clouds. It is our atmosphere that gives us the ability to live on Earth. But what is the stuff of the sky? Where did it come from? What is it made of? Understanding the atmosphere means understanding the blanket of air above Earth.

Lesson Objectives

- Compare the layers of the atmosphere according to properties such as temperature and composition.
- Explain how air density is related to both temperature and pressure.

PREPARE

Approximate lesson time is 60 minutes.

Advance Preparation

- The lamp must provide sufficient heat for the experiment. If you can, find the type of blub, of any wattage, that will provide the heat. If you cannot find one bulb that will heat efficiently, try arranging a number of blubs until the experiment works. Be creative in finding a heat source that does the job.

Materials

For the Student

> Atmospheric Temperatures
> Air Bag
> bags, paper grocery (2)
> household item - block of wood or soup can
> household item - needle
> meter stick
> lamp - incandescent
> scissors, round-end safety
> string
> tape - masking

Optional

> Air Pressure and Wind
> barometer
> stick
> compass

Keywords and Pronunciations

air pressure: The weight of air in the atmosphere pressing down on Earth. At sea level, the air pressure is 14 pounds per square inch.

altitude: The height of an object. The altitude of the weather balloon was 45,000 feet.

atmosphere: Air that surrounds Earth and other planets. The atmosphere is a blanket of gases.

density: How tightly the matter of an object is packed together. The density of lead is greater than the density of water.

exosphere (EK-soh-sfeer): The top layer of the Earth´s atmosphere. Beyond the exosphere is true outer space.

mesosphere (MEZ-uh-sfeer): A layer of the Earth´s atmosphere between the stratosphere and thermosphere, which lies between 30 and 50 miles above the Earth. The mesosphere is above the ozone layer, but it has little or no ozone itself.

ozone (OH-zohn): A form of oxygen present in a small layer in the Earth´s atmosphere, between 12 and 30 miles above the Earth. The ozone layer protects us from deadly ultraviolet rays from the sun.

photosynthesis (foh-toh-SINT-thuh-suhs): The process by which plant cells convert light energy from the sun into chemical energy. During photosynthesis, plants use the sun´s energy to make glucose out of carbon dioxide and water, releasing oxygen. Photosynthesis means "putting together with light."

stratosphere: A layer of the atmosphere about 7 to 30 miles above the Earth´s surface. Airplanes fly in the stratosphere because there are not many storms or clouds in this layer.

thermosphere: A layer of the Earth's atmosphere about 50 to 400 miles above the Earth's surface. Sunlight strikes the thermosphere directly and makes it very hot.

troposphere (TROH-puh-sfihr): The layer of the atmosphere closest to the Earth. Almost all of Earth's weather occurs in the troposphere.

LEARN

Activity 1: Earth's Atmosphere *(Online)*

What is the stuff of the sky? Where did it come from? What is it made of? Understanding the atmosphere means understanding the blanket of air over Earth. Explore atmospheric gases and layers, temperature and pressure. Discover the explosive way our atmosphere came into being.

Activity 2: Up Here in the Atmosphere *(Offline)*

The average temperatures of the atmosphere change a lot from layer to layer. Study and interpret a graph that shows these temperature differences.

Activity 3: Air Bag *(Online)*

Explore one of the basic causes of wind on Earth. Perform an experiment to see how heat affects air. This simple experiment shows an important scientific principle—hot air rises, creating a vacuum below it. Other air rushes to take its place. This is the basis for wind and weather.

ASSESS

Lesson Assessment: The Atmosphere *(Online)*

You will complete an online assessment covering the main objectives of this lesson. Your assessment will be scored by the computer.

LEARN

Activity 4: Optional: Investigate Air Pressure and Wind *(Offline)*

This activity is OPTIONAL. It's provided for enrichment or extra practice, but not required for completion of this lesson. You may skip this activity.

Could you predict the weather better than a meteorologist? Meteorologists use scientific equipment to gather data about air pressure, wind, and weather. With a few simple tools, you can make observations that may help you predict a change in weather, too.

Name _____   Date _____

The Atmosphere
Atmospheric Temperatures

Like the layers of the ocean, the layers in the Earth's atmosphere differ in certain ways. But the differences in the layers of the atmosphere have to do mostly with pressure and temperature. As you increase in altitude (height above sea level), pressure and temperature change in interesting ways. Pressure keeps decreasing, but the temperature rises and falls.

This graph displays temperature and pressure data for each layer in the atmosphere. But the graph is not complete. Read the descriptions of each layer, then follow the directions to complete the graph.

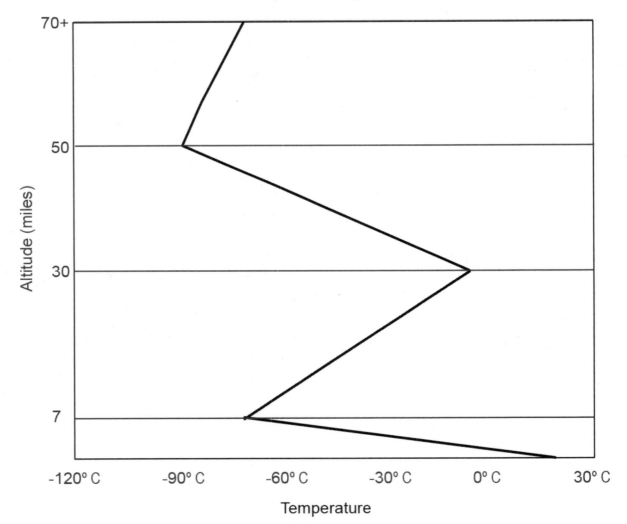

Troposphere:

The troposphere is the lowest layer of the atmosphere, and reaches from 0 to 7 miles. All weather happens in the troposphere. Air pressure is greatest here, too. A space shuttle traveling through the atmosphere would begin its journey in the troposphere.

Label the region of the troposphere on the graph and draw weather occurring there.

Thermosphere:

Lying between 50 miles and 400 miles, the thermosphere leads into the emptiness of space. The air here is very thin.

Label the region of the thermosphere on the graph. Notice the rising temperatures.

Stratosphere:

A layer about 7 miles to 30 miles above Earth, the stratosphere is interesting because it contains a layer of ozone. Ozone filters out radiation from the sun that is harmful to organisms on Earth. Ozone keeps temperatures in the stratosphere nearly the same for about 6 miles, then they rise.

Label the region of the stratosphere on the graph. Where temperatures in this layer are highest, label a layer of ozone. Jets fly in the lower region of the stratosphere. Draw a jet flying there.

Mesosphere:

Rising temperatures in the stratosphere drop again in the layer above it, the mesosphere. With no ozone and little atmospheric pressure, the mesosphere has the coldest temperatures in the atmosphere, from 0 to −80°C. Still, meteors from space begin to burn up when they travel through the mesosphere.

Label the region of the mesosphere on the graph. Draw a few bright meteors traveling through this region.

Think About It:

Watch a clock for two minutes. This is how long it takes for a space shuttle to reach the thermosphere from Earth. Eight minutes more and the shuttle will leave the thermosphere for the exosphere and space beyond.

Layer	Distance Above Earth	Time to Reach
Troposphere	0 miles	0 seconds
Stratosphere	10 miles	30 seconds
Mesosphere	30 miles	75 seconds
Thermosphere	50 miles	2 minutes

1. How long would it take for the shuttle to travel through half of the distance to the thermosphere?

   _____

2. How long would it take the shuttle to travel through three quarters of the distance to the thermosphere?

   _____

Name _____   Date _____

The Atmosphere
Air Bag

Atmospheric layers differ in their density. Air can heat up or cool down, and thus can become denser and less dense. You can observe some of the properties of air density with this simple investigation.

Materials:

meter stick
needle
tape
soup can
scissors
string
2 paper grocery bags
incandescent lamp

Procedure

1. Open the grocery bags and poke a hole in the center of each bag's bottom.

2. Cut two strings of equal length.

3. Tie a knot at the end of each string.

4. Have an adult help you use a needle to thread the string through the inside of the bag. The long end of the string should poke through the bottom of the bag.

5. Tie the loose ends one on each side 3 cm from the ends of the meter stick. The opening of the bag should be facing down, as shown.

6. Tape the soup can on the corner of a table so the stick can move freely without obstructions. Make sure the meter stick is perfectly balanced on the can.

7. Place the lamp under one of the bags, but not touching the bag. Turn it on.

8. Watch for about 2–3 minutes to see what happens.

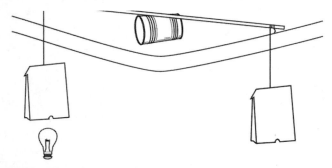

What happens?

The lamp produces heat and warms up the air in the bag. As the air warms up, it replaces the cold, denser air in the bag. Then the bag above the lamp will rise. This process demonstrates that warm air is less dense than cold air. Since cold air is denser than warm air, the cold air will fall as the warm air rises up.

What does this have to do with the atmosphere?

The air in your room is atmospheric air. Air surrounding the whole world behaves no differently than the air in your bag. When the sun heats up the air, it becomes less dense and rises. As it rises, other air has to come in and take its place. The result is wind, and wind is the result of different air densities all over the world.

Air is a gas, which is a form of matter. As you can see in this demonstration, air has mass. The higher you go in the atmosphere, the less air is present. Since there is less air pushing down from above, air pressure is less as height increases.

Close to Earth, in the troposphere, the movement of cold, denser air and warm, less dense air has an effect on the weather we experience. You will study more about these effects in the next lesson.

Name _____   Date _____

The Atmosphere
Air Pressure and Wind

Do you remember in which layer of the atmosphere weather occurs? The troposphere is the layer where we experience Earth's weather. Farmers, mariners, and other people whose jobs require them to work outside may be very concerned about the weather. They pay attention to air pressure, wind direction, and clues to changes in the weather.

A change in air pressure almost always means there will be a change in the weather. Make some observations to see if wind direction changes on days when there is a change in air pressure.

Materials

barometer
stick
string
compass

Procedure

1. Find a nearby outdoor spot where you can measure pressure and wind direction twice a day—in the morning and in the evening.

2. Use the barometer to measure the pressure. Barometers measure pressure in millibars, or millimeters of mercury. Changes in air pressure push the mercury up or down in the barometer. Do your best to record this measurement on the chart.

3. Tie the string to the stick. Push the stick in the ground, string end up.

4. Walk around the stick until the string is blowing toward you.

5. Move the compass so the needle points north.

6. Look at the compass and the string and estimate from which direction the wind is blowing. Record this measurement in the chart.

7. Repeat steps 2–7 twice a day for one week at about the same time every day.

Date	Time	Pressure	Wind Direction

Analysis

1. Describe how the barometric pressure changed each day.

   _____

   _____

   _____

2. Describe how the wind direction changed each day.

   _____

   _____

   _____

3. Did the wind direction change more on days when air pressure was changing or when air pressure stayed the same?

   _____

   _____

   _____

Conclusion

Write a short paragraph explaining what you learned about the relationship between pressure, pressure change, and wind direction. How might you use this information?

_____

_____

_____

_____

_____

_____

_____

_____

Student Guide
Why the Wind Blows

When the sun strikes the Earth, the Earth heats up unevenly. There is more heat in one place than in another. This difference in temperature is one cause of wind. *Wind* is the way in which heat gets distributed throughout the atmosphere.

Lesson Objectives

- Describe the circulation of air and the transfer of heat between the equator and the poles.
- Explain how winds occur.
- Explain that air moves from regions of high density to regions of low density.

PREPARE

Approximate lesson time is 60 minutes.

Materials

For the Student

> Demonstrating the Coriolis Effect
> household item - brass fastener
> posterboard or tagboard - different colors (2)
> ruler, metric
> scissors, round-end safety
> string
> Understanding Earth's Winds

Keywords and Pronunciations

convection current: Circulating air caused when warm air rises and cool air sinks. Convection currents occur throughout the world.

Coriolis Effect: the resulting movement of air or water caused by the Earth´s rotation

LEARN

Activity 1: Atmosphere and Weather *(Online)*

Activity 2: The Coriolis Effect *(Offline)*

Demonstrate the Coriolis Effect that is responsible for the wind patterns all over Earth.

Activity 3: Understanding Earth's Winds *(Offline)*

Review the different winds and geographical features related to circulation of air around Earth as winds.

ASSESS

Lesson Assessment: Why the Wind Blows *(Offline)*

You will complete an offline assessment covering the main objectives of this lesson. Your learning coach will score this assessment.

Name _____   Date _____

Why the Wind Blows
Demonstrating the Coriolis Effect

What happens when the rotating Earth meets moving air? Air that would simply blow from north to south gets deflected, or bent away into other paths. The Coriolis Effect is the term used to describe these air movements. The effect may be hard to understand from our viewpoint on the ground, but it is very easy to demonstrate.

Materials:

poster board 22" x 28", 2 pieces, different colors
scissors
pen
ruler
brass fastener

Procedure:

1. Cut a strip 1 inch wide and 22 inches long from one of the pieces of poster board. Keep this piece of poster board for step 3.

2. Using the same piece of poster board, draw the largest circle possible.

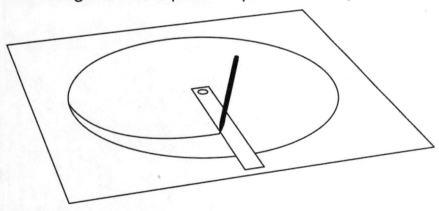

3. Cut out the circle.

4. Put the circle over the other piece of poster board.

5. Use the brass fastener to attach the strip through the center of the circle so the circle turns freely.

6. Have a partner turn the circle slowly in either direction.

7. Use the pen to draw a straight line all the way down one edge of the strip.

8. Remove the strip and observe your line.

What happens to the line?

_____

_____

_____

Imagine the line is moving air and the circle is Earth. As the "Earth" rotated, the "air" was deflected from its straight path into a curved path. You've just seen the Coriolis Effect!

Name _____   Date _____

Why the Wind Blows
Understanding Earth's Winds

Understanding wind might be easier with a different view of Earth. Down here on the ground, we can do little more than feel the wind, see its effects, and tell in which direction it is blowing.

1. Study the map of the Earth. How would the wind blow if the Earth did not rotate?

_____

_____

2. Tell how you learned in the last lesson that warm air is less dense than cold air.

_____

_____

In this imaginary large convection cell, you'd find warm air constantly rising at the equator and cold air constantly sinking as it cools on its way back to the poles.

3. You know that the Earth rotates. What have you learned about the effect of a rotating Earth on a path of moving air?

_____

_____

4. What is the name of this effect?

_____

This effect creates small convection cells of air. And even in these small convection cells, less dense warm air rises and denser cold air sinks.

So, even if the rotation of the Earth complicates the direction the wind blows, you can still see regular patterns of wind all over Earth. The winds even have names.

5. Use the map to review the movement of air and the winds on Earth. You may use the Explore activity to help you.

- Label the equator and the North and South Poles.
- Locate and label a convection cell.
- Draw arrows in the cell to show how air moves inside it. Label warm air and cold air in the cell.
- Draw arrows to show the following winds and label each one.

In the Northern Hemisphere:

Polar Easterlies
Westerlies
Trade Winds

In the Southern Hemisphere:

Polar Easterlies
Westerlies
Trade Winds

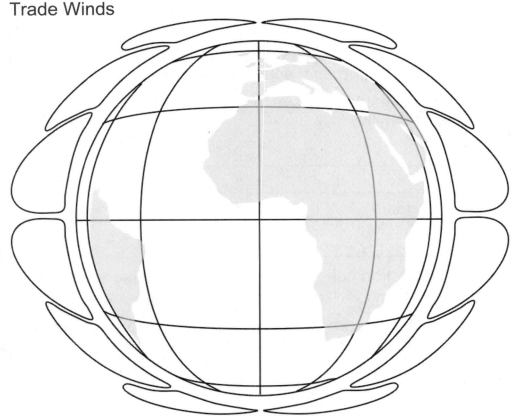

Student Guide
Humidity, Dew, and Frost

Many things are happening in our atmosphere. Two important events are the evaporation and condensation of water in the air. The terms *humidity* and *dew point* describe characteristics of water in the air. They tell at what point water vapor will condense into a liquid or solid. Learn about relative humidity, and measure it using a tool called a *psychrometer*.

Lesson Objectives

- Determine relative humidity.
- Define *humidity* as the amount of water vapor in the air and the *dew point* as the temperature at which water vapor in the air will condense.
- Describe how dew and frost form.

PREPARE

Approximate lesson time is 60 minutes.

Advance Preparation

- The Find Your Relative Humidity activity works best with two thermometers. You may want to try to locate a second one.

Materials

For the Student

> Find Your Relative Humidity
> gauze
> household item - electric fan (If needed, use an extension cord to plug the fan in.)
> rubber band
> thermometer, Celsius/Fahrenheit
> tape - masking
> water

Keywords and Pronunciations

dew: Drops of water that condense from the air onto cool surfaces during the night. In the early morning, drops of dew on plants can sparkle like stars.

frost: The depositing of water vapor from the air onto a surface cooler than 32 degrees F, creating solid ice crystals.

humidity: The amount of water vapor in the air. When the humidity is high, a hot day can feel even hotter.

psychrometer (siy-KRAH-muh-tuhr): A tool used to measure relative humidity by comparing the temperature readings on a dry-bulb and wet-bulb thermometer. Use a psychrometer to learn how much water is in the air.

LEARN

Activity 1: Water in the Air *(Online)*

In this lesson you will learn about water vapor in the air and its remarkable effects on your life. It is the source of clouds, dew, and precipitation such as rain and snow. Humidity is the amount of water in the air, so let's begin there.

Activity 2: Find Your Relative Humidity *(Offline)*

You do not necessarily need a psychrometer to tell that it is humid out. A sweaty body can easily give you a clue. For example, if you play outside on a cool day with low humidity, you'll find that you stay cool and dry. On a cool day with high humidity, you may find that you sweat more than normal and can't cool off as easily. This is because there is much more moisture in the air, and the sweat from your body cannot evaporate as quickly. On a day with high humidity, such as 90 percent, and a high temperature, very little water vapor can enter the atmosphere. Sweat will stay on your skin; it will not evaporate. You can't cool off because heat is not drawn away from your body, so you feel hot and sticky.

People generally feel uncomfortable when the temperature and humidity are unusually high. Knowing the humidity can help you predict how comfortable or uncomfortable you will be during the day. This activity will show you how to find the relative humidity in your area.

ASSESS

Lesson Assessment: Humidity, Dew, and Frost *(Offline)*

You will complete an offline assessment covering the main objectives of this lesson. Your learning coach will score this assessment.

LEARN

Activity 3: Optional: The Father of Cool: Willis Haviland Carrier *(Online)*

This activity is OPTIONAL. It's provided for enrichment or extra practice, but not required for completion of this lesson. You may skip this activity.

On a sweltering hot summer day, you'll want to thank Willis Haviland Carrier for his "cool" invention. Learn about Carrier's Apparatus for Treating Air, otherwise known as the air conditioner.

Activity 4: Optional: ZlugQuest Measurement *(Online)*

Name _____   Date _____

Humidity, Dew, and Frost
Find Your Relative Humidity

Weather reports always provide the relative humidity for the day. Relative humidity compares the actual amount of water vapor in the air with the greatest amount of water vapor the air can hold at that temperature. A wet-dry bulb psychrometer is a tool you can use to find relative humidity.

Materials

thermometer
tape
gauze
electric fan (If needed, use an extension cord to plug the fan in.)
rubber band
water

1. Find a place outside with a flat surface, such as a step or table.

2. Tape the thermometer to the surface with the numbers facing up. The end of the thermometer should extend about 2.5 cm over the edge of the surface.

3. Blow the fan on the thermometer until the temperature stops falling.

4. Write down the temperature below.

5. Quickly cover the thermometer with the wet gauze. Secure it with the rubber band.

6. Repeat steps 2 and 3.

7. Subtract the temperature of the wet thermometer from the temperature of the dry one.

8. Look at the humidity table. Find the dry thermometer temperature on the left and follow it to the right. Find the difference between the two thermometers at the top and follow it down. Where the row and column meet is a number. That number is the relative humidity and is expressed as a percentage.

9. Compare your measurement to today's weather report.

Dry Bulb Temperature:_____

Wet Bulb Temperature:_____

SUBTRACT:_____

NOTE: The illustration shows an example of a wet thermometer and an example of a dry thermometer, but you will use the same thermometer for both trials.

Difference Between Dry and Wet Bulb (°C)

Dry Bulb Reading (°C)	1	2	3	4	5	6	7	8	9	10	12	14	16	18	20
2	84	68	52	37	22	8									
4	85	70	56	42	29	26	3								
6	86	73	60	47	34	22	11								
8	87	75	63	51	39	28	18	7							
10	88	76	65	54	44	33	23	14	4						
12	89	78	67	57	47	38	29	20	11	3					
14	89	79	69	60	51	42	33	25	17	9					
15	90	80	71	62	54	45	37	29	22	14					
18	91	81	73	64	56	48	41	33	26	19	6				
20	91	82	74	66	58	51	44	37	30	24	11				
22	91	83	75	68	60	53	46	40	34	27	16	5			
24	92	84	76	69	62	55	49	43	37	31	20	9			
26	92	85	77	70	64	57	51	45	39	34	23	14	4		
28	92	85	78	72	65	59	53	47	42	37	26	17	8		
30	93	86	79	73	67	61	55	49	44	39	29	20	12	4	
32	93	86	80	74	68	62	56	51	46	41	32	23	15	8	1
34	93	87	81	75	69	63	58	53	48	43	34	26	18	11	5
36	93	87	81	75	70	64	59	54	50	45	36	28	21	14	8
38	94	88	82	76	71	65	60	56	51	47	38	31	23	17	11
40	94	88	82	77	72	66	62	57	52	48	40	33	26	19	13
42	94	88	83	77	72	67	63	58	54	50	42	34	28	21	16
44	94	89	82	78	73	68	64	59	55	51	43	36	29	23	18

1. What is the relative humidity today?

_____

2. What does relative humidity compare?

_____

_____

_____

3. What is happening when the relative humidity of the air is 50%?

_____

_____

4. Would you be more comfortable playing in weather that is 15°C at 98% relative humidity or 21°C degrees at 20% relative humidity? Explain your answer.

_____

_____

_____

5. Explain why you get hotter and stickier in humid weather than in dry weather.

_____

_____

_____

6. When will the humidity be higher—when there is a small difference or a great difference between the temperatures of the two thermometers? Use the chart to help you find the answer.

_____

7. Do your observations match the weather report? Do they describe the way the humidity outside feels to you today?

_____

_____

_____

Student Guide
Clouds and Precipitation

Now that you know that water vapor is in the air, it's easy to understand how clouds and precipitation form. Condensation of water vapor is responsible for both! Discover what particles in the air around you are the beginnings of clouds. Learn to associate cloud types with weather conditions.

Lesson Objectives

- Explain how clouds form and identify common cloud types according to their height and appearance.
- Identify types of precipitation (rain, snow, sleet, hail) and explain how they form.

PREPARE

Approximate lesson time is 60 minutes.

Advance Preparation

- Complete the Out of the Air lab sheet from the Particles in Air up through the observations section 5 days before the lesson. Complete the Observations, Analysis, and Conclusion on the day of the lesson.
- Have your student complete the cloud observations from the Beyond White and Fluffy activity 5 days before the lesson.

Materials

For the Student

> Out of the Air
> marker
> petroleum jelly
> index cards - 3 x 5 (6)
> knife - plastic or butter
> plastic wrap
> tape - masking - masking
> Beyond White and Fluffy

Keywords and Pronunciations

cirrus (SIHR-uhs)

cirrus cloud (SIHR-uhs): A high, wispy cloud made of ice crystals. The cirrus clouds looked like feathers in the sky.

condensation nucleus: A small particle in the air that acts as a nucleus around which water droplets form. You might say that a condensation nucleus is the core, kernel, or seed of a raindrop.

cumulonimbus clouds (kyoo-myuh-luh-NIM-buhs): Tall, dark, puffy clouds that bring heavy storms. If you see cumulonimbus clouds, a storm may be coming your way.

cumulus (KYOO-myuh-luhs)

cumulus cloud (KYOO-myuh-luhs): A round, fluffy, white cloud that usually shows up in fair weather. The children imagined they saw the shapes of animals in the cumulus clouds.

nuclei (NOO-klee-iy)

precipitation: Rain, snow, sleet, or hail that falls to Earth. My friend left India because there was too much precipitation during the rainy season.

stratus cloud: A low, gray cloud that usually brings rain. As they watched the stratus clouds move, they suspected that rain might not be too far behind.

LEARN

Activity 1: Moisture in the Air *(Online)*

Activity 2: Particles in the Air *(Offline)*

Search for particles in the air that may serve as condensation nuclei for hovering clouds. Explore how certain types of particles affect air quality. Learn how particles affect precipitation in your neighborhood.

Activity 3: Beyond White and Fluffy *(Offline)*

Are you tired of finding images of bunnies and sailboats in cloud shapes? Try your hand at scientific observations of clouds. You'll see more than just a fluffy cloud bunny or a puffy cloud sailboat.

ASSESS

Lesson Assessment: Clouds and Precipitation *(Offline)*

You will complete an offline assessment covering the main objectives of this lesson. Your learning coach will score this assessment.

Name _____   Date _____

Clouds and Precipitation
Out of the Air

The story of every cloud has the same beginning—the condensation of water vapor around particles in the air. These particles are called condensation nuclei. They come from many things floating around in the air, such as soil, pollen, factory smoke, ash, salt from the ocean, dust from volcanoes, and even bacteria.

Once water molecules make it onto a nucleus, other water molecules will join in, bumping and clinging to form water droplets. Several water droplets may collect and form a cloud.

Find out what particles in your air are providing nuclei to water vapor.

Materials:

index cards – 6 (3 x 5)
plastic wrap
petroleum jelly (small container)
butter or plastic knife
masking tape
marker

Procedure:

1. Select four outdoor locations and an indoor location to place five index cards.

2. Number the back of each card from 1 to 6.

3. Tape Card 1 securely in its location. Write the location in the chart.

4. Spread a thin layer of petroleum jelly on the card. (Be careful with the indoor card!)

5. Leave the card in its location for five days.

6. Repeat steps 3 through 6 for Cards 2, 3, 4, and 5.

7. Spread petroleum jelly on Card 6, and then cover it with plastic wrap. Set it aside.

8. After five days, collect all the cards and compare them to the card covered with plastic wrap.

Scientist Notebook

Remember that a *variable* in an experiment is what is changed. Scientists change variables to see the effect of the change on something else. What is the variable in this investigation?

_____

_____

Now you will learn that there are two kinds of variables—dependent and independent.

The *independent variable* is what the experimenter changes in an experiment. In this case, the thing that is changed is the location of the cards.

The *dependent variable* is what happens because of the independent variable. In this activity, something will happen because you have placed the cards in different locations. The "thing" that will happen is the dependent variable. It "depends" on something else. Circle what you think the dependent variable is in this experiment. It helps to think of what best completes this sentence:

Placing the cards in different locations will have an effect on

_____

_____

- the amount of particles attached to the card
- the types of clouds present in the sky
- the amount of sunlight each card receives

A third part of investigating is the *control*. The control is what you compare all of your results to. To compare your results to something, you must not allow anything to happen to it or change it in any way. Which index card do you think you will compare your results to? The card wrapped in plastic will not attract any particles. When you are finished, you will compare your outdoor and indoor cards to this card. This card is the control.

Observations

Record the appearance of each card on the chart.

Card	Location	Any particles?	Description of particles (textile fibers, stone dust, wood)
1			
2			
3			
4			
5			
6	Covered in plastic		

Analysis

1. When compared to the control, which card showed the most particles? In what location was this card?

_____

2. When compared to the control, which card showed the least particles? In what location was this card?

_____

3. Think about the particles you see on your card. Could these be considered pollution? Is it safe to breathe in these particles if they are in the air?

_____

4. Could all the particles on your card be possible condensation nuclei for raindrops?

_____

Conclusion

In your Science Notebook, write a paragraph about what possible condensation nuclei you found from this investigation. Then describe how clouds form around condensation nuclei.

Name _____   Date _____

Clouds and Precipitation
Beyond White and Fluffy

The types of clouds you see are different in appearance, altitude, and the ways they form. Over the next five days, observe the clouds you see in the sky, if any. Make a note of their appearance and observe the weather for the day. When you have learned about how clouds form and cloud types in the lesson, you can then identify the clouds you saw.

Copy the chart below into your Science Notebook, leaving enough space to write your observations. Observe the clouds in the sky each day. Describe them according to the characteristics listed on the chart. Cloud observations generally include words such as thick, thin, well-defined edges, hair-like, towering, or in sheets, but you may use your own words as well.

Days	Today's Weather	Thickness	Edges	Shape	Draw a Sketch
Day 1					
Day 2					
Day 3					
Day 4					
Day 5					

When you complete the lesson, add a column to your chart labeled Cloud Type. Name the types of clouds you saw that day. Use cloud descriptions and the weather you described to help you identify them.

Student Guide
Severe Weather

You know the destruction hurricanes, tornadoes, and severe thunderstorms can bring. Maybe you've even been in these storms yourself. Strong winds can topple trees and destroy buildings. Air may seem harmless, since it's invisible and easy to breathe. But certain changes in air pressure can mean the difference between a calm, clear sky and one full of threatening clouds. Learn what conditions are ideal for the formation of these storms. Try tracking the path of some famous hurricanes.

Lesson Objectives

- Describe how thunderstorms, tornadoes, and hurricanes form.
- Describe the characteristics of thunderstorms, tornadoes, and hurricanes.

PREPARE

Approximate lesson time is 60 minutes.

Keywords and Pronunciations

cumulonimbus clouds (kyoo-myuh-luh-NIM-buhs): Tall, dark, puffy clouds that bring heavy storms. If you see cumulonimbus clouds, a storm may be coming your way.

cumulus cloud (KYOO-myuh-luhs): A round, fluffy, white cloud that usually shows up in fair weather. The children imagined they saw the shapes of animals in the cumulus clouds.

hurricane: A powerful storm that has strong winds rotating around a low-pressure center. The hurricane left a wide path of destruction as it passed over south Florida.

monsoon: A seasonal storm of rain and wind. The monsoon season in India has huge amounts of rain.

nuclei (NOO-klee-iy)

prime meridian (priym muh-RIH-dee-uhn): the imaginary vertical line, running north to south, from which longitude is measured; the prime meridian runs right through England

tornado: A powerful, narrow, funnel-shaped wind that creates a path of destruction where it touches down to Earth. The state of Oklahoma is often struck by tornadoes.

LEARN

Activity 1: Storms *(Online)*

Fierce winds, heavy rain, and crashing lightening—these are some of the exciting things you'll experience if you encounter sever weather. Find out how high-pressure and low-pressure air interact to bring about intense thunderstorms, huge hurricanes, and towering tornadoes.

Activity 2: Hurricane Tracker! *(Online)*

Studies of hurricanes involve tracing the path of these powerful storms from sea to land. This is called *hurricane tracking*. Explore some of the most severe hurricanes. Uncover their destructive paths.

ASSESS

Lesson Assessment: Severe Weather *(Online)*

You will complete an online assessment covering the main objectives of this lesson. Your assessment will be scored by the computer.

LEARN

Activity 3: Optional: Real-Life Hurricane Discovery and Destruction *(Online)*

This activity is OPTIONAL. It's provided for enrichment or extra practice, but not required for completion of this lesson. You may skip this activity.

Witness for yourself the greatness and destruction of hurricanes. View video clips of super storms.

Student Guide
Fronts and Forecasts

Every day, when we watch a weather person on TV, we hear of warm and cold fronts and the weather they will bring. What are fronts, and how can we tell where they are and what they will do? Will knowing this make us better weather forecasters ourselves?

Lesson Objectives

- Identify the four types of fronts (cold, warm, stationary, and occluded) and describe how air masses interact.
- Identify tools meteorologists use to measure weather data.
- Interpret weather maps to forecast the weather.

PREPARE

Approximate lesson time is 60 minutes.

Materials

For the Student

> Weather Forecasting
> Weather Map
> Weather Symbols

Keywords and Pronunciations

forecast: A prediction of weather conditions based on scientific data. Checking the weather forecast before taking a trip can be very helpful.

front: A boundary between two different air masses. The cold front rushed in from the west, and we had severe thunderstorms last night.

meteorologist (mee-tee-uh-RAH-luh-jist): A scientist who studies the weather. The meteorologist predicted rain, so we carried umbrellas.

meteorology (mee-tee-uh-RAH-luh-jee): The study of weather. My brother went to college to study French, but he got interested in weather and started studying meteorology instead.

occluded front (uh-KLOOD-uhd): A type of front in which fast-moving cold air meets a warm front, bringing mild weather. Since there was an occluded front, we knew it was a good time for a picnic.

stationary front: A front in which there is a boundary between air masses that does not move. The weather person on TV was describing a stationary front that had remained in one place for a number of days.

LEARN

Activity 1: Weather Front Approaching! *(Online)*

Activity 2: And Now to You with the Weather... *(Offline)*

Ever heard a weather forecast predict snow, but awakened to a sunny day? Forecasts may sometimes seem like mistakes, but they are more often correct because they use a scientific process. Use simple weather data to create a forecast. You might end up feeling sympathetic to your local meteorologist!

ASSESS

Lesson Assessment: Fronts and Forecasts *(Online)*

You will complete an online assessment covering the main objectives of the lesson.

LEARN

Activity 3: Optional: ZlugQuest Measurement *(Online)*

Name _____   Date _____

Fronts and Forecasts
Weather Forecasting

All weather forecasts begin with observations of weather conditions everywhere on Earth. Often people complain that weather forecasts are not accurate, or that they cannot be given more than about 5 days in advance. The reason for this is that small differences in the atmosphere can cause big differences in weather – differences that occur only a few days later. For this reason, meteorologists cannot predict the weather for more than two weeks ahead with good accuracy.

There are different methods forecasters use to make weather predictions, depending on how much information is available to them. The best method uses computer models to analyze and interpret data from weather stations. The computer gives information about thing such as pressure, temperature, precipitation, and humidity, which the forecaster uses to make a prediction.

Using computers is the best way to predict weather, but it does not predict weather perfectly because it is based on models and not the real thing.

View the map and read the forecast tips below. Answer the questions based on what you have learned about fronts and weather forecasting.

Forecasting Tips

- If there are cloudy skies during daytime, forecast lower temperatures than normal.
- If there are cloudy skies at night, forecast higher temperatures. Clouds trap heat from exiting the Earth's surface.
- Forecast warmer temperatures for a windy night than a less windy night.
- If there is a lot of water vapor in the air and a cold front is approaching, precipitation is most likely on its way, too.
- A change in air pressure means there will most likely be a change in weather. Falling air pressure generally means rain. Rising air pressure generally means clearing skies.
- The closer the temperature and the dew point temperature, the higher the humidity.

Read the weather map and the current conditions for each city. Pay particular attention to fronts, symbols, and temperature, pressure, and humidity data. Then write a forecast for the next day in each city including temperature, cloud cover, humidity, and precipitation amount, if any.

Current conditions in Billings, MT

Cloud cover: Sunny, fair skies
75°F
Dew point 62°F
Humidity 64%
Pressure: 30.05 inches and steady
Wind: 6 miles per hour, different directions
Tonight: Scattered thunderstorms, 59°F

Forecast:

_____
_____
_____

Current conditions in Los Angeles, CA

Cloud cover: Mostly cloudy
65°F
Dew point 58°F
Humidity 78%
Pressure: 30.03 inches and rising
Wind: 5 mph from the east
Tonight: partly cloudy, 62°F

Forecast:

_____
_____
_____

Current conditions in Seattle, WA

Cloud cover: Cloudy
57°F
Dew point 52°F
Humidity 82%
Pressure: 30.31 inches and rising
Wind: 8 mph from the northwest
Tonight: Clear, 53°F

Forecast:

_____

_____

_____

Current conditions in Dallas, TX

Cloud cover: Partly cloudy
95°F
Dew point 69°F
Humidity: 40%
Pressure: 30.01 inches and falling
Wind: calm
Tonight: Mostly cloudy, 76°F

Forecast:

_____

_____

_____

Current conditions in Tampa, FL

Cloud cover: Cloudy, light rain
75°F
Dew point 73°F
Humidity 94%
Pressure: 29.90 and falling
Wind: 6 mph from the southwest
Tonight: Thunderstorms, 81°F

Forecast:

_____

_____

_____

Name _____   Date _____

Fronts and Forecasts
Weather Map

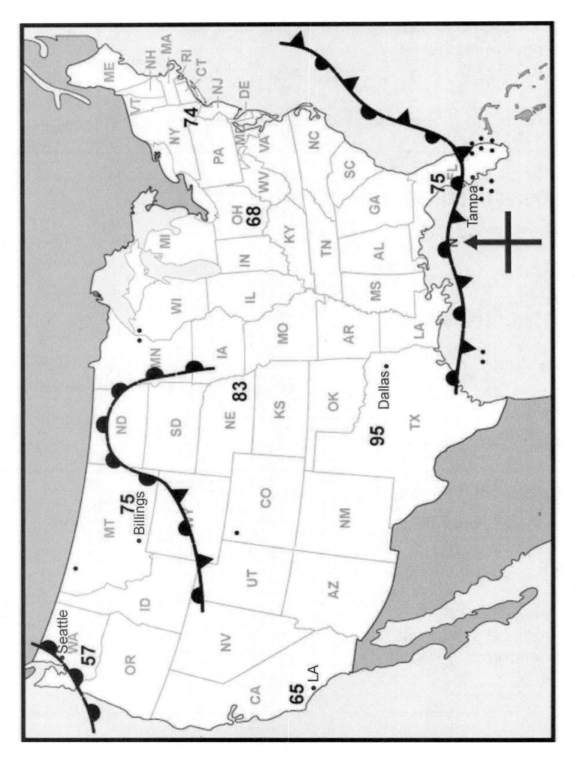

Name _____   Date _____

Fronts and Forecasts
Weather Symbols

These symbols are used all over the world so that meteorologists can understand the weather even if they do not speak the same language. They are used to create surface observations, or a display describing local weather conditions. Meteorologists can use these symbols to understand the weather quickly.

Cloud Coverage				
No Clouds	1/8 or less	2/8	3/8	4/8
5/8	6/8	7/8	overcast	sky obscured

General		Wind Speeds		Cloud Types	
'	Drizzle	◎	Calm	⌐⌐	Cirrus
•	Rain	—	1-2 knots	⌐⌐	Dense Cirrus
••	More Rain	⌐	3-7 knots	⌐	Cirrus, hook shaped, spreading over the whole sky
✳	Snow	⌐	8-12 knots	⌐⌐	Cirrus over the whole sky and getting thicker
✳✳	More Snow	⌐	13-17 knots	⌐⌐	Veil of cirrus covering the whole sky
∇	Showers	⌐	18-22 knots	⌐	Fair weather cumulus
℟	Thunderstorms	⌐	23-27 knots	⌐	Towering cumulus
△	Hail	⌐	28-32 knots	—	Stratus
∞	Haze	⌐	33-37 knots	- - -	Broken stratus
≡	Fog	⌐	38-42 knots	⌐	Cumulus with anvil top
⌢	Rainbow	⌐	43-47 knots		
⌓	Dew	⌐	48-52 knots		

A knot is equal to 0.5 m/s, or 1.15 mph.

Temperature in degrees Fahrenheit.

This number refers to the amount of pressure at sea level. It is measured in millibars.

Current weather conditions. This means lots of rain.

This number refers to the dew point temperature in degrees Fahrenheit.

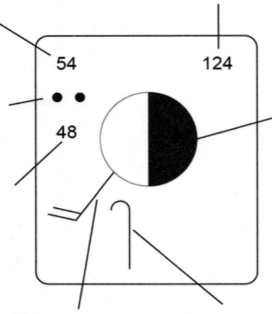

54   124

48

Cloud cover: This symbol tells about the cloud cover when the observation was taken. The sky was half-covered with clouds.

Wind barb: This symbol tells wind speed and direction. The wind was blowing from the southwest at 18-22 knots.

Cloud type: The clouds on this day were cirrus clouds.

Use the symbols to make a surface observation of weather based on these conditions:

Cloud cover: 3/8
Cloud type: Fair weather cumulus
Wind speed and direction: 3-7 knots, northeast
Rainbow
Temperature: 73 degrees Fahrenheit
Dew point temperature: 48 degrees Fahrenheit
Sea level pressure: 282

Student Guide
Climate

Have you ever been in a desert or seen a picture of a desert? How about a tropical rain forest? These areas exist because of the climate there. Find out what climates are, why they exist, and how they change.

Lesson Objectives

- Describe tropical, temperate, and polar climate types.
- Distinguish between *weather* and *climate* and describe some factors that influence climate (such as latitude, topography, prevailing winds, and oceans).
- Locate regions of a particular climate on a map.

PREPARE

Approximate lesson time is 60 minutes.

Materials

For the Student

> World Climates
> World Climates - Map

Keywords and Pronunciations

Wladimir Köppen (VLAH-dee-mihr KOU-puhn)

altitude: The height of an object above the Earth's surface. The altitude on the top of the mountain was so high that it became difficult for me to breathe.

climate: The usual weather pattern in a certain area for many years. Because the climate in coastal India is very hot, tourists usually stay in air-conditioned hotels.

latitude (LA-tuh-tood): The distance north or south of the equator by degrees. In high latitude regions, temperatures are usually below freezing.

precipitation: moisture, such as rain, snow, sleet, and hail, that falls from the atmosphere to the earth

topography (tuh-PAH-gruh-fee)

tundra (TUN-druh)

weather: The changing conditions of temperature, pressure, humidity, precipitation, and wind in an area. When the weather is rainy, it´s a good idea to carry an umbrella.

LEARN

Activity 1: Climates of the World (*Online*)

Activity 2: World Climates (*Offline*)

Print the activity sheet and use it to compare the climates of some of the world's major cities.

ASSESS

Lesson Assessment: Climate (*Online*)

You will complete an online assessment covering the main objectives of the lesson.

Name _____   Date _____

Climate
World Climates

Complete this sentence: These four factors affect the temperature and precipitation of an area: _____,

_____, _____, and _____.

The table below lists high and low temperature data for some major world cities.

City	High Temperature (°C)	High Temperature (°F)	Low Temperature (°C)	Low Temperature (°F)
Bangkok, Thailand	29.0	84.2	25.5	77.9
Buenos Aires, Argentina	23.5	74.3	10.0	50.5
Cairo, Egypt	27.9	82.2	13.8	56.8
Fairbanks, AK, USA	16.9	62.4	-23.3	-9.8
Nice, France	22.8	73.0	7.2	45.0
Quebec, Canada	19.2	66.6	-12.0	10.4
Stockholm, Sweden	17.2	63	-3.5	25.7
Sydney, Australia	22.0	71.8	11.8	53.2
Tiksi, Russia	6.6	43.9	-31.3	-24.2

Locate these cities on your map. Study the areas around them to determine factors that may contribute to these temperatures listed. Then answer the questions on the next page.

1. Study the climate zone map in this lesson. Then list which cities are in each climate zone:

   A. Tropical:

   _____

   B. Drylands:

   _____

   C. Subtropical:

   _____

   D. Continental:

   _____

   E. Polar:

   _____

2. What city had the warmest temperatures?

   _____

3. What city had the coldest temperature?

   _____

4. Which cities may be affected by topography?

   _____

Write a paragraph in your science notebook explaining how latitude, distance from an ocean, and topography affect an area's climate. Do the following in your paragraph:

- Give an explanation of latitude and topography.
- Describe the two effects of oceans on climates
- Use at least four of the cities from the table as examples.
- Describe the climate zones of the four example cities.

Name _____   Date _____

Climate
World Climates Map

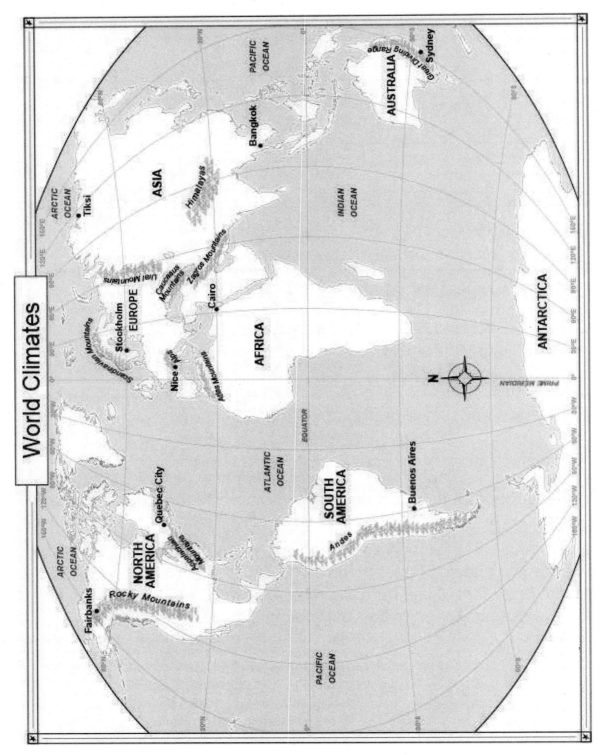

Student Guide
Climates and Change

Has the climate in your area always been the way it is now? Can you imagine what it might be like in the future or what it might have been like in the past? At some time in the past, your neighborhood may have been buried under two miles of ice, and it might develop into a desert in the future. How and why do climates change?

Lesson Objectives

- Describe the *greenhouse effect.*
- Describe how El Niño contributes to climate trends.
- Explain the contributing factors leading to global warming.

PREPARE

Approximate lesson time is 60 minutes.

Materials

For the Student

> Global Warming Data
> The Greenhouse Effect Debate
> household item - clock or watch
> household item – jar
> household item - sunlamp

Optional

> Modeling the Greenhouse Effect
> household item - thermometer (2)

Keywords and Pronunciations

El Niño (el NEEN-yoh): A current of warm water in the Pacific Ocean that occurs every few years and runs southward along the western coast of South America. El Niño causes major weather changes all over the world.

greenhouse effect: the rise in earth's temperature caused by carbon dioxide and other gases in the atmosphere; many scientists are concerned about whether the greenhouse effect will change the earth in the future

oceanic (oh-shee-A-nihk)

Pangaea (pan-JEE-uh): The name of the huge landmass that was the only continent on Earth millions of years ago. Pangaea broke apart, splitting into the continents we have today.

LEARN

Activity 1: How Climates Change *(Online)*

Activity 2: Dangerous or Not? *(Online)*

What's your opinion about the greenhouse effect? Some say we should worry, but others say we don't need to worry. Read the facts, then decide for yourself.

ASSESS

Lesson Assessment: Climates and Change *(Online)*

You will complete an online assessment covering the main objectives of this lesson. Your assessment will be scored by the computer.

LEARN

Activity 3: Optional: Model the Greenhouse Effect *(Offline)*

This activity is OPTIONAL. It's provided for enrichment or extra practice, but not required for completion of this lesson. You may skip this activity.

Our atmosphere allows heat and light to reach Earth and warm its surface. Gases in our atmosphere trap escaping heat, creating a greenhouse effect. Model the greenhouse effect by examining the effects of trapping heat inside a glass jar.

Name _____   Date _____

Climates and Change
The Greenhouse Effect Debate

When studying controversial issues, it is very important to know the difference between fact and opinion. There are many opinions on the greenhouse effect, but not all are based on fact. Before you make any decisions, it is important to know which is which.

A fact is a statement that can be checked with a scientific study, such as, "Carbon dioxide levels are 15% higher now than they were in 1950."

This statement is an opinion: "It is too early to restrict the use of fossil fuels." Opinions are based on feelings and desires, and cannot be checked scientifically.

It is also important to understand that not all statements of fact are true. They may seem true, but they could be based on false information. For this activity, though, we are just concerned with understanding the difference between statements based on facts or statements that are opinions.

Read the statements below. For each statement, mark:

O = if you think the statement is an opinion

F = if you think the statement is a fact

? = if you cannot judge

_____ Plants grow better when the carbon dioxide content of the air around them is increased.

_____ Most of the increase in greenhouse gases over the last 100 years is from burning fossil fuels.

_____ A 1°C change in the average global temperature might create another Little Ice Age in North America.

_____ People concerned about the environment are using the greenhouse effect to stop businesses from growing.

_____ People should be allowed to adjust to global warming how they want, without the government getting involved.

_____ It would be a disaster if the greenhouse effect caused sea levels to rise.

_____ Energy conservation reduces the production of greenhouse gases.

Summary of Viewpoints:

Below are viewpoints from both sides of the greenhouse effect debate. Read each view and choose one to research and present as your argument.

(a) The Greenhouse Effect Is Real

Industry, with its factories and the like, burns fossil fuels and puts more carbon dioxide in the air. The carbon dioxide becomes trapped, which is causing the Earth's temperature to rise. The hot summers of the 1980s and 1990s already show this happening.

(b) The Greenhouse Effect Is Exaggerated

The level of carbon dioxide in the air is a result of people burning fossil fuels. Factories also release sulfur dioxide. Sulfur dioxide makes "cool clouds" that counteract the effect of carbon dioxide. Anyway, the computer models of the climate that predict the greenhouse effect can't be trusted because we do not know enough about the atmosphere to make good computer models.

(c) The Greenhouse Effect Will Be Harmless

There may be a greenhouse warming of the planet but it is important to think about what effect it will have on the growth of plants in a carbon dioxide (CO_2) enriched environment. Increased CO_2 is good for plants. The plants grow larger and flower more. If there are more plants, then there will be less soil erosion and more food. Stopping CO_2 production is like "cutting our own throats" because it will increase world hunger.

(d) The Greenhouse Effect Will Result in Disaster

The global warming will cause the sea level to rise so much that coastlines and low coral islands, such as the Marshall Islands, will "go under." The polar ice caps will melt and flood rivers. Plants may grow better with increased CO_2 but, in years of drought, they will grow less because of excessive heat. Russia and Canada will become warmer and will have to grow new and different crops. This might be good for them, but if the climate changes too quickly, they won't be able to keep up and the ecosystem will collapse.

(e) Immediate Action Is Required

The longer we wait, the longer it will take to fix or even change the effects of CO_2 and greenhouse gases. Because we have not had a lot of hot summers, people think there is no problem—but the Earth could have a 3°C–4°C of warming before anything is done.

(f) Action Is Not Needed

The CO_2 in our air is increasing. Studies of gas trapped in glacial ice from many years ago show a rise in this gas in the air we breathe. But there is no good evidence that it is CO_2 that is causing global warming. Newspapers that want to print a good, scary story influence people's opinions. If we stop using fossil fuels, we will be stopping progress. If an earthquake hits California and Nicaragua, for example, more people will die in Nicaragua because California has better structures for protection. Why? Both use available resources, and Californians have the advantage.

Name _____   Date _____

Climates and Change
Global Warming Data

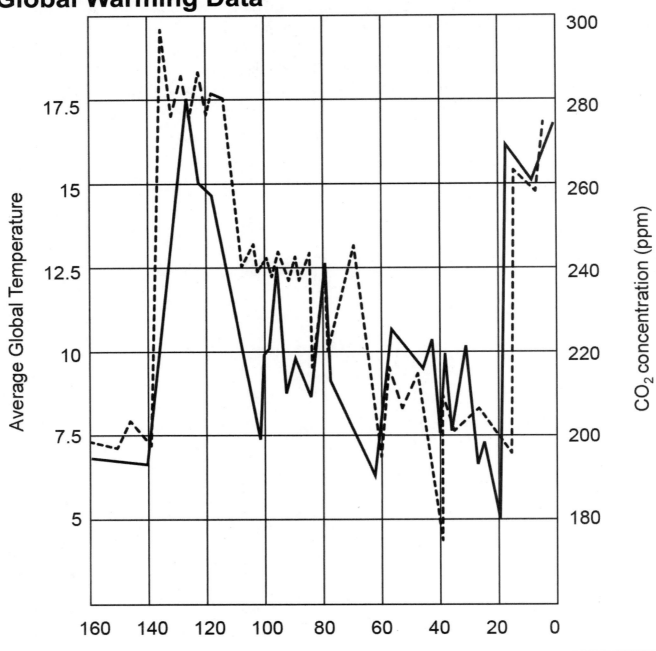

Thousands of years ago

Dotted line = CO2 concentration
Solid = Temperature change in C

Name _____   Date _____

Climates and Change
Modeling the Greenhouse Effect

Describe how El Nino contributes to climate trends.

By modeling the greenhouse effect, you can understand what happens in our atmosphere as a result of increased carbon dioxide.

Materials:

2 thermometers
jar
clock or watch
Optional: sunlamp

Procedure:

1. Find a spot in direct sunlight or place the two thermometers a few inches apart under the sunlamp.

2. Wait three minutes. Record the temperatures on both thermometers and the time.

3. Place the jar over one of your thermometers. Make sure there is no shadow over the uncovered thermometer. (It is okay to stand the thermometer up inside the jar.)

4. Every minute, for 10 minutes, record the readings on both thermometers.

Observations

Time	Temperature on Covered Thermometer	Temperature on Uncovered Thermometer
Start		
1		
2		
3		
4		
5		
6		
7		
8		
9		
10		

What Happened

The air over the uncovered thermometer is constantly changing – as the air gets warm it is replaced by cooler air. Air in the jar cannot circulate throughout the room. It gets warmer and warmer. In the atmosphere, sunlight passing through the atmosphere warms the Earth's surface. Greenhouse gases, such as carbon dioxide, trap heat radiating back off the Earth. This warming is called the greenhouse effect.

Both the atmosphere and the jar allow light to enter but trap that energy when it is changed to heat.

Student Guide

Earth's Atmosphere: Unit Review and Assessment

You have learned a lot about the atmosphere! You learned what it is made of and what causes wind and precipitation. You also learned how to predict weather and to think about climate changes that result from natural causes or because of human actions. Draw together your new knowledge, and complete the Unit Review and Assessment.

Lesson Objectives

- Define *humidity* as the amount of water vapor in the air and the *dew point* as the temperature at which the air cannot hold any more water vapor.
- Describe possible causes of climate changes (such as El Niño and the greenhouse effect) and their potential effects on climate.
- Describe some properties of the atmosphere, such as its composition, density, and pressure. Explain how air density is related to both temperature and pressure.
- Distinguish between *weather* and *climate* and describe some factors that influence climate (such as latitude, altitude, and ocean currents).
- Explain how clouds form and identify common weather patterns associated with different types of clouds.
- Explain that the uneven heating of the Earth's surface transfers heat through convection currents in the atmosphere.
- Identify sources of air pollution.
- Identify the five layers of the atmosphere: troposphere, stratosphere, mesosphere, thermosphere, and exosphere.
- Identify the three main types of storms and describe the air movements that produce them.
- Identify types of fronts and explain how air masses interact in cold and warm fronts.
- Identify types of precipitation (rain, snow, sleet, hail) and explain how each is formed.
- Interpret weather maps to forecast the weather.
- Identify types of precipitation (rain, snow, sleet, hail) and explain how they form.

PREPARE

Approximate lesson time is 60 minutes.

Materials

For the Student

Question Review Table

LEARN

Activity 1: Be a Meteorologist *(Online)*

ASSESS

Unit Assessment: Earth's Atmosphere *(Offline)*

You will complete an offline assessment covering the main objectives of this unit. Your learning coach will score this assessment.

LEARN

Activity 2: Unit Assessment Review Table *(Online)*

If you earned a score of **less than 80%** on the Unit Assessment, complete the activity.

If you earned a score of **80% or greater**, you may skip this activity.

Let's prepare to retake the Unit Assessment:

- Print the Question Review Table
- Identify the questions that you answered incorrectly
- Complete the appropriate review activities listed in the table.

Note: This will guide you through the process of using the Unit Assessment Review Tables. You may skip this video if you've already viewed it in another unit or course. As always, check in with your student's teacher if you have any questions.

Activity 3: Optional: ZlugQuest Measurement *(Online)*

Name _____   Date _____

Earth's Atmosphere: Unit Review and Assessment
Question Review Table

Before you retake the Unit Assessment, use the table to figure out which activities you should review.

Circle the numbers of the questions that you missed on the Unit Assessment. Review the activities that correspond with these questions.

Question	Lesson	Review Activity
1, 2, 3, 4	The Atmosphere	Explore: Earth's Atmosphere
		Investigate Air Pressure
		Up Here in the Atmosphere
		Air Bag
5, 6	Why the Wind Blows	Explore: Atmosphere and Weather
		The Coriolis Effect
		Understanding Earth's Winds
7, 8, 9	Humidity, Dew, and Frost	Explore: Water in the Air
		Find the Relative Humidity
		The Father of Cool: Willis Haviland Carrier
10, 11	Clouds and Precipitation	Beyond White and Fluffy
		Moisture in the Air
		Particles in the Air
12, 13, 14, 15, 16, 17	Clouds and Precipitation	Moisture in the Air

Question	Lesson	Review Activity
18, 26, 27	Climates and Change	Dangerous or Not?
		How Climates Change
		Human Actions and Greenhouse Gases
19, 21	Severe Weather	Real-Life Hurricane Discovery and Destruction
		Storms
		Hurricane Tracker!
22, 23	Fronts and Forecasts	And Now to You with the Weather
24, 25	Climate	Climates of the World
		World Climates

Student Guide

The Solar System: Planets and Orbits

Can you name the eight planets in our solar system? Take an adventure in outer space as you learn about them. You'll find that the planets are different sizes and distances from the sun. Let's blast off!

Lesson Objectives

- Name the planets of the solar system in order, starting at the sun.
- Name the largest planet and the smallest planet in our solar system.
- State that the force of gravity keeps the planets in orbit around the sun.
- Apply the concept of rotation to explain how celestial bodies move across the sky.
- Define revolution as the period in which a planet makes one complete orbit around the sun.
- Define rotation as the period in which a planet makes one complete turn on its axis.
- Recognize that the planets in the solar system revolve around the sun in elliptical orbits.

PREPARE

Approximate lesson time is 60 minutes.

Advance Preparation

- For this Science activity you will need the following food items:
- honeydew melon
- cantaloupe
- apples - 2
- cherries - 2
- small raspberry
- pea
- If these items are expensive to buy or difficult to find due to the season, use substitutes of similar size.

Materials

For the Student

Earth's Axis
Earth Year
Lunar Earth Orbit
Moving Shadows
Reveal Earth Revolution
Season's Songs
Eating Your Way Through the Solar System
Planet Clues

Keywords and Pronunciation

axis: A line, real or imaginary, that runs through the middle of an object. The Earth spins completely on its axis once a day.

asteroid (AS-tuh-royd)**:** A rocky object larger than a meteoroid but less than about 1,000 km in greatest dimension, orbiting the sun. Most asteroids orbit the sun between the orbits of Mars and Jupiter.

comet: A large, icy object that orbits the sun and may develop a "tail" when it comes near the sun.

gravity: The attraction between two bodies due to their mass. Gravity provides the force that keeps us planted firmly on the Earth.

meteoroid: A small, rocky object, less than about 100 meters in greatest dimension. Meteoroids can move through the solar system and sometimes hit the surfaces of other bodies in the solar system, such as planets and moons.

orbit: The path of one body around another. The Earth moves in an orbit around the sun. Used also to refer to the motion itself. The Earth orbits the sun.

orbit (OR-bit)**:** the path any object in space takes as it goes around another

orbital plane: a plane is a flat surface extending infinitely in all directions; an orbital plane is the plane that an object orbits around

period of rotation: the time it takes for a planet, or another object, to make one complete turn on its axis

perpendicular: in a vertical position, straight up and down

revolution (re-vuh-LOO-shuhn)**:** the travelling of the Earth or another body around the Sun; one complete revolution of the Earth takes one year

rotation: the spinning of an object such as the Earth on its axis; one complete rotation of the Earth takes one day

solar system: The sun and the planets, moons, asteroids, meteoroids, comets, and dust particles that are in orbits around the sun.

Uranus (YUR-uh-nuhs)

LEARN

Activity 1: The Planets *(Online)*

Activity 2: Rotation and Revolution *(Online)*

One earth year is equal to about 365 days, the amount of time it takes for earth to orbit the sun.

But think about Neptune, where one year, the amount of time it takes for Neptune to orbit the sun, is equal to about 164 earth years. Imagine how many things can happen in a Neptune year!

Let's take a closer look at the movement of planets in our solar system.

Activity 3: Eat Your Way Through the Solar System (*Offline*)

Safety

This lesson involves eating or working with food. Check with your doctor, if necessary, to find out whether your student will have any allergic reaction to the food.

Activity 4: May I Have Your Order, Please? (*Offline*)

ASSESS

Lesson Assessment: The Solar System: Planets and Orbits (*Online*)

You will complete an online assessment covering the main objectives of the lesson.

Reveal: Earth's Axis

Earth's axis is tilted by 23.5 degrees and runs through the planet from the North Pole to the South Pole.

The animation shows the Earth running on its axis or revolving on its axis.

Reveal: Earth Year

An animation shows Earth revolving around the sun. Earth's orbital path is labeled with dates and each quarter of the path is labeled with a season of the year – winter, spring, summer, and autumn. The tilt of Earth causes a different area of Earth to face the sun most directly in each season. In spring, it is the area near the North Pole. In autumn, it is the area near the South Pole.

Reveal: Lunar Earth Orbit

Animation shows Earth rotating on its axis and revolving around the sun. As Earth follows its orbital path, the moon follows an orbital path around Earth. The moon continues to revolve around Earth, moving with Earth as Earth revolves around the sun.

Name _____   Date _____

The Solar System: Planets and Orbits
Moving Shadows

In this activity, you will explore how the earth rotates with respect to the sun, and how the size and shape of a shadow change with the position of the sun.

Question

Write a question about a light's position and the shadow of an object.

Answer:

Hypothesis

Write a hypothesis based on your question.

Answer:

Materials

- Clock
- Pencil
- Small object that stands on its own (such as a water bottle)
- Meter stick
- Flat open area outside such as a sidewalk or playground
- A sunny day
- Chalk
- Flashlight

Procedure

Set Up

1. Measure the height of your object.

2. Describe the shape of your object.

3. Place the object on the ground.

Shadow Measurements from the Sun

1. Use the meter stick to measure the length of the shadow from the base of the object to the tip of the shadow.

2. Write down the direction of the shadow. Is the shadow pointing to the east or west?

3. Stand behind your object and point your arm at the sun. Describe the angle made by your arm and the ground. Is it a small angle, or a 90° angle (the sun directly overhead, your arm pointing straight up in the air)? Write down the position of the sun.

4. Describe the shape of the shadow. You may trace the shape of the shadow on the ground with chalk.

5. You will measure the shadow of your object every 2 hours beginning at 8 a.m. At each time of day, write down the position of the sun, the length of the shadow, the direction of the shadow, and the shape of the shadow.

Shadow Measurement from the Flashlight

1. Place the object on a table.

2. Hold the flashlight directly overhead.

3. Measure the length of the shadow, and describe the shape of the shadow.

4. Move the flashlight to the side of the object, so that the flashlight points at an angle through the object to the ground.

5. Measure the length of the shadow, and describe the shape of the shadow.

6. Move the flashlight to a lower angle (the flashlight is closer to the ground).

7. Measure the length of the shadow, and describe the shape of the shadow.

Data

For each time of day, fill in the position of the sun, length of shadow (in centimeters), direction of the shadow, and shape of the shadow.

Sunlight

Time of Day	Position of Sun	Length of Shadow (cm)	Direction of Shadow	Shape of Shadow
8 am	Answer:	Answer:	Answer:	Answer:
10 am	Answer:	Answer:	Answer:	Answer:
12 noon	Answer:	Answer:	Answer:	Answer:
2 pm	Answer:	Answer:	Answer:	Answer:
4 pm	Answer:	Answer:	Answer:	Answer:
6 pm	Answer:	Answer:	Answer:	Answer:

Flashlight at an angle

Flashlight position	Length of Shadow	Direction of Shadow	Shape of Shadow
Directly overhead	Answer:	Answer:	Answer:
Angle close to the ground	Answer:	Answer:	Answer:
Angle closer to the ground	Answer:	Answer:	Answer:

Analysis

Position of the Sun

1. Describe how the position of the sun changed throughout the day.

Answer:

Length of Shadow

2. Describe how the length of the shadow changed throughout the day.

Answer:

3. Describe how the length of the shadow changed as the flashlight changed position.

Answer:

Direction of the shadow

4. Describe how the direction of the shadow changed throughout the day.

Answer:

5. Describe how the direction of the shadow changed as the sun changed position.

Answer:

Shape of shadow

6. Describe how the shape of the shadow changed throughout the day.

Answer:

7. Describe how the shape of the shadow changed as the flashlight changed position.

Answer:

Questions

1. Was your hypothesis correct? Why or why not?

Answer:

2. How does the change in position of the sun affect the size of the shadow?

Answer:

3. Does the change in position of the flashlight have the same effect on shadow size as the sun?

Answer:

4. How does the change in position of the sun affect the shape of the shadow?

Answer:

5. Does the change in position of the flashlight have the same effect on shadow shape as the sun?

Answer:

6. What direction does the sun appear to move across the sky? How do you know?

Answer:

7. What causes the sun to appear to move across the sky?

Answer:

Reveal: Earth Revolution

This is an animation of Earth revolving around the sun along its orbital path.

Reveal: Season's Songs

Hands playing a piano keyboard

Back:
The seasons of the year have been used as inspiration to create music. Antonio Vivaldi, an Italian composer and violinist, composed a piece of music called "The Four Seasons." Visit the website listed at the end of this lesson to hear some of Vivaldi's compositions.

Name _____ Date _____

The Solar System: Planets and Orbits
Eating Your Way Through the Solar System

The planets in our solar system vary in size. To see just how different they are, compare them to the foods in the following list:

Jupiter - a honeydew melon
Saturn - a cantaloupe
Neptune and Uranus - two large apples
Earth and Venus - two cherries
Mars - a raspberry
Mercury - a pea

If the planets were the sizes of the foods on this list, the sun would be as big as a large van. Place all the food items on a large, flat surface. Cut out the pictures of the planets and glue them onto index cards. Then match each food item to the picture of the planet it represents. Tape the card onto the food item, or in the case of the smaller planets, glue the food items onto the index cards.

What is the smallest planet?

_____

What is the largest planet?

_____

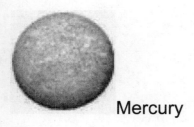

Mercury

Venus

Earth

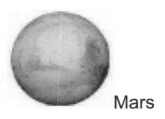

Mars

Jupiter

Saturn

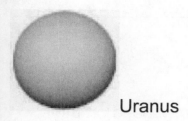 Uranus

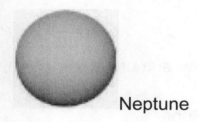 Neptune

Name _____   Date _____

The Solar System: Planets and Orbits

Planet Clues

Use the clues below to help place your food "planets" in order, based on their distance from the sun.

Clue 1: Earth, Jupiter, Mercury, Venus, and Mars are the five planets closest to the sun.

Clue 2: Saturn is closer to Earth than Neptune.

Clue 3: Long ago, astronomers found that Mercury and Venus are the only two planets closer to the sun than Earth.

Clue 4: Neptune, Uranus, Saturn, and Jupiter are the four planets farthest from the sun.

Clue 5: Uranus is between Saturn and Neptune.

Clue 6: Copernicus knew that the six planets closest to the sun are Mars, Earth, Jupiter, Saturn, Mercury, and Venus.

Clue 7: There are six planets between Mercury and Neptune.

Did you place all eight planets in the correct order?

Student Guide

The Sun

When you look up in the sky on a bright sunny day, what do you see? The sun! The sun is by far the biggest thing in the whole solar system. It's also the solar system's major source of energy. You have learned about the sun's relationship with Earth and the moon. Now learn more about the sun itself.

Lesson Objectives

- State that the sun is the major source of energy on Earth.
- Identify the major layers of the sun: core, photosphere, and corona.
- Describe patterns of daily changes in length and direction of shadows, day and night, or the seasonal appearance of some stars in the night sky.

PREPARE

Approximate time is 60 minutes.

Materials

For the Student

Shadow Graphing Assignment
My Solar System Book

Keywords and Pronunciations

aurora borealis (uh-ROR-uh bor-ee-A-luhs)

core: The center of the sun. The sun's energy comes from nuclear reactions fusing, which happen deep inside its core.

corona (kuh-ROH-nuh)**:** The outer atmosphere of the sun. If you drew a cartoon of the sun as a circle with flames all around it, the corona would be those flames.

photosphere: The bright surface of the sun. If you drew a cartoon of the sun as a circle with flames all around it, the photosphere would be the circle.

solar system: The sun and the planets, moons, asteroids, meteoroids, comets, and dust particles that orbit the sun. Gravity keeps all the planets of the solar system from leaving the sun.

LEARN

Activity 1: The Sun *(Online)*

Activity 2: Sun Rise, Sun Set *(Online)*

You will be given the task to find a reliable website using specific keywords to collect data and graph the day and time of sunrise.

Activity 3: My Solar System Book *(Online and Offline)*

Print the My Solar System Book if you have not already done so.

ASSESS

Lesson Assessment: The Sun *(Online)*

You will complete an online assessment covering the main objectives of the lesson.

Name _____ Date _____

Assignment
Shadow Graphing

In this activity, you will graph data to show the changes in shadow length over the course of a day. A mailbox is about 45 inches tall. Use the data table that includes the shadow length of a mailbox at different times of day to create a graph. Then answer the questions using your graph.

Sunlight

Time of Day	Length of Mailbox Shadow in Inches
8 am	132
10 am	52
12 noon	24
2 pm	15
4 pm	31
6 pm	67
8 pm	215

1. What time did you expect the mailbox to have the shortest shadow?

   _____

   _____

2. Why might the shortest shadow occur at a different time?

   _____

   _____

3. This mailbox is located on the borders between Michigan, Ohio, and Indiana. If the location of the mailbox was right on the equator, what would you expect the mailbox height to be at noon? Why?

   _____

   _____

Name _____   Date _____

My Solar System Book
The Sun

_____

_____

_____

_____

_____

_____

_____

_____

_____

Student Guide
The Inner Planets

You have learned that eight planets orbit the sun. The four planets closest to the sun are similar in many ways, but they also have big differences. Begin your planetary journey by visiting these inner planets to learn what they're like.

Lesson Objectives

- Recognize the common characteristics of the inner planets.
- Identify each of the four inner planets by their characteristics.
- Name the inner planets of the solar system: Mercury, Venus, Earth, and Mars.

PREPARE

Approximate lesson time is 60 minutes.

Advance Preparation

- Have on hand the pages about the sun that your student created in the previous lesson, The Sun. Also, gather the pages of My Solar System Book from earlier lessons in this unit.
- For today's lesson you will need the pictures of the planets on index cards, which you used in the first lesson of the unit.

Materials

For the Student

    My Solar System Book
    Planet Distances Chart

Keywords and Pronunciation

terrestrial: Earth-like, made mainly of rock and metal, with a solid surface. The terrestrial surface of the planet made it easy for the astronauts to walk there.

LEARN

Activity 1: The Inner Planets *(Online)*

Activity 2: My Solar System Book, Part 2 *(Offline)*

Activity 3: Make a Model of the Solar System *(Offline)*

ASSESS

Lesson Assessment: The Inner Planets *(Online)*

You will complete an online assessment covering the main objectives of this lesson. Sit with your Learning Coach in case you need help. The assessment will be scored by the computer.

Name _____   Date _____

My Solar System Book
Venus

_____

_____

_____

_____

_____

_____

_____

_____

_____

_____

Mercury

_____
_____
_____
_____
_____
_____
_____
_____
_____
_____

Mars

_____

_____

_____

_____

_____

_____

_____

_____

_____

_____

Earth

Name _____   Date _____

Planet Distances Chart

Planet	Average distance from the sun (1.609 miles = 1 km)	Distance from sun on toilet paper 30,100,000 km/sheet (18,700,000 mi / sheet)
Mercury	58,000,000 km	1.9
Venus	108,000,000 km	3.6
Earth	150,000,000 km	5.0
Mars	228,000,000 km	7.6
Jupiter	778,000,000	26
Saturn	1,426,000,000 km	47
Uranus	2,877,000,000 km	96
Neptune	4,508,000,000 km	150

Student Guide
The Outer Planets

Continue your planet journey as you travel farther away from the sun to the outer planets. See what makes these planets different from the inner planets, and how they compare to one another.

Lesson Objectives

- Identify the characteristics of the outer planets.
- Identify the common characteristics of the gas giants (Jupiter, Saturn, Uranus, and Neptune).
- Name the outer planets: Jupiter, Saturn, Uranus, and Neptune.

PREPARE

Approximate lesson time is 60 minutes.

Advance Preparation

- Have on hand the pages about the sun and the inner planets that your student created in the previous lessons. Also, gather the pages of My Solar System Book from the previous lessons.
- Have on hand the toilet-paper strips representing the distances from the sun of the inner planets. For today's lesson you will need the planets cards you used in the first lesson of the unit. Also, gather the previous work of the toilet-paper model.

Materials

For the Student

My Solar System Book
Planet Distances Chart

Keywords and Pronunciation

asteroid (AS-tuh-royd)**:** A rocky object that orbits the sun, mostly found between Mars and Jupiter, and that is larger than meteoroids but less than about 1,000 km in length or diameter.

Charon (KAIR-uhn)

comet: A large, icy object that orbits the sun and develops a "tail" when it is near the sun.

meteor: A chunk of rock that falls from space through the Earth´s atmosphere.

meteorite (MEE-tee-uh-riyt)**:** A meteoroid that falls to Earth.

meteoroid: A small, rocky object, less than about 100 meters in length or diameter.

Uranus (YUR-uh-nuhs)

LEARN

Activity 1: Far Out! *(Online)*

Activity 2: My Solar System Book, Part 3 *(Offline)*

Activity 3: Make a Model of the Solar System, Part 2 *(Offline)*

ASSESS

Lesson Assessment: The Outer Planets *(Online)*

You will complete an online assessment covering the main objectives of this lesson.

Name _____   Date _____

My Solar System Book
Saturn

_____

_____

_____

_____

_____

_____

_____

_____

_____

_____

Jupiter

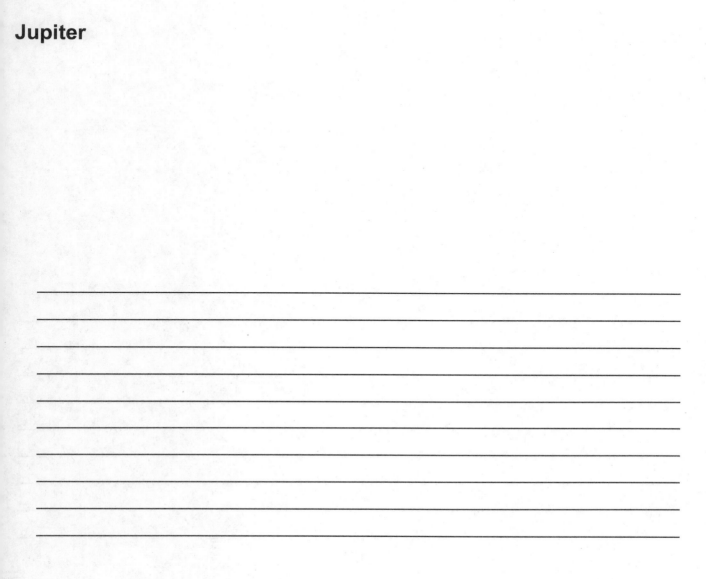

Neptune

_____

_____

_____

_____

_____

_____

_____

_____

_____

_____

Uranus

_____

_____

_____

_____

_____

_____

_____

_____

_____

Name _____   Date _____

Planet Distances Chart

Planet Name	Average distance from the sun (1.609 miles = 1 km)	Distance from sun on toilet paper 30,100,000 km/sheet (18,700,000 mi / sheet
Mercury	58,000,000 km	1.9
Venus	108,000,000 km	3.6
Earth	150,000,000 km	5.0
Mars	228,000,000 km	7.6
Jupiter	778,000,000	26
Saturn	1,426,000,000 km	47
Uranus	2,877,000,000 km	96
Neptune	4,508,000,000 km	150

Student Guide
Stars of the Night Sky

When you look up on a clear night, the sky seems to sparkle with millions of tiny white lights. Almost all these white lights are stars up in space. The stars may look tiny, but they are actually huge. Explore stars and learn how something so big can look so small.

Lesson Objectives

- Recognize that the brightness of a star in the sky depends on the star's light-energy output as well as its distance from the Earth.
- Recognize that stars are classified according to their brightness.
- Recognize that the brightness of a star in the sky depends on the star's light-energy output as well as its distance from the Earth.
- Recognize that stars are classified according to their brightness.
- Explain that differences in the apparent brightness of the sun compared to other stars is due to their relative distances from Earth.

PREPARE

Approximate time is 60 minutes.

Advance Preparation

Have on hand a 40-watt bulb and a 100-watt bulb for this lesson.

Keywords and Pronunciations

astronomer: A scientist who studies matter and objects that are outside Earth's atmosphere, including their physical and chemical properties. Johnny dreamed of becoming an astronomer so he could participate in making new discoveries about the stars.

Hans Lippershey (hahnts LIHP-uhrs-hiy)

Hipparchus (hih-PAHR-kuhs)**:** ancient Greek astronomer and mathematician who created an extensive star catalog and developed trigonometry

star: a hot ball of glowing gases in space; our sun is a star that is similar to many stars we see at night

LEARN

Activity 1: Stars in Space *(Online)*
Activity 2: Star Bright *(Offline)*
Safety

The light bulb will become hot after a short amount of use. Allow time for it to cool before taking it out of the lamp.

ASSESS

Lesson Assessment: Stars of the Night Sky *(Online)*

You will complete an online assessment covering the main objectives of the lesson.

Student Guide
Constellations: Star Patterns

Are you a sky watcher? Sky watchers like to study the night sky and all the stars. Back in ancient times, sky watchers used their imaginations to see that certain stars form patterns that look like a bear, a hunter, a dog, or other animals, people, and objects. Explore the night sky as you learn about some of the star patterns called *constellations*.

Lesson Objectives

- Recognize some bright stars (Polaris, Sirius, Betelgeuse, and Rigel).
- Recognize some well-known constellations (Little Dipper, Big Dipper, and Orion).
- Recognize that the Earth's rotation makes the constellations appear to revolve in the sky, or move across it.
- Describe patterns of daily changes in length and direction of shadows, day and night, or the seasonal appearance of some stars in the night sky.

PREPARE

Approximate time is 60 minutes.

Advance Preparation

Be sure to have stickers of gold stars on hand for this activity.

Materials

For the Student

> Constellation Dance Assignment
> Stars of the Night Sky

Keywords and Pronunciations

Betelgeuse (BEE-tl-joos)

constellation: A group of stars that forms a pattern in the sky; Orion is a constellation

Orion (uh-RIY-uhn)

Polaris (puh-LAIR-uhs): A star directly above the North Pole in line with the Earth's axis; also called the North Star

Ptolemy (TAH-luh-mee): A Greek astronomer and mathematician who lived in ancient Egypt and who named many of the constellations

Rigel (RIY-juhl)

Sirius (SIHR-ee-uhs)

star: A hot ball of glowing gases; the sun is the star closest to the Earth

LEARN

Activity 1: Constellations *(Online)*

Activity 2: Sky Umbrella *(Offline)*

ASSESS

Lesson Assessment: Constellations: Sky Patterns *(Offline)*

You will complete an online assessment covering the main objectives of this lesson. Sit with your Learning Coach in case you need help. The assessment will be scored by the computer.

LEARN

Activity 3: Twinkling Star *(Offline)*

Name _____   Date _____

Assignment
Constellation Dance

In this activity you will see how constellations change position in the sky at different times of year. Take a look at the big dipper in September, which is the season of fall in North America. Complete the graphs for winter, spring, and summer and answer questions about the pattern you see for the Big Dipper.

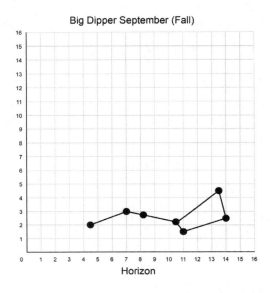

Big Dipper September (Fall)

Horizon

x-axis or horizon	y-axis
4.5	2
7	3
8.25	2.75
10.5	2.25
11	1.5
14	2.5
13.5	4.5

1. What do you notice about the position of the Big Dipper in relation to the horizon?

_____

_____

_____

_____

2. Use the coordinates to complete the graph that represents the Big Dipper's position in the sky during winter.

Big Dipper December (Winter)

Horizon

x-axis or horizon	y-axis
15	1
14	5
14.5	6.5
14.75	10
16	10.75
15.5	15
14	14.5

3. How has the position of the Big Dipper changed from fall to winter? Why has the position changed?

_____

_____

_____

_____

4. Use the coordinates to complete the graph that represents the Big Dipper's position in the sky during spring.

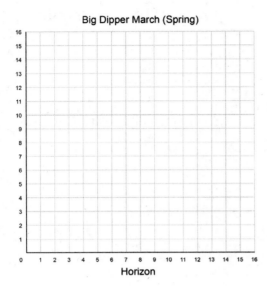

Big Dipper March (Spring)

x-axis or horizon	y-axis
14.5	14
12	12.75
10.5	13.25
8.75	13.5
7.75	15.25
4.75	14.5
5.5	12.25

5. How has the appearance of the Big Dipper changed in spring?

_____

_____

_____

_____

6. Use the coordinates for the Big Dipper in the summer and complete the graph.

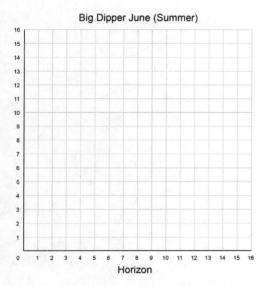

Big Dipper June (Summer)

Horizon

x-axis or horizon	y-axis
2	15.5
3	12
2.5	10
2.5	7
1	6
1.5	1.5
3	2.5

7. How has the position changed in summer? What pattern does the Big Dipper follow throughout a year?

_____

_____

_____

_____

8. What if some stars dip below the horizon at certain times of the year? Does that mean the stars have disappeared? Why or why not?

_____

_____

_____

_____

Name _____   Date _____

Constellations: Star Patterns

Stars of the Night Sky

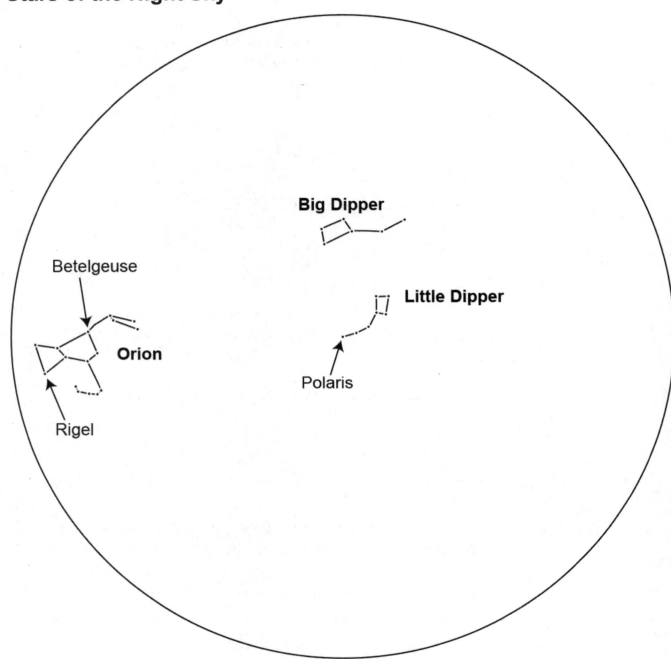

Student Guide
Galaxies

Our solar system contains a star and many planets, as well as meteoroids, asteroids, and comets. But our solar system is itself part of something even bigger—a galaxy. And galaxies are grouped as well. See how scientists have used high-powered telescopes to learn about galaxies—including ours, the Milky Way—and more.

Lesson Objectives

- State that our solar system is part of the Milky Way galaxy.
- State that telescopes magnify the appearance of some distant objects in the sky and collect enough light from very dim objects to make them visible.

PREPARE

Approximate lesson time is 60 minutes.

Advance Preparation

- You will need the book *Galaxies* by Seymour Simon for the optional activity in this lesson.

Materials

For the Student

Spiral Pattern

Keywords and Pronunciation

Andromeda (an-DRAH-muh-duh)

elliptical (ih-LIP-tih-kuhl)

galaxy: An enormous group of stars, dust, and gas all held together by gravity. The Milky Way is just one of many galaxies in our universe.

Milky Way: The galaxy that includes our solar system, with the sun, Earth, and other planets, and many billions of other stars. Ashley was amazed to learn that the Milky Way is a swirling collection of billions of stars, including our own sun.

LEARN

Activity 1: What Is a Galaxy? *(Online)*

Activity 2: Make a Model of the Milky Way Galaxy *(Offline)*

ASSESS

Lesson Assessment: Galaxies *(Online)*

You will complete an online assessment covering the main objectives of this lesson. Your assessment will be scored by the computer.

LEARN

Activity 3: More About Galaxies *(Offline)*

Safety

As usual, you may wish to preview any books listed in this lesson.

Name _____ Date _____

Galaxies
Spiral Pattern

Student Guide

Gravity and Motion at the Earth's Surface

What goes up, must come down! You work with and against gravity every day. If you play soccer, you know that if you kick the ball high up into the air it will come back to the field. As you run across the field, you are pushing against the pull of gravity to do so. Gravity on Earth is always pulling you down.

Lesson Objectives

- Define weight as the product of an object's mass and the gravitational force on it.
- Recognize that the pull decreases as the masses move farther apart, and increases as the mass of either increases.
- State that any two masses have a gravitational pull between them, but this pull is easily noticeable only if the mass of at least one is very great.
- State that near the Earth's surface, objects with no other force acting on them accelerate downward at a constant rate.
- Explain that the gravitational force exerted by Earth on objects is directed down.

PREPARE

Approximate time is 60 minutes.

Advance Preparation

Be sure to have stickers of gold stars on hand for this activity.

Materials

For the Student

> Gravity on Planet Earth
> baking dish
> bottle, plastic - 2-liter, with cap
> coins - loose, same kind as roll
> coins - roll
> spring scale
> string
> tape - masking
> water

Optional

> household item - flour
> balance

Keywords and Pronunciations

acceleration: Any change in velocity. An airplane taking off and a horse on a carousel moving at constant speed are both experiencing acceleration.

Galileo Galilei (gal-uh-LEE-oh gal-uh-LAY-ee)

gravity: An attractive force exerted on any object with mass by any other object. If you drop a glass, it falls toward the floor because gravity is acting on it.

mass: The amount of matter in an object, or a measure of how hard it is to change an object′s speed or direction. The mass of the ball was 50 grams, and Earth′s gravity acted on this mass.

weight: The force on a mass due to gravity. The weight of the astronauts on Earth was six times their weight on the moon.

LEARN

Activity 1: Weight, Weight, Gravity (Online)

Gravity pulls you toward the center of the Earth and the Earth toward the sun. But a gravitational force exists between any two objects, not just very large ones. There's a force of gravity between you and your bed, between two pencils, even between two atoms. How does gravity operate on Earth?

Activity 2: Gravity on Planet Earth (Offline)

How much force does Earth exert on objects at its surface? Use a spring scale to find out.

Activity 3: Gravitational Forces (Online)

Access and read *Big Universe: Gravity*. You will learn that gravity always pulls down toward the center of celestial objects.

ASSESS

Lesson Assessment: Gravity and Motion at the Earth's Surface (Online)

You will complete an online assessment covering the main objectives of this lesson.

Name _____   Date _____

Gravity and Motion at the Earth's Surface
Gravity on Planet Earth

Mass and Weight

Consider this: The gravitational force of the Earth on a 1-kilogram mass is 9.8 newtons (N).

If a watermelon has a mass of 10 kilograms, it is attracted to Earth by a force of 9.8 N/kg. So the weight of the watermelon is 9.8 + 9.8 + 9.8 + 9.8 + 9.8 + 9.8 + 9.8 + 9.8 + 9.8 + 9.8 or 10 kg × 9.8 N/kg. And that means its weight is 98 N.

Suppose you knew something weighed 44N and wanted to find its mass. You could divide: 44 N ÷ 9.8 N/kg = about 4.5 kg.

This is easy to practice with water. One milliliter (mL) of water has a mass of 1 g. So 1000 mL of water (or 1 liter) will have a mass of 1 kg.

1. Fill an empty 473 mL (16 oz) bottle with water (to about the same level as an unopened bottle).

2. Cap the bottle and tie a string around the neck.

3. Loop the other end of the string around the spring scale.

4. Hold the spring scale in the air to measure the weight of the water.

Write the weight of the water in newtons: _____ N
Divide by 9.8 N/kg.
Write the water's mass in kilograms: _____ kg

Well done!

Investigation Idea:

In calculating the water's mass, we've made a scientific error. You really found the mass of the bottle, water, and string. Because the bottle and string are light, including them in our measurements did not make too much difference.

To find the mass of the water alone, you need to subtract the mass of the string and bottle. With a pan balance, you can try to find the mass of the bottle and string, then subtract to find the mass of the water alone.

Gravity Pulls at a Constant Rate

You learned that gravity pulls all unsupported objects down toward Earth with an acceleration of 9.8 meters/second^2. This means that all objects, whether a watermelon or a piece of string, will fall toward Earth with this same acceleration (disregarding air friction).

Use the spring scale to find the weight of a roll of coins in newtons:

_____

Divide by 9.8 N/kg.

Write the mass of the roll of coins in kilograms: _____ kg

Divide the mass by the number of coins in the roll to find the mass of just one coin: _____ kg

Let's re-create an experiment that is very much like some tests Galileo might have done.

1. Place a metal pan on the floor.

2. Hold a single coin in each hand.

3. Drop them at the same time from the same height and listen for them to land.

4. Tape two coins together.

5. Hold two coins in one hand and a single coin in the other.

6. Drop them as before and listen for them to land.

7. Now hold an entire roll of coins in one hand and a single coin in the other.

8. Drop them as before and listen for them to land.

You should notice that in each case the coins hit the pan at the same time.

Student Guide

The Solar System and Beyond: Unit Review and Assessment

Review what you have learned about the solar system, stars, constellations, the Milky Way galaxy, and other galaxies, as you prepare to take the Unit Assessment.

Lesson Objectives

- Demonstrate mastery of the skills taught in this unit.
- Name the planets of the solar system in order, starting at the sun.
- Recognize that the brightness of a star in the sky depends on the star's light-energy output as well as its distance from the Earth.
- State that our solar system is part of the Milky Way galaxy.
- Distinguish objects inside the solar system from objects outside the solar system.
- Identify the major layers of the sun: core, photosphere, and corona.
- Recognize some bright stars (Polaris, Sirius, Betelgeuse, and Rigel).
- Recognize some well-known constellations (Little Dipper, Big Dipper, and Orion).
- Recognize that stars are classified according to their brightness.
- State that telescopes magnify the appearance of some distant objects in the sky and collect enough light from very dim objects to make them visible.
- State that the force of gravity keeps the planets in orbit around the sun.

PREPARE

Approximate lesson time is 60 minutes.

LEARN

Activity 1: Planets, Stars, and Galaxies *(Online)*

ASSESS

Unit Assessment: The Solar System and Beyond *(Offline)*

You will complete an offline assessment covering the main objectives of this unit. Your learning coach will score this assessment.

Student Guide
Atoms and Elements

How is it possible to know about something that no one can see? These are the challenges faced by scientists who study atoms. We know about atoms because we can see how they behave. Everything is made of atoms, and the way things are depend on the properties of the atoms that make them up. Explore atoms and their subatomic parts.

Lesson Objectives

- Identify the three main parts of atoms as protons, electrons, and neutrons, and that protons have a positive charge, electrons a negative charge, and neutrons have no charge at all.
- Describe the current model of the atom as a positively charged nucleus containing the protons and neutrons surrounded by electrons moving in certain regions within an electron "cloud."
- Recognize that atoms of each element are exactly alike.
- State that atoms of different elements have different masses depending on the number of protons, electrons, and neutrons, but that most of the mass comes from the protons and neutrons.
- Describe the current model of the atom as a positively charged nucleus containing the protons and neutrons surrounded by electrons moving in certain regions within an "electron cloud".

PREPARE

Approximate lesson time is 60 minutes.

Materials

For the Student

    At the Electron Hotel

Keywords and Pronunciations

Erwin SchrÃdinger (EHR-veen SHROH-ding-ur)

atom: A tiny particle that is the fundamental building block of any substance. The properties of the atom determine the properties of the element made up of only those atoms.

electron: A tiny part of an atom with a negative electric charge. In an atom, electrons form a cloud around the nucleus.

neutron: A particle in the nucleus of an atom, which has no electric charge. Atoms contain neutrons, electrons, and protons.

nucleus (NOO-klee-uhs)**:** The core of an atom made up of protons and neutrons. Electrons form a cloud around the nucleus of an atom.

---

proton: A tiny part of the nucleus of an atom, which has a positive electric charge. The number of protons determines the chemical properties of the atom.

subatomic: Particles that make up atoms. Protons, electrons, and neutrons are subatomic particles.

LEARN

Activity 1: Element-ary Science *(Online)*

Activity 2: At The Electron Hotel *(Offline)*

Visit The Electron Hotel to learn a thing or two about how electrons are placed in their own atomic "rooms," called *shells*.

ASSESS

Lesson Assessment: Atoms and Elements *(Offline)*

You will complete an offline assessment covering the main objectives of this lesson. Your learning coach will score this assessment.

Name _____   Date _____

Atoms and Elements

At the Electron Hotel

An atom's electrons are arranged in energy levels called *shells*. Which shell an electron is in depends on how much energy it has. Exactly how are these electrons arranged? Let's pay a visit to The Electron Hotel to find out.

The Electron Hotel is a happening place for atoms. It's an especially cool place to stay because there is plenty of room for electrons. Like any hotel, though, there are rules—in particular, at The Electron Hotel there are certain rules for where protons, electrons, and neutrons can be.

Imagine you work at the reception desk at The Electron Hotel. You have been given the following rules for atoms and data for floors. Study them carefully.

Electron Hotel Rules

Rule 1: Protons and neutrons must stay in the lobby (nucleus) at all times.

Rule 2: Electrons must stay in the floors above the lobby. (nucleus)

Rule 3: Each floor can hold only a certain number of electrons.

Rule 4: One floor must be full before you place electrons on the next highest floor.

> 1st floor holds 2 electrons
> 2nd floor holds 8 electrons
> 3rd floor holds 18 electrons
> 4th floor holds 32 electrons

On a cold day, in walks an atom of sodium (symbol = Na). Sodium needs a place to stay. Sodium has 11 electrons. The picture below shows the floors sodium would fill at The Electron Hotel. Notice that the third floor isn't full. That's okay. Count the electrons to make sure there are 11. Then, try placing fluorine (symbol = F) into the hotel.

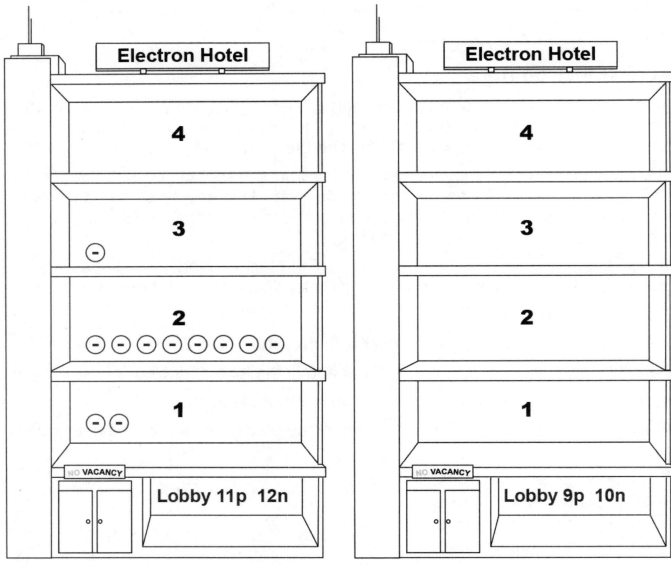

Sodium: 11 p, 12 n, 11 e   Fluorine: 9 p, 10 n, 9 e

You know that, in real atoms, electrons are not arranged on floors. In the current model of atoms, the lobby is the atom's nucleus and the floors are really energy levels. Electrons move around the nucleus in energy levels, creating an electron cloud. Here's another way to show how electrons move around a nucleus. Study it, and then sketch electrons in their energy levels for the following atoms. Stick to the rules of The Electron Hotel!

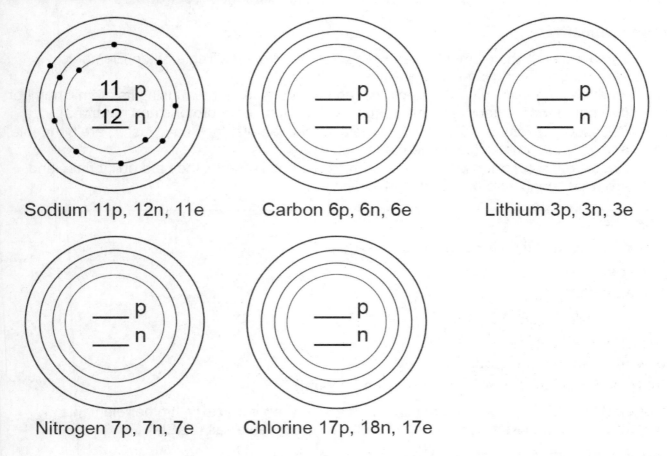

Sodium 11p, 12n, 11e

Carbon 6p, 6n, 6e

Lithium 3p, 3n, 3e

Nitrogen 7p, 7n, 7e

Chlorine 17p, 18n, 17e

Student Guide
The Periodic Table of Elements

The Periodic Table of the Elements is a tool that has information on more than 100 known elements. A quick glance at this table and you'll know element names, symbols, numbers, and parts. By the time you finish, you'll be ready to adopt an element of your own.

Lesson Objectives

- Explain that all the elements are organized in the Periodic Table of the Elements according to their chemical properties.
- Find the number of protons, electrons, and neutrons in an atom using its atomic number (the number of protons) and mass number (the number of protons and neutrons).
- Describe the common properties of metals (for example, they have luster, are bendable, and are good conductors of heat and electricity).
- Describe the common properties of nonmetals (for example, they are dull, brittle, and are poor conductors of heat and electricity).

PREPARE

Approximate lesson time is 60 minutes.

Materials

For the Student

    Atomic Calculations
    Periodic Table of the Elements

Keywords and Pronunciations

Dimitry Mendeleev (dih-MEE-tree men-duh-LAY-uhf)

halogen (HA-luh-juhn)**:** An element that forms a salt when it reacts with other elements. Chlorine, a halogen, reacts with sodium to form common table salt (NaCl)

Jons Jakob Berzelius (youns YAH-kawp buhr-ZAY-lee-uhs)

malleable (MA-lee-uh-buhl)**:** Able to be hammered out. Aluminum is so malleable that it can be hammered out into a thin foil.

metal: An element that is shiny, a good conductor of electricity, and malleable. Aluminum is a metal.

metalloid (MEH-tl-oyd)**:** An element that contains properties of both metals and nonmetals. Silicon is a metalloid.

noble gas: An element that is unreactive and rarely forms compounds with other elements. Helium is a noble gas.

nonmetal: An element that is dull, a poor conductor of electricity, and brittle. Oxygen, the most abundant element in the Earth´s crust, is a nonmetal.

LEARN

Activity 1: The Periodic Table *(Online)*

Activity 2: Atomic Calculations *(Offline)*

The Periodic Table of the Elements is very useful to scientists because it contains a lot of information in a small space. Use the periodic table to find the number of protons, electrons, and neutrons in an atom of any element.

Activity 3: Adopt an Element *(Online)*

Make an element your very own! Adopt an element and find out as much as you can about your new chemical friend.

Select the arrow to begin the activity on the next screen.

ASSESS

Lesson Assessment: The Periodic Table of Elements *(Offline)*

You will complete an offline assessment covering the main objectives of this lesson. Your learning coach will score this assessment.

LEARN

Activity 4: More Elemental Stuff *(Online)*

Did you know that hydrogen once turned a superhero into a proton? Or that sodium was a superhero in a 1963 comic? Look at the Periodic Table of Comic Books to see where elements have turned up in comic book history. Take a quiz on your periodic table knowledge if you're ready.

Safety

The Periodic Table of Comic Books site (referenced in the Beyond the Lesson activity) shows snippets of comic book stories that may include fighting.

The Periodic Table of Elements

Periodic table with atomic number, symbol, name, atomic mass and family

Group headers: Group 1A (1), Group 2A (2), 3 (Group 3B), 4 (Group 4B), 5 (Group 5B), 6 (Group 6B), 7 (Group 7B), 8 (Group 8B), 9 (Group 8B), 10 (Group 8B), 11 (Group 11B), 12 (Group 12B), Group 3A (13), Group 4A (14), Group 5A (15), Group 6A (16), Group 7A (17), Group 8A (18)

Period 1
- 1 H, Hydrogen, 1.008, Hydrogen
- 2 He, Helium, 4.003, Noble Gas

Period 2
- 3 Li, Lithium, 6.94, Alkali Metal
- 4 Be, Beryllium, 9.012, Alkali Earth Metal
- 5 B, Boron, 10.811, Metalloid
- 6 C, Carbon, 12.011, Other Nonmetal
- 7 N, Nitrogen, 14.007, Other Nonmetal
- 8 O, Oxygen, 15.999, Other Nonmetal
- 9 F, Fluorine, 18.998, Halogen
- 10 Ne, Neon, 20.18, Noble Gas

Period 3
- 11 Na, Sodium, 22.99, Alkali Metal
- 12 Mg, Magnesium, 24.305, Alkali Earth Metal
- 13 Al, Aluminum, 26.982, Other Metal
- 14 Si, Silicon, 28.086, Metalloid
- 15 P, Phosphorus, 30.974, Other Nonmetal
- 16 S, Sulfur, 32.065, Other Nonmetal
- 17 Cl, Chlorine, 35.453, Halogen
- 18 Ar, Argon, 39.948, Noble Gas

Period 4
- 19 K, Potassium, 39.098, Alkali Metal
- 20 Ca, Calcium, 40.078, Alkali Earth Metal
- 21 Sc, Scandium, 44.956, Transition Metal
- 22 Ti, Titanium, 47.88, Transition Metal
- 23 V, Vanadium, 50.942, Transition Metal
- 24 Cr, Chromium, 51.996, Transition Metal
- 25 Mn, Manganese, 54.938, Transition Metal
- 26 Fe, Iron, 55.847, Transition Metal
- 27 Co, Cobalt, 58.933, Transition Metal
- 28 Ni, Nickel, 58.693, Transition Metal
- 29 Cu, Copper, 63.546, Transition Metal
- 30 Zn, Zinc, 65.39, Transition Metal
- 31 Ga, Gallium, 69.723, Other Metal
- 32 Ge, Germanium, 72.61, Metalloid
- 33 As, Arsenic, 74.922, Metalloid
- 34 Se, Selenium, 78.96, Other Nonmetal
- 35 Br, Bromine, 79.904, Halogen
- 36 Kr, Krypton, 83.8, Noble Gas

Period 5
- 37 Rb, Rubidium, 85.468, Alkali Metal
- 38 Sr, Strontium, 87.62, Alkali Earth Metal
- 39 Y, Yttrium, 88.906, Transition Metal
- 40 Zr, Zirconium, 91.224, Transition Metal
- 41 Nb, Niobium, 92.906, Transition Metal
- 42 Mo, Molybdenum, 95.94, Transition Metal
- 43 Tc, Technetium, 97.907, Transition Metal
- 44 Ru, Ruthenium, 101.07, Transition Metal
- 45 Rh, Rhodium, 102.906, Transition Metal
- 46 Pd, Palladium, 106.42, Transition Metal
- 47 Ag, Silver, 107.868, Transition Metal
- 48 Cd, Cadmium, 112.411, Transition Metal
- 49 In, Indium, 114.818, Other Metal
- 50 Sn, Tin, 118.71, Other Metal
- 51 Sb, Antimony, 121.76, Metalloid
- 52 Te, Tellurium, 127.6, Metalloid
- 53 I, Iodine, 126.904, Halogen
- 54 Xe, Xenon, 131.29, Noble Gas

Period 6
- 55 Cs, Cesium, 132.905, Alkali Metal
- 56 Ba, Barium, 137.327, Alkali Earth Metal
- 57-71 Lanthanoids
- 72 Hf, Hafnium, 178.49, Transition Metal
- 73 Ta, Tantalum, 180.948, Transition Metal
- 74 W, Tungsten, 183.84, Transition Metal
- 75 Re, Rhenium, 186.207, Transition Metal
- 76 Os, Osmium, 190.23, Transition Metal
- 77 Ir, Iridium, 192.22, Transition Metal
- 78 Pt, Platinum, 195.08, Transition Metal
- 79 Au, Gold, 196.967, Transition Metal
- 80 Hg, Mercury, 200.59, Transition Metal
- 81 Tl, Thallium, 204.383, Other Metal
- 82 Pb, Lead, 207.2, Other Metal
- 83 Bi, Bismuth, 208.98, Other Metal
- 84 Po, Polonium, 208.982, Metalloid
- 85 At, Astatine, 209.987, Metalloid
- 86 Rn, Radon, 222.018, Noble Gas

Period 7
- 87 Fr, Francium, 223.02, Alkali Metal
- 88 Ra, Radium, 226.025, Alkali Earth Metal
- 89-103 Actinoids
- 104 Rf, Rutherfordium, 261, Transition Metal
- 105 Db, Dubnium, 262, Transition Metal
- 106 Sg, Seaborgium, 263, Transition Metal
- 107 Bh, Bohrium, 264, Transition Metal
- 108 Hs, Hassium, 265, Transition Metal
- 109 Mt, Meitnerium, 268, Transition Metal
- 110 Ds, Darmstadtium, 269, Transition Metal
- 111 Rg, Roentgenium, 272, Transition Metal
- 112 Cn, Copernicium, 277, Transition Metal
- 114 Fl, Flerovium, [unkown], New Discovery
- 116 Lv, Livermorium, [unkown], New Discovery

Period 6, Group 2 — Lanthanide Series
- 57 La, Lanthanum, 138.906, Transition Metal
- 58 Ce, Cerium, 140.115, Transition Metal
- 59 Pr, Praseodymium, 140.908, Transition Metal
- 60 Nd, Neodymium, 144.24, Transition Metal
- 61 Pm, Promethium, 144.913, Transition Metal
- 62 Sm, Samarium, 150.36, Transition Metal
- 63 Eu, Europium, 151.965, Transition Metal
- 64 Gd, Gadolinium, 157.25, Transition Metal
- 65 Tb, Terbium, 158.925, Transition Metal
- 66 Dy, Dysprosium, 162.5, Transition Metal
- 67 Ho, Holmium, 164.93, Transition Metal
- 68 Er, Erbium, 167.26, Transition Metal
- 69 Tm, Thulium, 168.934, Transition Metal
- 70 Yb, Ytterbium, 173.04, Transition Metal
- 71 Lu, Lutetium, 174.967, Transition Metal

Period 7, Group 2 — Actinide Series
- 89 Ac, Actinium, 227.028, Transition Metal
- 90 Th, Thorium, 232.038, Transition Metal
- 91 Pa, Protactinium, 231.036, Transition Metal
- 92 U, Uranium, 238.029, Transition Metal
- 93 Np, Neptunium, 237.048, Transition Metal
- 94 Pu, Plutonium, 244.064, Transition Metal
- 95 Am, Americium, 243.061, Transition Metal
- 96 Cm, Curium, 247.07, Transition Metal
- 97 Bk, Berkelium, 247.07, Transition Metal
- 98 Cf, Californium, 251.08, Transition Metal
- 99 Es, Einsteinium, 252.083, Transition Metal
- 100 Fm, Fermium, 257.095, Transition Metal
- 101 Md, Mendelevium, 258.1, Transition Metal
- 102 No, Nobelium, 259.101, Transition Metal
- 103 Lr, Lawrencium, 262, Transition Metal

Name _____   Date _____

The Periodic Table of Elements

Atomic Calculations

It would be hard to find a tool as useful as The Periodic Table of the Elements. In addition to displaying the name, symbol, atomic number, and atomic mass of more than 100 known elements, the Periodic Table contains much more information that can be quickly read.

In an electrically balanced atom, the number of protons and electrons is the same. The atomic number on the Periodic Table tells you the number of protons an element has in the nucleus of any one atom. Therefore, the atomic number also tells you the number of electrons in any one atom. Study the illustration below.

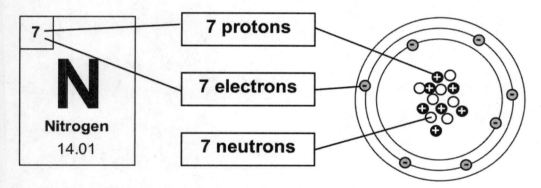

An atom of nitrogen has the same number of protons and electrons. How many neutrons does it have?

Figuring out the number of neutrons requires an easy extra step. At the bottom, under the element symbol, is a number. That number is the atomic mass. Remember that most of the mass in an atom comes from protons and neutrons in the nucleus. Round the atomic mass to the nearest whole number: 14, in this case. Then subtract the number of protons: 7. This number is often close to one or more common isotopes of the element. In some cases, however, an element has many different isotopes and therefore many different numbers of neutrons. The number at the bottom of the square gives you the average atomic mass of all the isotopes.

14 mass – 7 protons = 7 neutrons

Try this for yourself. Color the protons in this oxygen atom. Draw the electrons. Write the number of protons, electrons, and neutrons.

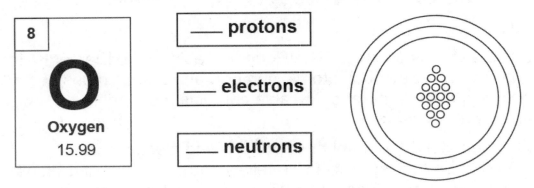

| 8 |
| O |
| Oxygen |
| 15.99 |

_____ protons

_____ electrons

_____ neutrons

Write the number of protons, electrons, and neutrons in each atom.

| 3 |
| Li |
| Lithium |
| 6.94 |

Protons: _____

Electrons: _____

Neutrons: _____

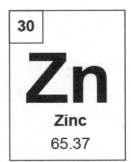

| 30 |
| Zn |
| Zinc |
| 65.37 |

Protons: _____

Electrons: _____

Neutrons: _____

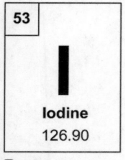

Protons: _____

Electrons: _____

Neutrons: _____

Use the Periodic Table to identify each element. Write the symbol, name, atomic number, and atomic mass in each square.

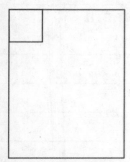

Protons: 29
Electrons: 29
Neutrons: 35

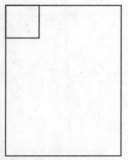

Protons: 14
Electrons: 14
Neutrons: 14

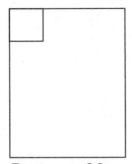

Protons: 82
Electrons: 82
Neutrons: 125

Use the Periodic Table to identify each element. Subtract the number of protons from the mass number to find the neutrons.

Atomic Mass (rounded)	Protons and Electrons	Neutrons	Element
12	6		
24	12		
31		16	
59		32	
	17		
197	79		
	88		

Student Guide
Compounds and Molecules

Elements and now compounds! It takes just over 100 elements to make millions of compounds. Elements join together chemically in special ways. Learn how to read and write a chemical formula and make compound models.

Lesson Objectives

- Use the chemical formula of a compound to identify the elements from which it is composed, and determine the number of each type of atom in the compound.
- Define a *compound* as a substance made of two or more elements.
- Explain that the properties of a compound differ from those of the elements that make up the compound.
- Recognize that elements combine in certain specific proportions to form compounds.

PREPARE

Approximate lesson time is 60 minutes.

Materials

For the Student

    Modeling Molecules

Keywords and Pronunciations

subscript: The number displayed to the bottom right of a symbol that tells how many atoms of that element are present in a compound. In the chemical formula H_2O, the number 2 is the subscript.

LEARN

Activity 1: Elements Get Together—Chemically (*Online*)
Safety

Keep your student away from poisonous products.

Activity 2: Modeling Molecules (*Offline*)

A chemical formula is used to show what elements and the number of atoms of that element that are in a compound. Study chemical formulas and name the elements in each. Use clay and a key to make models of compounds based on their chemical formulas.

ASSESS

Lesson Assessment: Compounds and Molecules *(Offline)*

You will complete an offline assessment covering the main objectives of this lesson. Your learning coach will score this assessment.

LEARN

Activity 3: Surrounded by Compounds *(Online)*

What compounds can be found in a loaf of bread? How about cocktail sauce or shampoo? Search for compounds in foods or products you use each day.

Name _____   Date _____

Compounds and Molecules

Modeling Molecules

Write the name and amounts of each element in each formula.

1. NaCl _____

2. H_2SO_4 _____

3. $CuSO_4$ _____

4. $C_6H_{12}O_6$ _____

Write the chemical formula for each molecule pictured below.

Choose from the following:

H_2S C_2H_5OH

Fe_2O_3 CO_2

CH_4 H_2O

NH_3

          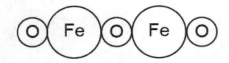

_____   _____   _____

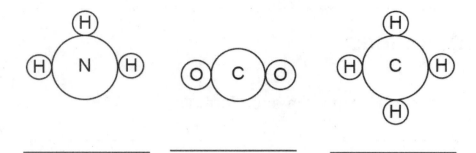

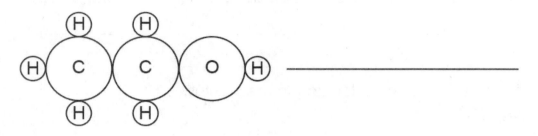

_____   _____   _____

_____

Use clay and the key to make a model of one molecule of each compound. Use resources from this lesson to make sure the atoms are arranged correctly in each molecule.

KEY:

Blue = oxygen

Yellow = nitrogen

Green = hydrogen

Red = carbon

N_2

O_2

H_2O

CO_2

NH_3

CH_4

Challenge Models:

Can you arrange the atoms in the correct way?

C_3H_8

$C_6H_{12}O_6$

Student Guide
Chemical Reactions

Exploding firecrackers, fizzing antacid tablets, and burning wood. What do these have in common? They are all examples of chemical reactions. Emission of light and heat energy, bubbles, fizzing, and formation of a new solid are all clues that a chemical reaction has taken place. Observe a chemical reaction that produces a green blob and work with chemical equations.

Lesson Objectives

- Identify the reactants and products in a chemical equation.
- Match chemical equations to word equations.
- Recognize that for every chemical reaction the number of atoms of each element must be the same for both the reactants and the products.
- Recognize that in chemical reactions the original atoms rearrange themselves into new combinations, and that the resulting products have properties differing from those of the reacting compounds.

PREPARE

Approximate lesson time is 60 minutes.

Advance Preparation

- Prepare iron acetate. Remove any soap from the steel wool with water. Fill one half of a jar with steel wool. Add vinegar so that is covers the steel wool. Label the jar "Iron Acetate." Leave the jar undisturbed for 5 days.

Materials

For the Student

Reaction!
ammonia
jar - small (2)
steel wool
vinegar
safety goggles
spoon - tablespoon
Chemical Equations
Periodic Table of the Elements
household item - calculator
household item - crayons, 64 box
household item - paper

Keywords and Pronunciations

Antoine Lavoisier (AN-twahn lahv-WAHZ-yay)

LEARN

Activity 1: Chemical Reactions *(Online)*

Activity 2: Reaction! *(Offline)*

If you've ever wanted to be a chemist in a laboratory, this investigation is for you. You won't cure diseases, but you'll cause a chemical reaction that will leave you with a great green blob.

Safety

Wear safety goggles during this activity.

Do not smell, taste, or touch any of the reactants or products.

Wash all remaining solutions down the sink with lots of water after the activity.

Activity 3: Chemical Equations *(Offline)*

Instructions

Just like math problems, chemical equations show what happens when two or more things are added together. Practice writing chemical equations.

ASSESS

Lesson Assessment: Chemical Reactions *(Online)*

You will complete an online assessment covering the main objectives of the lesson.

Name _____   Date _____

Chemical Reactions

Reaction!

Investigate a chemical reaction by joining together two reactants to form a new product.

Materials:

Vinegar

Steel wool

Household ammonia

Tablespoon

Two small jars

LAB SAFETY: Wear safety goggles during this activity. Do not smell, taste, or touch any of the reactants or products.

Procedure:

1. Use water to remove any soap from the steel wool.

2. Label one jar Iron Acetate. Fill it halfway with steel wool.

3. Add enough vinegar to cover the steel wool.

4. Cover the jar securely with the lid.

5. Leave the jar undisturbed for 5 days.

6. Pour 1 tablespoon of the liquid iron acetate into the second jar.

7. Add 1 tablespoon of ammonia and stir.

Observations:

1. Describe what happened during this chemical reaction.

_____

_____

2. What clues did you see that told you a reaction had taken place?

_____

_____

The equation for this reaction is:

ammonium hydroxide + iron acetate $\rightarrow$ ammonium acetate + iron hydroxide

You can see there was a change of materials but nothing new was produced. The hydroxide, ammonium, acetate, and iron are still there, but the recombination of their atoms produced a completely new substance.

3. What are the reactants?

_____

_____

4. What are the products?

_____

_____

5. If you were to find the mass of the products and reactants, what differences, if any, would you find?

_____

_____

Name _____   Date _____

Chemical Reactions

Chemical Equations

Chemical equations are a shorthand way of describing chemical reactions. A chemical equation is not finished, though, until it is balanced. A balanced equation has *the same number of atoms on the reactants' side as it has on the products' side*. Students are encouraged to refer to the Periodic Table as a resource to complete the activity.

1. Count the number of atoms of each element on each side of the equation.

2. Use coefficients to balance the numbers of atoms.

3. Check your work by counting the numbers of atoms on each side of the equation again.

   (a) $\_H_2 + O_2 \rightarrow \_H_2O$ (water)

   (b) $\_Na + Cl_2 \rightarrow \_NaCl$ (sodium chloride)

   (c) $\_Fe + O_2 \rightarrow \_FeO$ (iron oxide)

   (d) $\_C + \_H_2O \rightarrow C_6H_{12}O_6$ (glucose)

   (e) $\_CO_2 + \_H_2O \rightarrow C_6H_{12}O_6 + \_O_2$ (glucose and oxygen)

With practice, you can learn to write chemical equations. Read the word equations below, then write their chemical equations. Make sure your equations balance. Chemical formulas that you may need are also listed.

   (f) Nitrogen and hydrogen yield ammonia.

   Nitrogen: N_2

   Hydrogen: H_2

   Ammonia: NH_3

   _____

(g) Magnesium and oxygen yield magnesium oxide.

Magnesium: Mg

Oxygen: O_2

Magnesium oxide: MgO

(h) Bromine and potassium iodide yield potassium bromide and iodine.

Bromine: Br_2

Potassium Iodide: KI

Potassium bromide: KBr

Iodine: I_2

Challenge

Below is the chemical equation for photosynthesis, the process by which plants use energy from the sun to make food. Rewrite the equation for photosynthesis and balance it, if you can.

$$CO_2 + H_2O + light \rightarrow C_6H_{12}O_6 + O_2$$

The Periodic Table of Elements

Periodic table with atomic number, symbol, name, atomic mass and family

Period 1
- Group 1A: 1 H, Hydrogen, 1.008, Hydrogen
- Group 8A: 2 He, Helium, 4.003, Noble Gas

Period 2
- Group 2A: 3 Li, Lithium, 6.941, Alkali Metal
- 4 Be, Beryllium, 9.012, Alkali Earth Metal
- Group 3A: 5 B, Boron, 10.811, Metalloid
- Group 4A: 6 C, Carbon, 12.011, Other Nonmetal
- Group 5A: 7 N, Nitrogen, Other Nonmetal
- Group 6A: 8 O, Oxygen, Other Nonmetal
- Group 7A: 9 F, Fluorine, Halogen
- Group 8A: 10 Ne, Neon, 20.180, Noble Gas

Period 3
- 11 Na, Sodium, 22.99, Alkali Metal
- 12 Mg, Magnesium, 24.305, Alkali Earth Metal
- 13 Al, Aluminum, 26.982, Other Metal
- 14 Si, Silicon, 28.086, Metalloid
- 15 P, Phosphorus, 30.974, Other Nonmetal
- 16 S, Sulfur, 32.06, Other Nonmetal
- 17 Cl, Chlorine, 35.453, Halogen
- 18 Ar, Argon, 39.948, Noble Gas

Period 4
- 19 K, Potassium, 39.098, Alkali Metal
- 20 Ca, Calcium, 40.078, Alkali Earth Metal
- 21 Sc, Scandium, 44.956, Transition Metal
- 22 Ti, Titanium, 47.88, Transition Metal
- 23 V, Vanadium, 50.942, Transition Metal
- 24 Cr, Chromium, 51.996, Transition Metal
- 25 Mn, Manganese, 54.938, Transition Metal
- 26 Fe, Iron, 55.847, Transition Metal
- 27 Co, Cobalt, 58.933, Transition Metal
- 28 Ni, Nickel, 58.693, Transition Metal
- 29 Cu, Copper, 63.546, Transition Metal
- 30 Zn, Zinc, 65.39, Transition Metal
- 31 Ga, Gallium, 69.723, Other Metal
- 32 Ge, Germanium, 72.61, Metalloid
- 33 As, Arsenic, 74.922, Metalloid
- 34 Se, Selenium, Other Nonmetal
- 35 Br, Bromine, Halogen
- 36 Kr, Krypton, 83.8, Noble Gas

Period 5
- 37 Rb, Rubidium, 85.468, Alkali Metal
- 38 Sr, Strontium, 87.62, Alkali Earth Metal
- 39 Y, Yttrium, 88.906, Transition Metal
- 40 Zr, Zirconium, 91.224, Transition Metal
- 41 Nb, Niobium, 92.906, Transition Metal
- 42 Mo, Molybdenum, 95.94, Transition Metal
- 43 Tc, Technetium, 97.907, Transition Metal
- 44 Ru, Ruthenium, 101.07, Transition Metal
- 45 Rh, Rhodium, 102.906, Transition Metal
- 46 Pd, Palladium, 106.42, Transition Metal
- 47 Ag, Silver, 107.868, Transition Metal
- 48 Cd, Cadmium, 112.411, Transition Metal
- 49 In, Indium, 114.818, Other Metal
- 50 Sn, Tin, 118.71, Other Metal
- 51 Sb, Antimony, 121.76, Metalloid
- 52 Te, Tellurium, 127.6, Metalloid
- 53 I, Iodine, 126.904, Halogen
- 54 Xe, Xenon, 131.29, Noble Gas

Period 6
- 55 Cs, Cesium, 132.905, Alkali Metal
- 56 Ba, Barium, 137.327, Alkali Earth Metal
- 57–71 Lanthanoids
- 72 Hf, Hafnium, 178.49, Transition Metal
- 73 Ta, Tantalum, 180.948, Transition Metal
- 74 W, Tungsten, 183.84, Transition Metal
- 75 Re, Rhenium, 186.207, Transition Metal
- 76 Os, Osmium, 190.23, Transition Metal
- 77 Ir, Iridium, 192.22, Transition Metal
- 78 Pt, Platinum, 195.08, Transition Metal
- 79 Au, Gold, 196.967, Transition Metal
- 80 Hg, Mercury, 200.59, Transition Metal
- 81 Tl, Thallium, 204.383, Other Metal
- 82 Pb, Lead, 207.2, Other Metal
- 83 Bi, Bismuth, 208.98, Other Metal
- 84 Po, Polonium, 208.982, Metalloid
- 85 At, Astatine, 209.987, Metalloid
- 86 Rn, Radon, 222.018, Noble Gas

Period 7
- 87 Fr, Francium, 223.02, Alkali Metal
- 88 Ra, Radium, 226.025, Alkali Earth Metal
- 89–103 Actinoids
- 104 Rf, Rutherfordium, 261, Transition Metal
- 105 Db, Dubnium, 262, Transition Metal
- 106 Sg, Seaborgium, 263, Transition Metal
- 107 Bh, Bohrium, 264, Transition Metal
- 108 Hs, Hassium, 265, Transition Metal
- 109 Mt, Meitnerium, 268, Transition Metal
- 110 Ds, Darmstadtium, 269, Transition Metal
- 111 Rg, Roentgenium, 272, Transition Metal
- 112 Cn, Copernicium, 277, Transition Metal
- 114 Fl, Flerovium, [unknown], New Discovery
- 116 Lv, Livermorium, [unknown], New Discovery

Lanthanide Series — Period 6, Group 2
- 57 La, Lanthanum, 138.906, Transition Metal
- 58 Ce, Cerium, 140.115, Transition Metal
- 59 Pr, Praseodymium, 140.908, Transition Metal
- 60 Nd, Neodymium, 144.24, Transition Metal
- 61 Pm, Promethium, 144.913, Transition Metal
- 62 Sm, Samarium, 150.36, Transition Metal
- 63 Eu, Europium, 151.965, Transition Metal
- 64 Gd, Gadolinium, 157.25, Transition Metal
- 65 Tb, Terbium, 158.925, Transition Metal
- 66 Dy, Dysprosium, 162.5, Transition Metal
- 67 Ho, Holmium, 164.93, Transition Metal
- 68 Er, Erbium, 167.26, Transition Metal
- 69 Tm, Thulium, 168.934, Transition Metal
- 70 Yb, Ytterbium, 173.04, Transition Metal
- 71 Lu, Lutetium, 174.967, Transition Metal

Actinide series — Period 7, Group 2
- 89 Ac, Actinium, 227.028, Transition Metal
- 90 Th, Thorium, 232.038, Transition Metal
- 91 Pa, Protactinium, 231.036, Transition Metal
- 92 U, Uranium, 238.029, Transition Metal
- 93 Np, Neptunium, 237.048, Transition Metal
- 94 Pu, Plutonium, 244.064, Transition Metal
- 95 Am, Americium, 243.061, Transition Metal
- 96 Cm, Curium, 247.07, Transition Metal
- 97 Bk, Berkelium, 247.07, Transition Metal
- 98 Cf, Californium, 251.08, Transition Metal
- 99 Es, Einsteinium, 252.083, Transition Metal
- 100 Fm, Fermium, 257.095, Transition Metal
- 101 Md, Mendelevium, 258.1, Transition Metal
- 102 No, Nobelium, 259.101, Transition Metal
- 103 Lr, Lawrencium, 262, Transition Metal

Student Guide

Acids and Bases

What's sour, corrosive when strong, and contains the element hydrogen? An acid is. What's bitter and slippery when wet? A base is. A substance may be an acid, a base, or it may be neutral. Find out about the properties of acids and bases. Use an indicator and the pH scale to find out if common substances are acids or bases.

Lesson Objectives

- Use the pH Scale to determine whether a solution is acidic or basic.
- Describe properties of acids (for example, acids taste sour, are corrosive, and contain the element hydrogen).
- Describe properties of bases (for example, bases taste bitter and feel slippery when dissolved in water).
- Demonstrate mastery of the skills taught in this lesson.

PREPARE

Approximate lesson time is 60 minutes.

Materials

For the Student

Testing Acids and Bases
ammonia - weak
aspirin tablet
cup, plastic (8)
lemon juice
litmus paper
milk of magnesia
soft drink
vinegar - white
graduated cylinder
soap
spoon
tape - masking
food - head of red cabbage
strainer - or sieve

Optional

coffee filter
household item - food processor or knife
household item - saucepan or 500 mL beaker
jar, storage
rubbing alcohol

Keywords and Pronunciations

acid: A substance that is characterized by sour taste and has a pH of less than 7. Ascorbic acid is found in citrus fruits such as lemons and oranges.

ascorbic (uh-SKOR-bihk)

base: compound that produces hydroxide ions in solution with water, reacts with an acid to form a salt, captures hydrogen ions, and donates an electron pair to form a chemical bond

bases: substance that is characterized by a bitter taste, slippery feel, and a pH of greater than 7.

indicator: A dye that can be used to show the pH level of a solution. Litmus paper contains an indicator.

neutralize: To reduce the acidity of a substance with a base, and vice versa. Antacid tablets neutralize the acid in your stomach.

pH: A scale that measures the acidity or baseness of a solution. A substance is classified as an acid if it has a pH of less than 7.

LEARN

Activity 1: Acids and Bases *(Online)*

Activity 2: Testing Acids and Bases *(Offline)*

Litmus paper is an indicator that turns red in the presence of an acid and blue in the presence of a base. Use litmus paper to test solutions for this property.

You will need your safety goggles. Do not smell or taste any of the solutions you test in this activity.

Safety

Wear safety goggles. Do not taste or smell any of the solutions used in this activity.

ASSESS

Lesson Assessment: Acids and Bases *(Offline)*

You will complete an offline assessment covering the main objectives of this lesson. Your learning coach will score this assessment.

LEARN

Activity 3: Optional: Cabbage Juice Indicator *(Offline)*
Instructions

Follow the directions to make a cabbage juice indicator.

1. Chop the red cabbage.

2. Bring 500 ml water to boil in a saucepan.

3. Add the cabbage to the boiling water and carefully remove from heat.

4. Let the saucepan stand for 30 minutes.

5. Strain the liquid-cabbage mixture and discard the cabbage.

6. For storage, make a solution of the cabbage liquid and alcohol, using 1 part alcohol to 5 parts cabbage liquid.

Label carefully to prevent accidents. The cabbage liquid can also be stored by freezing in ice cube trays.

To use as an indicator, add a drop or two of cabbage juice to the substance to be tested. Try re-testing some of the solutions used in the lesson. Observe the color change.

You can also use cabbage juice to make a homemade kind of litmus paper. Another testing method is to soak a filter paper in cabbage liquid. Place on wax paper or paper plate to dry. Cut the dry paper into rectangular strips. The strips can be dipped into substances for testing

Name _____   Date _____

Acids and Bases
Testing Acids and Bases

Litmus paper is a tool chemists use to determine whether a solution is an acid, a base, or is neutral. It is dipped into a solution and then removed. If the color of the litmus changes to red, the solution is acidic. If it changes to blue, it is basic. If it does not change color, the solution is neutral.

Use litmus paper as an indicator to test for acids and bases.

Hypothesis

From the following list of materials, predict which are acids and which are bases: white vinegar, lemon juice, weak ammonia solution, liquid soap, soft drink, milk of magnesia, aspirin, water.

_____

_____

_____

Materials

litmus paper	lemon juice
8 plastic cups	weak ammonia solution
graduated cylinder	liquid soap
spoon	soft drink
masking tape	milk of magnesia
white vinegar	aspirin tablet
water	eyedropper

LAB SAFETY: Wear safety goggles during this activity. Do not smell or taste any of the solutions you test.

Procedure

1. Use masking tape to make a label for each cup: vinegar, lemon juice, ammonia, liquid soap, soft drink, milk of magnesia, aspirin, water.

2. Crush the aspirin tablet in 120 mL of water.

3. Use the cylinder to add 5 mL of each solution to the cups.

4. Use the eyedropper to place a few drops of a solution between your thumb and forefinger, then rub your fingers together. Does the solution feel slippery?

5. Wash your hands.

6. Dip one piece of litmus paper into the first cup. Record your results on the chart.

7. Repeat the test for each cup with a new piece of litmus paper each time.

Science Notebook:

Identify the variables in your experiment. Remember, the independent variable is what the experimenter changes in an experiment. The dependent variable is what happens because of the change.

Independent Variable: _____

Dependent Variable: _____

Solution	Slippery Feel	Litmus Paper Color	Acid, Base, or Neutral?
White Vinegar			
Lemon Juice			
Ammonia			
Liquid Soap			
Soft Drink			
Milk of Magnesia			
Water			
Aspirin			

Conclusion

1. Check your hypothesis. Which substances did you predict correctly?

_____

_____

2. If you predicted any incorrectly, explain why you think this happened.

_____

_____

Investigation Idea

Wet a cotton swab with your saliva. Touch the saliva to the paper to find out if your saliva is acidic or basic.

Student Guide

Identification of Compounds

Elements are made of atoms. Elements combine to form compounds. Compounds can combine with other compounds to make even more compounds! Certain tests can be used to determine what elements or compounds are present in the product of a chemical reaction. Try an iodine test for starch and observe flame tests for certain metals.

Lesson Objectives

- Describe one method of identifying a compound or element in a product of a chemical reaction.
- Name four types of evidence of a chemical reaction: Change in temperature, color change, release of a gas, and the formation of a precipitate.

PREPARE

Approximate lesson time is 60 minutes.

Advance Preparation

- If you don't already have it, you will need iodine for the Starch Search activity.

Materials

For the Student

Starch Search
household item - apple
iodine - Lugol's iodine solution or iodine tincture
potato - white
bread
plate, paper

Keywords and Pronunciations

precipitate (prih-SIH-puh-tayt): A solid that forms as a result of a chemical reaction. A white solid precipitate may form when aluminum chloride is added to a substance that contains aluminum.

residue: A substance left over as a result of a chemical reaction. The black residue left over from burning fossil fuels or wood is carbon.

LEARN

Activity 1: Identifying Compounds *(Online)*

Activity 2: Starch Search *(Offline)*

Searching for starch takes a matter of seconds with iodine. Iodine is a quick reactor to the presence of starch. Look for a color change in iodine to figure out whether a potato, piece of bread, or an apple contain starch.

Safety

Wear safety goggles during the Starch Search activity.

Activity 3: Flame Tests *(Online)*

Flame tests can be used to figure out whether a compound contains certain metals. It is not safe to do a flame test unless you are in a lab with lab equipment. It is safe, however, to see pictures of flame tests. See three different flame tests and then answer a series of questions about them.

ASSESS

Lesson Assessment: Identification of Compounds *(Offline)*

You will complete an offline assessment covering the main objectives of this lesson. Your learning coach will score this assessment.

Name _____ Date _____

Identification of Compounds
Starch Search

Certain tests can tell whether a particular compound is in a reactant or product. One of those tests is a starch test. Iodine can be used to detect starch in foods.

Hypothesis:

Predict which foods contain starch: apple, bread, and/or potato.

_____

_____

Materials:

1 apple

1 potato

1 slice of bread

iodine

plate

LAB SAFETY:

Wear safety goggles during this experiment.

Procedure:

1. Cut a slice of the apple, potato, and bread.

2. Put the slices on a plate with space between them.

3. Place 2 to 3 drops of iodine on each piece.

4. Record your observations on page 2.

Science Notebook

The *independent variable* is what an experimenter changes in an experiment. The *dependent variable* is what happens because of the change. Identify both variables.

IV: _____

DV: _____

Observations

Describe how the iodine reacted when placed on each of the foods.

_____

_____

_____

_____

Analysis:

Which foods contain starch?

_____

_____

Conclusion:

Describe the method you used to find out whether there was a certain compound in a substance.

_____

_____

_____

Investigation Idea:

Some people try to lose weight by eating a low-starch diet. Test other foods of your choice for the presence of starch. Test foods you eat most of the time. Do you have a starchy diet? Are some foods starchier than others?

Student Guide

Molecules of Life

You know that compounds make up the stuff around you, but did you ever stop to think that you are made of compounds, too? Living things contain compounds made from just four main elements. Learn about the three classes of compounds necessary for survival and how you can take them into your body as food.

Lesson Objectives

- Define inorganic compounds as those that do not usually contain the element carbon.
- Define organic compounds as carbon-based, such as those produced by living things and certain others produced in chemistry laboratories.
- Describe the functions of proteins, lipids, and carbohydrates in human nutrition.
- Recognize that living organisms are composed of mainly just a few elements: carbon, hydrogen, oxygen, and nitrogen.

PREPARE

Approximate lesson time is 60 minutes.

Materials

For the Student

Carbohydrates, Proteins, and Lipids
Molecular Models
clay - blue
clay - green
clay - red
clay - yellow
toothpicks

Keywords and Pronunciations

carbohydrates (kahr-boh-HIY-drayts)**:** Substances made from carbon, oxygen, and hydrogen that provide energy to the body in the form of glucose. Pasta, bread, and rice are foods high in carbohydrates.

lipid (LIH-puhdz)**:** Substances that include fats and oils and provide the body with energy and material to build hormones. Lipids are found in foods containing fat.

proteins: Substances built from amino acids that function in many ways in the body. Proteins provide the body with material for forming new cells, skin, and muscles.

LEARN

Activity 1: The Molecules of Our Lives *(Online)*

Activity 2: Review Carbohydrates, Proteins, and Lipids *(Offline)*

Certain compounds are very important to you personally. Your body needs carbohydrates, proteins, and lipids for energy and to carry out processes. Review the structures and functions of these compounds.

Activity 3: Molecular Models *(Offline)*

Eating is fun—and necessary, too! We must eat in order to get nutrients, such as carbohydrates, proteins, and lipids, into our bodies. Learn how we interact with these organic molecules and build molecular models of each type.

ASSESS

Lesson Assessment: Molecules of Life *(Offline)*

You will complete an offline assessment covering the main objectives of this lesson. Your learning coach will score this assessment.

Name _____   Date _____

Molecules of Life
Carbohydrates, Proteins, and Lipids

Use the table to compare carbohydrates, proteins, and lipids. Then answer the questions.

Characteristics	Carbohydrates	Proteins	Lipids
Structure			
In what foods?			
Purpose in the body			

1. Organic compounds are found naturally in, or are produced by, living things and contain the element _____.

2. Compounds that do not come from living organisms and do not contain this element are called _____compounds.

3. What four elements are the main components of living things?

   _____

Name _____   Date _____

Molecules of Life

Molecular Models

Living organisms are made of just a few elements: carbon, hydrogen, nitrogen, and oxygen.

Carbohydrates are made of chains of sugars called *glucose*. The word *carbohydrate* comes from the fact that glucose is made of carbon and water. The formula for glucose is $C_6H_{12}O_6$. A diagram of a glucose molecule is shown below.

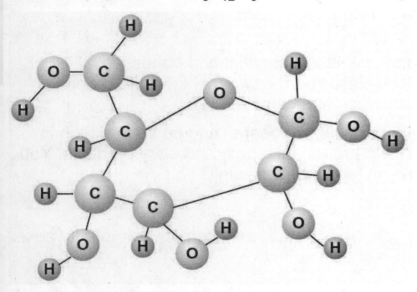

The body uses glucose to make energy. Glucose is a sugar. You may have been told to stay away from sugary foods, such as soda and candy bars, because they make you too energetic. The reason for this is that soda and candy bars contain simple sugars. Simple sugars are absorbed very quickly into your bloodstream, giving you lots of energy quickly. Your body secretes insulin to balance the sugar. A few hours later, your blood sugar drops and you may feel tired and irritable. This describes the "sugar high" and "low" you might feel after eating sweet things.

Complex carbohydrates take longer to enter the bloodstream. Foods such as pasta and breads contain complex carbohydrates, which are eventually broken down into simple sugars, but much more slowly than glucose breaks down.

When you look at a "Nutrition Facts" label on a food package, look for "Sugars" under the "Carbohydrates" section of the label. This shows the amount of simple sugars the product contains.

Proteins

Proteins are made of chains of amino acids. Amino acids provide your cells with "building material" to grow and develop. They are called *amino acids* because they have an amino group and an acid group. A model of an amino acid is shown below.

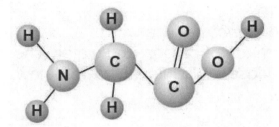

There are two different types of amino acids—essential and nonessential. Your body can make nonessential amino acids. Your body cannot make essential amino acids. You must eat foods that contain them.

Most vegetables are low in protein, but nuts, soybeans, and beans are high in protein. Other good sources of protein are meats, eggs, and dairy products. You can find information about proteins on food labels as well.

Lipids

Fats and oils are types of lipids. In the body, fats are broken down into fatty acids and glycerol. A fatty acid molecule is shown below.

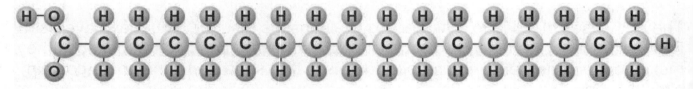

It is important to make fats a part of your diet. Fats are found in vegetable oil, shortening, or lard. These are often used in bread and pastries. Meat has animal fat. Fried food is cooked in fatty oils. Fats are greasy and slick.

Some vitamins will dissolve only in fat, so the only way to get these vitamins is to eat fat. Some fatty acids are essential, and you need them because your body cannot make them. Fats are also good sources of energy.

Make a Model

Use the diagrams, toothpicks, and clay to make a model of either a protein, carbohydrate, or lipid. Choose one to model. (You may do more than one if you have time.)

Red clay = oxygen atom

Blue clay = nitrogen atom

Yellow clay = hydrogen atom

Green clay = carbon atom

1. Compare the glucose and fatty acid molecule. Lipids store more energy in their bonds than carbohydrates do. Explain what happens to the leftover energy.

   _____

   _____

   _____

2. Make a list of what you have eaten today. Try to identify each as a carbohydrate, protein, or lipid (fat). Is your diet balanced?

Student Guide

Reaction Rates

Explore four ways by which you can increase the rate of a chemical reaction. Investigate two ways to speed things up—with a plop and a fizz!

Lesson Objectives

- Explain that all chemical reactions require a certain amount of energy in order to break existing bonds in the reactants and form new bonds in the products.
- Identify four ways to increase the rate of a chemical reaction (increase the temperature, surface area, concentration, and add a catalyst).
- Recognize that enzymes can act as catalysts to speed up chemical reactions in the human body.

PREPARE

Approximate lesson time is 60 minutes.

Advance Preparation

- You will need at least 6 fizzling antacid tablets, 3 balloons, and 3 plastic10-12oz bottles for the Quick Action Reaction activity. If you choose to complete the Flour Power activity, you will need a half gallon milk carton and rubber tubing.

Materials

For the Student

Quick Action Reaction
drinking glass - clear, 3
household item - cutting board
household item - fizzling antacid tablets (6)
household item - stopwatch
rock
thermometer, Celsius/Fahrenheit
balloon - 3 (blow up to stretch)
bottle, plastic - 10, 12 oz soda
graduated cylinder
paper
spoon
water - tap, cold
water - tap, hot
water - tap, room temperature

Keywords and Pronunciations

catalyst (KA-tl-uhst): A substance that increases the rate of a reaction but doesn't get used up. To speed the decomposition of hydrogen peroxide into water and oxygen, use manganese dioxide as a catalyst.

concentration: The amount of something packed into a given space. The concentration of students on the bus increased when Jared and Sonya got on.

enzymes (EN-ziym): A protein in the body. Some enzymes help break food down into usable nutrients during digestion. Enzymes in your saliva break down starch, starting the process of digestion.

surface area: The amount of space the outer face of an object takes up. To find the surface area of a rectangle, multiply the width times the height.

LEARN

Activity 1: Explore: Reaction Rates *(Online)*
Activity 2: Quick Action Reaction *(Offline)*

There are several ways you can speed up the rate of a chemical reaction. Investigate two of them now.

Safety

Wear safety goggles during the Quick Action Reaction activity.

Use caution when handling hot water.

ASSESS

Lesson Assessment: Reaction Rates *(Online)*

You will complete an online assessment covering the main objectives of the lesson.

Name _____   Date _____

Reaction Rates
Quick Action Reaction

Fill in the blanks to review four ways to speed up a chemical reaction.

1. A _____ speeds up a chemical reaction without being used up.
2. Increasing the _____ increases the energy at which atoms collide in a reaction.
3. Breaking up a substance into smaller pieces increases _____.
4. Packing more molecules into a certain space increases the _____ of a substance.

Try It!

Dropping an antacid tablet into a cup of water produces a lot of fizz—and a chemical reaction. The reaction of the tablet and water releases carbon dioxide gas. You can use this simple reaction to investigate ways to speed up reaction rates.

Investigation: Temperature and Reaction Rate

You can increase the rate of a chemical reaction by increasing the temperature of these reactants.

Hypothesis:

Predict how many times faster an antacid tablet will react in hot water than in cold water.

_____

Materials:

fizzing antacid tablets (such as those with sodium bicarbonate), 6

tap water

clear glasses, 3

balloons, 3 (blow up to stretch)

spoon

10 to 12 oz (248 to 340 mL) soda bottles, 3

stopwatch

thermometer

rock

cutting board

paper

graduated cylinder

Lab Safety:

Wear safety goggles during the activity. Use caution when handling hot water.

Procedure:

Hot Water

1. Run water from the hot tap until it is as hot as possible.

2. Fill a glass with 150 mL of hot water.

3. Use the thermometer to find and record the temperature of the water, then pour the water into one of the soda bottles.

4. Break an antacid tablet into about five pieces. Add it to the hot water bottle.

5. Have a partner immediately place a balloon over the mouth of the bottle. Start the timer. *Be quick!* The reaction takes less than 15 seconds.

6. Time how long it takes for the balloon to inflate. Record your observations.

Room-Temperature Water

7. Fill a glass with 150 mL of room-temperature water.

8. Repeat steps 3 to 6.

Cold Water

9. Fill a glass with 75 mL of water. Add ice to adjust the level to 150 mL. Stir the ice water for about 15 seconds.

10. Repeat steps 3 to 6. Leave the ice cubes in the water.

Scientist Notebook

Identify the independent variable (what is changed) and dependent variable (what will happen) in this investigation.

_____

_____

_____

Observations

Temperature of Water °C	Reaction Time in Seconds

Analysis

Make a line graph of your data.

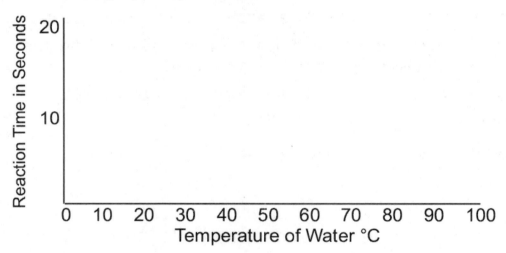

Conclusion

1. What happens to the rate of reaction as the temperature increases?

_____

2. How many times faster was the reaction in hot water than in cold water?

_____

3. How many seconds would it take for an antacid tablet to react with water at a temperature of 10°C? _____

4. If the temperature is doubled from 20°C to 40°C, the time for the rate of reaction will _____.

Investigation: Surface Area and Reaction Rate

Increasing the surface area of a reactant by breaking it up into pieces will expose more of the reactant so its molecules collide faster and more often.

Hypothesis:

Predict how much faster a ground-up antacid tablet will react compared to a whole tablet.

_____

_____

Materials

clear glasses, 3

fizzing antacid tablets (such as those with sodium bicarbonate), 3

rock

cutting board

stopwatch

paper

graduated cylinder

Lab Safety:

Wear safety goggles during the activity. Use caution when handling hot water.

Procedure

Whole Tablet

1. Fill a glass with 150 mL of room-temperature water.

2. Drop one whole antacid tablet into the water. Measure and record the time it takes to dissolve.

Tablet in Pieces.

3. Place one antacid tablet on paper and break it into about eight pieces of equal size.

4. Repeat step one.

5. Slide the broken tablet from the paper into the glass. Measure and record the time it takes to dissolve.

Powdered Tablet

1. Use the rock and cutting board to grind one tablet into a fine powder.

2. Transfer the powder into a glass (before adding water).

3. Add 150 mL of water to the glass. Measure and record the time the powder takes to dissolve.

Scientist Notebook

Identify the independent variable (what is changed) and dependent variable (what will happen) in this investigation.

_____

_____

Observations

Condition of Tablet	Reaction Time in Seconds
Whole	
Broken	
Powder	

Analysis

Make a bar graph of your data.

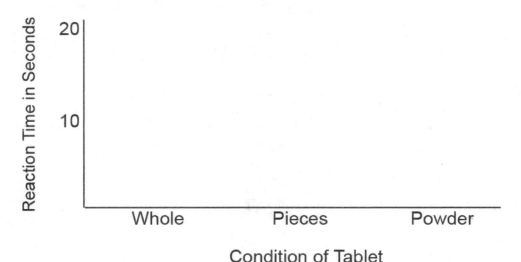

Conclusion

1. What happens to the rate of reaction as the particle size decreases?

_____

2. The rate of reaction for the powder was _____ faster than for the whole tablet.

3. Which has more of an effect on the rate of a reaction—particle size or temperature?

_____

_____

_____

_____

Student Guide

Chemistry: Unit Review and Assessment

You are familiar with atomic structure and the periodic table. Compounds, chemical reactions, and chemical equations you've also got down. You're ready to show your new skills in chemistry.

Lesson Objectives

- Explain that all the elements are organized in the Periodic Table of the Elements according to their chemical properties.
- Identify the three main parts of atoms as protons, electrons, and neutrons, and that protons have a positive charge, electrons a negative charge, and neutrons have no charge at all.
- Use the pH Scale to determine whether a solution is acidic or basic.
- Describe a *compound* as a substance made of two or more elements. Explain that the properties of a compound differ from those of the elements that make up the compound.
- Describe how reaction rates increase with temperature, surface area, concentration, and in the presence of a catalyst.
- Describe the common properties of metals and nonmetals.
- Describe the current model of the atom as a positively charged nucleus containing the protons and neutrons surrounded by electrons moving in certain regions within an "electron cloud".
- Explain that all chemical reactions require energy.
- Identify some common elements and compounds by both their chemical symbols and their formulas.
- Recognize that in chemical reactions the original atoms rearrange themselves into new combinations, and that the resulting products have properties differing from those of the reacting compounds.
- Recognize that the atoms of an element are exactly alike and that each element is made of only one kind of atom.
- Write chemical equations to show what happens in a chemical reaction.
- Find the number of protons, electrons, and neutrons in an atom using its atomic number (the number of protons) and mass number (the number of protons and neutrons).
- Define a *compound* as a substance made of two or more elements.
- Demonstrate mastery of the skills taught in this unit.
- Describe the common properties of metals (for example, they have luster, are bendable, and are good conductors of heat and electricity).
- Describe the common properties of nonmetals (for example, they are dull, brittle, and are poor conductors of heat and electricity).
- Name four types of evidence of a chemical reaction: Change in temperature, color change, release of a gas, and the formation of a precipitate.
- Recognize that atoms of each element are exactly alike.

- Recognize that enzymes can act as catalysts to speed up chemical reactions in the human body.
- Recognize that living organisms are composed of mainly just a few elements: carbon, hydrogen, oxygen, and nitrogen.
- Identify some parts of the human endocrine system and their function (pituitary gland, thyroid gland, adrenal gland, and pancreas).

PREPARE

Approximate lesson time is 60 minutes.

Materials

For the Student

Question Review Table

LEARN

Activity 1: Professor Pete and the Interview (Online)

ASSESS

Unit Assessment: Chemistry (Offline)

You will complete an offline assessment covering the main objectives of this unit. Your learning coach will score this assessment.

LEARN

Activity 2: Optional: Unit Assessment Review Table (Online)

If you earned a score of **less than 80%** on the Unit Assessment, complete the activity.

If you earned a score of **80% or greater**, you may skip this activity.

Let's prepare to retake the Unit Assessment:

- Print the Question Review Table.
- Identify the questions that you answered incorrectly.
- Complete the appropriate review activities listed in the table.

Note: This will guide you through the process of using the Unit Assessment Review Tables. You may skip this video if you've already viewed it in another unit or course. As always, check in with your student's teacher if you have any questions.

Activity 3: Optional: ZlugQuest Measurement (Online)

Name _____   Date _____

Chemistry: Unit Review and Assessment
Question Review Table

Before you retake the Unit Assessment, use the table to figure out which activities you should review.

Circle the numbers of the questions that you missed on the Unit Assessment. Review the activities that correspond with these questions.

Question	Lesson	Review Activity
1, 2	2: The Periodic Table of Elements	Explore: The Periodic Table
3, 5, 8, 11	1: Atoms and Elements	Explore: Elementary Science
4, 6	2: The Periodic Table of Elements	Explore: The Periodic Table Adopt an Element More Elemental Stuff
7	3: Compounds and Molecules	Explore: Elements Get Together – Chemically Modeling Molecules Surrounded by Compounds
9	4: Chemical Reactions	Explore: Chemical Reactions Reaction!
10	8: Reaction Rates	Explore: Reaction Rates
11, 12, 13, 14	1: Atoms and Elements	Explore: Element-ary Science At the Electron Hotel
15, 16	2: The Periodic Table	Explore: The Periodic Table Atomic Calculations Adopt an Element

Question	Lesson	Review Activity
17, 18, 19, 20, 21, 22	3: Compounds and Molecules	Explore: Elements Get Together Modeling Molecules
23	3: Compounds and Molecules	Explore: Elements Get Together
24, 25	5: Acids and Bases	Explore: Acids and Bases Testing Acids and Bases Cabbage Juice Indicator
26	6: Identification of Compounds	Explore: Identifying Compounds
27	8: Reaction Rates	Explore: Reaction Rates Quick Action Reaction Flour Power-Surface Area and Reactions
28	4: Chemical Reactions	Explore: Chemical Reactions Reaction!
29	6: Identification of Compounds	Starch Search
30	7: Molecules of Life	Explore: The Molecules of Our Lives Review Carbohydrates, Proteins, and Lipids Molecular Models

Student Guide
The Cell Theory

Compared to most scientific discoveries, ideas about cells began forming not that long ago. In the 1600s, people began wondering about what makes up living things. We now know that the smallest part of any living thing is a cell—with organelles that perform jobs much like the organs in your body. Learn the parts of plant and animal cells and their jobs.

All living things are made of cells. Cells are the "building blocks" of living things, from the leaves of a marigold to a duck's webbed feet. You'd think that cells would be tiny—and they usually are. But some cells are large enough for you to see and hold. Learn the cell theory and explore the basic parts of cells.

Lesson Objectives

- Identify the major structures of the cell (such as cell membrane, cytoplasm, and nucleus) and describe their functions.
- Describe the three major ideas of the cell theory.

PREPARE

Approximate lesson time is 60 minutes.

Materials

For the Student

  Did You Know?

Keywords and Pronunciations

Anton van Leeuwenhoek (AHN-tohn vahn LAY-ven-hook)

cell: The basic unit of life, of which all living things are made. Some organisms are made up of only one cell.

cell membrane: The flexible, double-layered covering of all cells. The cell membrane is composed of a double layer of molecules.

chloroplast (KLOR-uh-plast)**:** The "solar panel" of plant cells, in which energy from the sun is converted into stored chemical energy by the process of photosynthesis. Chloroplasts contain chlorophyll and are found in plant cells, but not in animal cells.

cytoplasm (SIY-tuh-pla-zuhm)**:** The jelly-like matter of a living cell that is outside the nucleus. Organelles are contained in cytoplasm.

endocrine (EN-duh-kruhn)

Francesco Redi (frahn-CHAYS-koh REHD-ee)

Matthias Schleiden (mah-TEE-uhs SHLIY-duhn)

---

nucleus (NOO-klee-uhs): The command center of plant and animal cells, which contains the information needed to direct activities for building, maintaining and operating the cell. Information in the nucleus determines which molecules the cell makes.

prokaryotes (proh-KAIR-ee-ohts)

Rudolf Virchow (ROO-dawlf FIHR-koh)

LEARN

Activity 1: What Are You Made Of? *(Online)*

Activity 2: Did You Know? *(Online)*

What's the difference between Hooke and Anton van Leeuwenhoek? Find out through a review of cells and their discovery with an interactive time line.

ASSESS

Lesson Assessment: The Cell Theory *(Offline)*

You will complete an offline assessment covering the main objectives of this lesson. Your learning coach will score this assessment.

Name _____ Date _____

The Cell Theory
Did You Know?

Did you know major cell discoveries have been taking place for hundreds of years? But that's not all! Use the lesson and the links in Lesson Resources to answer the questions and learn lesser-known facts about the development of the cell theory.

1. Did you know the first person to observe cells through a microscope thought they looked like tiny rooms? Who observed these cells?

_____

2. Did you know the inventor of the simple microscope kept how he made it a secret until he died? What is a simple microscope? Who invented it?

_____

_____

_____

3. Did you know that scientists once thought the "dark spot" in cells wasn't important? Name the Scottish botanist who paid attention to this spot and named it "nucleus."

_____

4. Did you know that the botanist who stated that plants are made of cells started his career as a lawyer? Who was that lawyer-turned-botanist?

_____

5. Did you know that it took longer to figure out that animals are also made of cells? Name the botanist who proposed this idea.

_____

6. Do you know the first two statements of the cell theory?

   Write them here:

   (a)

   _____

   _____

   (b)

   _____

   _____

7. Did you know the scientist who developed the third part of the cell theory was once challenged to a duel… of sausages? Who was this scientist?

   _____

8. What is the third statement of the cell theory?

   (c)

   _____

   _____

Cell Diagram

9. Draw a diagram of a cell that includes a nucleus, membrane, and cytoplasm.

Student Guide

Cell Organelles

Inside cells are parts, called organelles, which are responsible for carrying out the cell's life processes. Study cell organelles and their functions and make a model cell that you can eat.

Lesson Objectives

- Distinguish between plant and animal cells.
- Recognize the major cell organelles (for example, endoplasmic reticulum, ribosomes, Golgi bodies, chloroplasts, chromosomes, mitochondria, and vacuoles) and describe their functions.

PREPARE

Approximate lesson time is 60 minutes.

Advance Preparation

- You will need certain foods to make a cell model. These foods are prunes, mandarin oranges, grapes, a carrot, raisins, a tortilla, and a banana.
- Before the lesson, shred the carrot. Cut the shreds so they are small. Tear strips of tortilla and slice thin pieces of banana.

Materials

For the Student

This Is Your Life, Cell!
A Cell You Can Eat
bag, clear plastic (2)
food - carrot shreds
food - green grapes
food - Mandarin oranges
food - prunes
food - raisins
pot with lid
twist tie (2)
bowl - large mixing
gelatin - yellow
spoon
water - boiling

Keywords and Pronunciations

cell wall: The stiff structure outside the cell membrane in a plant cell that provides support for the cell. Animal cells do not have cell walls.

chloroplast (KLOR-uh-plast)**:** The "solar panel" of plant cells, in which energy from the sun is converted into stored chemical energy by the process of photosynthesis. Chloroplasts contain chlorophyll and are found in plant cells, but not in animal cells.

chromosomes (KROH-muh-sohms)**:** Thread-like structures containing protein and made of DNA, which itself contains the instructions for building, maintaining, and operating the cell

cytoplasm (SIY-tuh-pla-zuhm)**:** The jelly-like matter of a living cell that is outside the nucleus. Organelles are contained in cytoplasm.

endoplasmic reticulum (EN-doh-plaz-mihk rih-TIHK-kyuh-luhm)**:** An organelle that makes, stores, and transports molecules in the cell. Ribosomes are found in some parts of the endoplasmic reticulum.

Golgi (GOHL-jee)

Golgi bodies (GOHL-jee)**:** Organelles that package molecules to send elsewhere within a cell. Golgi bodies are named for Camillo Golgi, who first described the structures in 1898.

mitochondria (miy-tuh-KAHN-dree-uh)**:** "Power plants" in the cytoplasm, where energy is released to a usable form, for organisms to function. The singular is mitochondrion. Mitochondria are dense in muscle cells, which need plenty of energy to contract.

organelle (or-guh-NEL)**:** A differentiated structure within a cell—such as a mitochondrion, vacuole, or chloroplast—that performs a specific function. A mitochondrion is an organelle that changes chemical energy into a form that the cell can use.

ribosomes (RIY-buh-sohmz)**:** Organelles that produce protein for the cell. Ribosomes build proteins according to instructions from chromosomes.

vacuoles (VA-kyuh-wohls)**:** Organelles that store food, water, and wastes in a cell and help get rid of wastes. In a plant cell, a large central vacuole takes up most of the cell.

LEARN

Activity 1: Inside a Cell *(Online)*

Activity 2: This Is Your Life, Cell! *(Offline)*

If a cell had feelings, it would probably be grateful to all of its organelles for the many jobs they perform. Reunite a happy plant cell with its organelles by identifying the organelles based on their descriptions. Welcome to This Is Your Life, Cell!

Activity 3: A Cell You Can Eat *(Offline)*

At your next birthday party, why not serve your guests cytoplasm jello and chromosome carrot shreds? Review organelles by making a cell you can eat.

Safety

This lesson involves eating or working with food. Before beginning, check with your doctor, if necessary, to find out whether your student will have any allergic reaction to the food.

ASSESS

Lesson Assessment: Cell Organelles (*Online*)

You will complete an online assessment covering the main objectives of the lesson.

LEARN

Activity 4: Visit a Virtual Cell (*Online*)

Explore cells further with a look at a virtual cell. Select the arrow to continue.

Name _____   Date _____

Cell Organelles

This Is Your Life, Cell!

Read the script from This is Your Life, Cell! Fill in the blanks with the names of cell organelles. Use the Word Bank to help you.

Word Bank

Nucleus	Chloroplasts
Cell Membrane	Ribosomes
Mitochondria	Cytoplasm
Cell Wall	Chromosomes
Golgi Body	Endoplasmic Reticulum
Vacuole	

(Lights on, crowd cheers)

BART FRANKLIN, HOST: Welcome, kids, to "This is Your Life"—a show that's guaranteed to bring a smile to your face and a tear to your eye. I'm Bart Franklin, your always-smiling, always-talking host. Today our guest is Cell—a small little guy, but alive and kicking nonetheless. Cell is here to be reunited with his old friends, the organelles. How are you feeling, Cell?

CELL (*in a young voice*): Well, Bart, I can't believe I am here. I am so happy, I could split!

BART: Woah! That's pretty serious, kids! Do you know what happens when cells divide? More cells. We had better get this show started before we've got more than we can handle. But first, let's se e whom Cell's brought to the show. Cell?

CELL: Bart, I've brought some of my good friends today—there's Muscle Cell and Nerve Cell. I also brought Red Blood Cell, but he doesn't talk much on account of the fact that he doesn't have a nucleus.

BART: Well, that is a shame, Cell. Speaking of nucleus, would you believe we've got your pal Nucleus right here in the studio tonight?

CELL: No! Not old Nucleus!

BART: It's true. Now, before we've got double trouble on our hands, how about we begin?

CELL: Sure thing, Bart!

BART: Okay, Cell. Listen to this first mystery guest.

GUEST 1 (*in a rubbery, shaky voice*): Hi ya, Cell. I'm the guy that holds it all together for ya. I hold your nucleus, your chloroplasts, even your endoplasmic reticulum. I'm kinda jelly-like. Once, I helped you stretch out and sorta change shape because I give ya your shape. Do you remember me?

CELL (*thinking*): Hmmm… Jelly-like? Holds all my organelles? You must be
_____ !

BART: Excellent work. (*crowd claps*) Let's hear from mystery guest number two.

GUEST 2 (*in a hurried voice*): Oh, Cell, Cell, I could hardly come today—I was so busy changing chemical energy into something you can use. I am always changing energy, like changing a check into money at the bank. Tell me quickly who I am so I can get back to work.

CELL (*excited*): Oh, I remember you! You were always a powerhouse! You're
_____ !

BART: Two for two! (*crowd claps*) Okay, Cell, see if you can figure out this third mystery guest…

GUEST 3 (*in an intelligent voice*): Ah, yes, Cell. Long time, no diffusion. Well, in order for you to do your job, you need me to give you instructions. I have all of the genetic information in me inside a long molecule called DNA. Just who might I be?

CELL: Is that you, Nucleus?

BART: Oooooh, Cell, not this time. (*crowd gasps*) But I hang out with Nucleus. Try again. Think DNA and genetic information.

CELL (*with a smile*): It can't be…I thought you'd been copied long ago. Is it
_____ ?

BART: Thatta boy, Cell! (*crowd claps*) Be sure to save a hug for your old pal. (*crowd sighs*) Okay, Cell. Now things are going to get a little tough. We've got two organelles here this time because they are often found together. Listen closely to the next mystery guests!

GUEST 4 (*a tiny voice*): Cell, it is so good to see you. Just backstage I was talking to Chromosomes and we were remembering how I used to follow their instructions to put together proteins. You often find me in the folds of the next mystery guest.

GUEST 5 (*a deep voice from offstage*): Cell…some have described my looks as a maze, but you can't get lost in me. I let my buddy here stay within my membrane network. I also store and move molecules. I hope you know who I am, Cell, because it's been a long time and I sure miss ya.

CELL: Wow, this is a tough one, Bart. There's only one maze-like network I know that lets molecules in and out. It's _____. And that fourth guest that can be found there…that must be _____!

BART: Excellent job, Cell! Just look at the crowd cheering! (*clapping*) Since you did so well with two organelles last time, let's try that again. Plus, we're running out of time and we've got to show some commercials before our next guest, Mr. Zinc. He's getting quite unstable backstage. Let's hear from our next two mystery guests.

GUEST 6 (*a kind voice*): Cell! The flight here was terrible! I felt sick, but no one could tell because I am already green. Remember all those times you were hungry? I was able to take the sun's energy and change it into chemical energy so you were fed. It was not an easy job, but I was happy to do it for you all these years.

GUEST 7 (*a tough voice*): Cell, I've got some bumps and bruises and my back hurts from holding you up so rigidly for so long. I gave you your shape, remember? My feet hurt a little, too. Many times I thought about quitting, but I am loyal to you, Cell.

CELL (*about to cry*): Bart, I'd know those two anywhere. They are the reason I am a plant cell. Come on out here, _____ and _____!

BART: Aw, gee folks, isn't that sweet? Cell, we just got great news. One of your organelles was not able to make it today, but we've got her on the phone. Listen in carefully to this guest!

GUEST 8 (*a military voice*): Hello there, Cell! Hold on a second there—(*away from the phone*) hey molecules—get over here, please! It's time to package you up and send you to other areas. Quit moving around now, you've got a job to do! (*back on phone*) I'm sorry, Cell, there's a lot to do around here. Do you know who I am?

CELL: Is that you, Vacuole?

GUEST 8: Do I sound like a liquid bubble? I do a hard job for you Cell, packaging up molecules and sending them on their way. Try again!

CELL: Could it be you, _____?

BART: Cell! You've done it again. (*crowd cheers*) Okay, just two more to go. Next guest!

GUEST 9 (*with a British accent*): Hallo there, Cell! It's me, back here directing everyone else. Mitochondria, I do wish you would stay still. Goodness chromosomes, what *are* you doing? Very well. Cell, you know me. I direct all of your activities, like a command center inside you.

CELL: It's _____! How are you? Don't work too hard back there!

BART: He's done it again! Okay, Cell, we've got one more organelle here to see you today. Let's listen in and see if you can identify this last mystery guest.

GUEST 10 (*a motherly voice*): Oh Cell, Cell, Cell…without me, you'd have no shape. I protect you like a skin. I am the outermost layer of you, next to the wall. Remember when we looked like a rectangle, then sort of like a rounded rectangle? That was Cytoplasm and me! I also let things pass into and out of you. Do you remember me?

CELL (*in tears*): Could it be? I know that voice anywhere… Is that you, _____?

BART: You've done it! (*crowd cheers and claps*) Excellent, Cell. In just a moment we'll reunite you with all your cell organelles—except Golgi Body, of course. She wishes she could have been here today.

CELL: I can hardly wait.

BART: That's great, Cell. Before we go, have you got anything you'd like to say?

CELL: This has been amazing, Bart. When do I get to take my trip to Hawaii?

BART: Well, this isn't that kind of show, Cell. But we can reunite you with your organelles -- how about it, folks?

CELL: But I'd rather go to Hawaii!

BART: Cell, you're kind of rooted here. You live in an evergreen tree. I just don't think Hawaii is possible. But we have some nice parting gifts, including the board game version of "This is Your Life!" How about we get all your organelles out here for a great big hug—come one, gang! We need to cut to a commerical, be right back!

CELL: But I learned to hula!

(*lights go down*)

Name _____ Date _____

Cell Organelles
A Cell You Can Eat

Why do scientists make models? Models help us study things we can't easily see.

You can make a model of a cell using different fruits to represent different organelles. Study the chart. Fill in either the name of the cell organelle or its description. When you finish, make a cell you can eat!

Fruit	Cell Organelle	Description
Prune		Command center, directs cell activities
Gelatin	Cytoplasm	
Mandarin Oranges		Change chemical energy to a form that is usable by the cell
Green grapes	Chloroplasts	
Carrot shreds		Contains the genetic information for the cell in its DNA
Raisins	Ribosome	
Thin pieces of tortilla, stacked and crumpled		A maze-like network of membranes that store or move molecules in the cell
Thin slices of banana, stacked		Packages molecules to send to other places in the cell
Bag	Cell membrane	
Cup		Rigid, gives plant cells their shape

Make the Model

Materials

2 plastic sandwich bags	cup (8 oz)
carrot shreds	prune
twist ties	water
raisins	gelatin, yellow
boiling water	heat source
thin strips of tortilla, folded	Mandarin oranges
large mixing bowls	pot
thin slices of banana, stacked	green grapes
spoons	

Procedure

1. Leave one plastic bag open. This represents the cell membrane of an animal cell.

2. Place the second bag into the cup, completely lining the cup with a little extra sticking out from the top. This represents the cell membrane and cell wall of a plant cell.

3. Make gelatin following the directions on the packet.

4. Place the cell bag close to full with warm gelatin. This represents the cytoplasm.

5. Place the cell "organelles" into the bag: a prune to represent a nucleus with a few carrot shred chromosomes stuck inside, mandarin oranges for mitochondria, several banana slices stacked together for a golgi body, folded tortilla strips for endoplasmic reticulum, and raisins for ribosomes. Place a few "ribosomes" between the layers of "endoplasmic reticulum."

6. Close the "cell" using the twist tie.

7. Repeat steps 5 and 6 for the plant cell, adding grapes for chloroplasts.

8. Put them in the refrigerator to set.

Questions

1. What parts do plant and animal cells have in common? List all of them, not just those used in the model.

   _____

   _____

2. What parts are different between plant and animal cells? How does this affect what the cells do?

   _____

   _____

   _____

   _____

3. If you were looking at cells with a microscope, how would you know whether they came from a plant or an animal?

   _____

   _____

   _____

   _____

4. What types of cells have chloroplasts? What function do chloroplasts serve?

   _____

   _____

5. What information do chromosomes carry?

   _____

   _____

   _____

   _____

Student Guide
Diffusion, Osmosis, and Active Transport

And now, more activities from those busy cells! The movement of molecules is one of a cell's basic processes. How else could it be fed, pass nerve signals, or secrete hormones when they are needed? Explore diffusion, osmosis, and active transport: three ways cells are able to get particles in and out through their cell membranes. Make models to observe diffusion through a plastic "membrane" and osmosis through the cell membrane of an egg.

Lesson Objectives

- Recognize various ways in which molecules are transported across the cell membrane.
- Define *diffusion* as the process by which molecules move from areas of higher concentration to areas of lower concentration.
- Recognize that water moves through membranes by *osmosis*—diffusion of water through a semipermeable membrane.

PREPARE

Approximate lesson time is 60 minutes.

Advance Preparation

- The model cells you make in this lesson will need to stand overnight. You may start the lesson and come back to it the next day or prepare this activity ahead of time. Print the Diffusion Through a Membrane activity sheet for directions.
- Follow the directions in the Osmosis activity sheet to soak an egg in vinegar for at least two days. If, after two days, the shell is not completely dissolved or softened, leave the egg in vinegar an extra day.

Materials

For the Student

Diffusion Through a Membrane
bag, clear plastic - sandwich bags-no zipper
cornstarch - 5 mL (1 tsp)
drinking glass - 355 mL (12oz) (2)
iodine
measuring spoon - teaspoon
rock - small
eyedropper
graduated cylinder
measuring cup
spoon - mixing
string - 30 cm (2)
water

Osmosis
food - corn syrup
food - one raw egg
household item - clear 500 mL containers (2)
vinegar - 250 mL
graduated cylinder - 250 mL
spoon
tape - masking

Keywords and Pronunciations

cell membrane: The flexible, double-layered covering of cells. Cell membranes help control what goes in and out of cells.

cytoplasm (SIY-tuh-pla-zuhm): The jelly-like matter of a living cell that is outside the nucleus. Organelles are contained in cytoplasm.

diffusion: The process by which molecules tend to move from an area of higher concentration to an area of lower concentration. Diffusion of molecules from onions frying in the kitchen brings the smell to the living room.

osmosis (ahz-MOH-suhs): the diffusion of water across a semipermeable membrane

permeable (PUHR-mee-uh-buhl): Allowing molecules to pass or diffuse through. Any barrier or membrane that lets molecules through it is said to be permeable to those molecules.

semipermeable: Permeable to some molecules, but not to others. Cell membranes are semipermeable, permeable to water molecules, but not to larger molecules.

turgor (TUHR-guhr): outward force on the cell wall of a plant that results from water contained within the cell; turgid pressure helps keep a plant rigid.

LEARN

Activity 1: Moving Through Membranes *(Online)*
Activity 2: Diffusion Through a Membrane *(Offline)*

Not all barriers are molecule proof! In cells, diffusion involves molecules passing through a cell "barrier," or membrane, as well as from one place to another where no membrane exists. Observe the diffusion of iodine molecules using a model system.

Safety

Use caution when using a heat source and handling boiling water. Never leave your student unattended near boiling water.

Activity 3: Osmosis *(Offline)*

Sadly, putting a book under your pillow won't help you learn by osmosis. But you can observe how osmosis happens in other parts of your body—namely your cells.

ASSESS

Lesson Assessment: Diffusion, Osmosis, and Active Transport *(Online)*

You will complete an online assessment covering the main objectives of this lesson. Your assessment will be scored by the computer.

Name _____   Date _____

Diffusion, Osmosis, and Active Transport
Diffusion Through a Membrane

Diffusion takes place when molecules in a gas or liquid spread out, moving from a place where they are highly concentrated to a place where they are not as concentrated. You experience the result of diffusion when smells from a kitchen reach you in a faraway room. Where is the area of high concentration of smelly molecules? _____ Where is the area of low concentration of smelly molecules? _____

Diffusion also happens in cells as molecules move in and out through the cell membrane. You can make a model to see how this works.

Materials

water

plastic sandwich bag (not the zipper-close type), 2

cornstarch

iodine

cup, 355 mL (12 oz.), 2

graduated cylinder

measuring spoon

measuring cup

small rock

marker

Procedure

1. Fill both bags with 5 mL cornstarch and 120 mL water.

2. Add a small rock about the size of a golf ball to each bag.

3. Knot the top of the bags to close them.

4. Fill the cups halfway with water.

5. Add 10 drops of iodine to one of the cups. Label this Cup 1. The cup of plain water will be Cup 2.

6. Place the bags in the cup. Completely submerge the bag of cornstarch mixture.

7. Wait 15 minutes, then make your observations. While waiting, answer the questions.

Questions

Think about concentrations. A more concentrated substance has more "stuff" in a given amount of it. A less concentrated substance has less "stuff."

1. In which is starch more concentrated—the bag or the cup?

   _____

2. For Cup 1: In which is iodine more concentrated—the bag or the cup?

   _____

Substance	Starting Color	Color after 15 Minutes
Solution in Cup 1		
Bag in Cup 1		
Solution in Cup 2		
Bag in Cup 2		

Analysis

You know that iodine changes to a deep purple-black when it comes into contact with starch. Use your observations to answer the questions.

1. Which substance moved, the iodine or the starch? _____

2. How can you tell?

_____

_____

_____

_____

3. The plastic bag allowed which molecules to pass through—water, cornstarch, or iodine? _____

4. Diffusion happens when molecules move from areas of high concentration to areas of low concentration. Which substance diffused?

_____

5. What was the purpose of Cup 2? _____

6. Sketch Cup 1 and its bag below. Label the areas of high concentration and low concentration at the start for both starch and iodine. Use arrows to show how diffusion happened in this investigation.

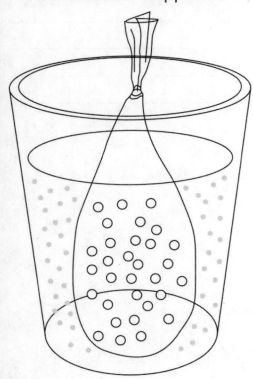

Conclusion

1. Explain how diffusion occurred in this investigation. Use your observations to write a detailed answer.

_____

_____

_____

_____

_____

_____

2. What would happen if you did this experiment again, but placed iodine in the bag and the cornstarch solution in the cup?

_____

_____

_____

3. Tell why it is not a good idea to store iodine in a plastic bag.

_____

_____

_____

_____

Name _____   Date _____

Diffusion, Osmosis, and Active Transport
Osmosis

A membrane that is *semipermeable* will let some things through, but not others. If water molecules are able to pass from a high-concentration area to a low-concentration area through membranes like this, we call it *osmosis*.

A key fact to remember about osmosis is that it involves the movement of water molecules. Diffusion involves liquid and gas molecules, but when you are thinking about osmosis, think about water.

Use an egg to see how osmosis works.

Materials

one raw egg

two clear 500 mL containers

plates, 2

250 mL vinegar

250 mL corn syrup

water

spoon

masking tape

marker

graduated cylinder

measuring cups

Procedure:

1. Use the masking tape and marker to label the containers A and B.

2. Pour 250 mL of vinegar into container A. Mark the level of the vinegar with a piece of masking tape.

3. Pour 250 mL of syrup into container B. Compare the levels of the liquids in containers A and B to make sure they are the same. Mark the level of the syrup with a piece of masking tape.

4. Place the egg into container A. Make sure it is completely covered. Cover both containers with plates or other lids.

5. After two days, use the spoon to very carefully remove the egg from container A. Rinse the egg and place it into container B.

6. Mark the new level of the vinegar in container A with masking tape.

7. Observe the egg the next day. Record its appearance in the Observations section on page 2.

8. Remove the egg and place it in water. Mark the new level of the syrup in container B with masking tape.

Observations

After two days in vinegar, what is the appearance of the egg?

_____

After another day in the syrup, what is the appearance of the egg?

_____

Was there more or less vinegar in container A after two days? _____

Was there more or less syrup in container B after one day? _____

Analysis

Follow directions *carefully* to answer the questions.

1. In container A, how can you tell that water from the vinegar moved into the egg?

   _____

   _____

   _____

   _____

2. In container B, how can you tell that water moved out of the egg?

   _____

   _____

   _____

   _____

3. The egg has many molecules in its cytoplasm, some of which are water. Why did water move into the egg in container A? Tell about the concentrations of water molecules.

_____

_____

_____

_____

4. Why did water move out of the egg in container B? Tell about the concentrations of water molecules.

_____

_____

_____

_____

Conclusions

1. What part of the egg controlled what moved into and out of the egg?

_____

2. What would happen if you left the egg you removed from the syrup in water? Explain your answer.

_____

_____

_____

_____

Student Guide

Photosynthesis and Respiration

All the energy that living organisms use begins with the sun. Without the sun, plants would not be able to make their own food. Without food, plants would die. And without plants, animals—including humans—would not survive. Study the processes of photosynthesis and respiration, which are the keys to the flow of energy in life. Investigate the process of photosynthesis using a common household plant.

Lesson Objectives

- Describe the process of *cellular respiration*.
- Describe the process of *photosynthesis* in plants.

PREPARE

Approximate lesson time is 60 minutes.

Advance Preparation

- Find a houseplant and a sunny location. Print Where are the Stomata? and follow the directions to set up the investigation. Coat the top sides of four leaves with a heavy layer of petroleum jelly. Coat the undersides of four other leaves with petroleum jelly. Place the plant in normal sunlight and water as usual for one week. Observe the plant during the lesson.
- You will need a sprig of elodea if you choose to do the Beyond the Lesson activity. You can buy elodea at a pet store or any other store that sells fish supplies.

Materials

For the Student

Yes, Teacher!
A Lot of Stomata
petroleum jelly
plant - with broad leaves
knife - butter
Exhale!
food - purple cabbage, head
household item - drinking straw
household item - heat source
jar - pint size-with lids (3)
plant - sprig of elodea
aluminum foil
bowl - mixing
water
water - distilled

Keywords and Pronunciations

chlorophyll (KLOR-uh-fil)**:** A special, large molecule that "captures" light energy and starts its change into chemical energy in the process of photosynthesis. Chlorophyll gives many plants their green color.

chloroplasts (KLOR-uh-plasts)**:** Structures in green plant cells that enable plants to produce their own food by converting light energy into chemical energy in molecules of glucose. Animal cells do not have chloroplasts.

mitochondria (miy-tuh-KAHN-dree-uh)**:** "Power plants" in the cytoplasm, where energy is released to a usable form, for organisms to function. The singular is mitochondrion. Mitochondria are dense in muscle cells, which need plenty of energy to contract.

photosynthesis (foh-toh-SINT-thuh-suhs)**:** The process by which plant cells convert light energy from the sun into chemical energy. During photosynthesis, plants use the sun´s energy to make glucose out of carbon dioxide and water, releasing oxygen. Photosynthesis means "putting together with light."

respiration: The process by which most living things convert the chemical energy in glucose into more accessible chemical energy in ATP. During respiration, cells break down glucose into carbon dioxide and water, using oxygen in the process. The overall process of cellular respiration is the reverse of photosynthesis.

stomata (STOH-muh-tuh)**:** Microscopic openings in the leaves of plants through which the plant takes in and releases gases. Stomata are found on the undersides of leaves.

LEARN

Activity 1: Energy Flows *(Online)*

Activity 2: Photosynthesis and Respiration Review *(Offline)*

Photosynthesis means "putting together with light." Now you will put together information using a pencil. Review photosynthesis and respiration.

Activity 3: Gas Exchange in Plants *(Offline)*

A photosynthesis "recipe" requires several ingredients: some carbon dioxide and water, a little sunlight, and a chemical reaction. What happens when a plant can't get all the ingredients it needs? See what happens when a change affects a plant's ability to "cook" its own food.

ASSESS

Lesson Assessment: Photosynthesis and Respiration *(Offline)*

You will complete an offline assessment covering the main objectives of this lesson. Your learning coach will score this assessment.

LEARN

Activity 4 Exhale! *(Offline)*

Did you know that plants as well as animals exhale carbon dioxide? During the day, plants use sunlight for photosynthesis. What happens at night when there's no sun? Test for the presence of carbon dioxide using a cabbage-juice indicator.

Safety

When using the drinking straw in the Beyond the Lesson activity, exhale only. Do not inhale or drink the indicator.

Name _____   Date _____

Photosynthesis and Respiration
Yes, Teacher!

Imagine you are responsible for teaching someone about photosynthesis and cellular respiration. Follow the directions to help prepare these notes and diagrams for your student. Afterward, make a colorful poster to help you teach your lesson.

Taking Notes

Start with the basics. Provide your students with a few notes about photosynthesis and respiration. Write the chemical equations for both processes below. Use the Word Bank to help you.

Word Bank

carbon dioxide	glucose
water	ATP
oxygen	+
→	energy
sunlight	

Photosynthesis:

_____

Respiration:

_____

Comparing

Once your students are familiar with photosynthesis and respiration, they should compare them. Comparing is a good way to see how things are either alike or different. Fill out the table to prepare for teaching your students how to compare photosynthesis and respiration.

Process	Where?	When?	Reactants?	Products?	Energy Source?	Ener Res
Photo-synthesis	In cells that have chlorophyll		Carbon dioxide, water			Ener store gluc
Respiration		All the time		Carbon dioxide, water	Energy in glucose	

Drawing a Diagram

Every student learns in a different way. Some may need to see a "picture" or diagram of a process before they understand it completely. Help prepare a diagram for your students.

The diagram below compares photosynthesis and respiration. Fill in the blanks in the diagram to complete the comparison.

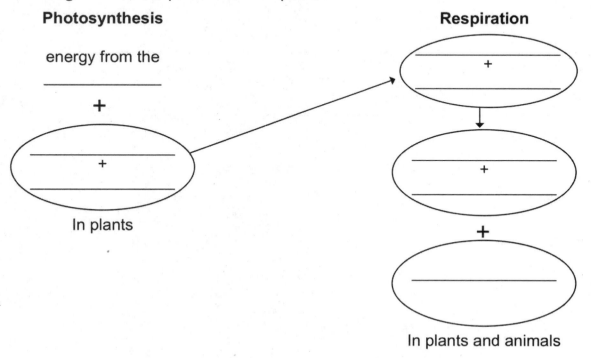

Teach Your Lesson

Use the answer key to check your answers in the Taking Notes, Comparing, and Drawing a Diagram sections. Next, make a poster to teach what you know about photosynthesis and respiration. Your poster should:

- Tell which processes happen in plants and which happen in animals
- List the products and reactants in both
- Explain where the energy comes from or goes to for both
- Use colors and pictures to explain what you are teaching

Share your poster with an adult. Use your poster to teach what you've learned about photosynthesis and respiration. Answer any questions the adult has after your lesson.

Name _____   Date _____

Photosynthesis and Respiration
A Lot of Stomata

Fill in the blanks to review gas exchanges in plants during photosynthesis.

_____ and _____ are the gases involved in photosynthesis. During photosynthesis, plants give off _____ and take in _____. What would happen if these gases could not be exchanged in plants?

Suppose you saw microscopic structures that looked like openings on the bottoms of plant leaves, but not on the tops. You wanted to know whether these structures were important in gas exchange for photosynthesis. You could use petroleum jelly to block the openings from taking in and giving off gases. Make a hypothesis that you can test in this experiment, using petroleum jelly to block the openings.

Hypothesis

Predict what will happen to the plant leaves if you coat the bottoms of a few leaves with petroleum jelly.

_____

_____

Predict what will happen if you coat the tops of some leaves.

_____

_____

Materials

potted plant

petroleum jelly

butter knife

Procedure

1. Coat the top of two leaves with a heavy layer of petroleum jelly.

2. Coat the undersides of two other leaves with a heavy layer of petroleum jelly.

3. Place the plant in an area where it will receive sunlight. Water the plant as normal.

4. Observe the leaves daily for 1 week.

Analysis

1. Which leaves were able to function well during the week? How could you tell?

_____

_____

2. Which leaves were not able to function well during the week? How could you tell?

_____

_____

3. What does this tell you about gas exchange and the tiny openings on the bottoms of plant leaves?

_____

_____

Conclusion

Tiny openings in plant leaves allow gases to move in and out. When the openings are blocked, the plant cannot receive carbon dioxide gas or give off oxygen, so it cannot photosynthesize. Those tiny openings are called *stomata*. Based on your investigation, how are stomata important?

_____

_____

_____

_____

_____

_____

Name _____   Date _____

Photosynthesis and Respiration
Exhale!

You now know that photosynthesis involves energy from sunlight. But what happens when the sun goes down? In the dark, plants can use oxygen and food the way animals do. They produce carbon dioxide. You can test for carbon dioxide with a cabbage juice indicator.

The cabbage juice indicator has a dye that turns red when mixed with any acid. Carbon dioxide combines with water to form a weak acid called *carbonic acid*. If the indicator turns red, you will know that carbon dioxide is present.

Materials

distilled water

sprig of elodea

3 pint jars with lids

straw

aluminum foil

head of purple cabbage

water

heat source

mixing bowl

Lab Safety:

When using the straw, exhale only. Do not inhale or drink the indicator.

Procedure

Make the Indicator

1. Cut the cabbage into small pieces. You may pull the leaves off and tear them.
2. Place the cabbage pieces into a 2-liter bowl.
3. Heat the distilled water. Add enough to fill the bowl.
4. Let the cabbage stand until the water cools.
5. Strain the liquid. Throw away the cabbage pieces and keep the blue liquid.

Use the Indicator

6. Rinse the jars with distilled water. Label them 1, 2, and 3.

7. Fill all three jars with equal amounts of cabbage juice.

8. Place an elodea plant in Jar 1. Seal the lid tightly and place it in bright sunlight.

9. Place an elodea plant in Jar 2. Close the lid tightly and cover the jar with aluminum foil. Place the jar in a location where it will not be disturbed.

10. Seal Jar 3 and place it in bright light.

11. After two days, observe the color changes in the jars.

Observations

1. Which jars showed a color change? _____

2. Use a straw to **EXHALE** into the cabbage juice in Jar 3 until a color change occurs. *Do not inhale or drink the cabbage juice.* What substance is added to the cabbage juice as you exhale?

_____

Conclusion

1. What can you conclude about the presence of carbon dioxide in the jars? Do plants give off carbon dioxide? Under what conditions?

_____

_____

2. In what process do plants give off carbon dioxide, which occurred in the dark?

_____

3. What process occurs in green plants in the light?

_____

4. Why didn't the elodea in the light give off carbon dioxide and change the color of the indicator?

_____

_____

Student Guide

Cells and Cell Processes: Unit Review and Assessment

Play Cell-ebrity Pranksters to review cell structures and processes. Review organelles, the movement of molecules, photosynthesis, and respiration. Then take the unit assessment.

Lesson Objectives

- Demonstrate knowledge and skills gained in this unit.
- Describe the three major ideas of the cell theory.
- Distinguish between plant and animal cells.
- Explain that different types of substances move across the cell membrane by means of diffusion, osmosis, and active transport.
- Explain that plant cells store energy through photosynthesis and that plant and animal cells release stored energy during respiration.
- Identify the major structures of cells and describe their functions (nucleus, cytoplasm, cell wall, cell membrane, chromosomes, mitochondria, and chloroplasts).
- Describe the process of *photosynthesis* in plants.
- Identify the major structures of the cell (such as cell membrane, cytoplasm, and nucleus) and describe their functions.
- Recognize various ways in which molecules are transported across the cell membrane.
- Define *diffusion* as the process by which molecules move from areas of higher concentration to areas of lower concentration.
- Demonstrate mastery of the skills taught in this unit.
- Explain that all the information an organism needs to live and reproduce is contained in its DNA.
- Recognize that water moves through membranes by osmosis—diffusion of water through a semipermeable membrane.
- Recognize the major cell organelles (for example, endoplasmic reticulum, ribosomes, Golgi bodies, chloroplasts, chromosomes, mitochondria, and vacuoles) and describe their functions.

PREPARE

Approximate lesson time is 60 minutes.

Materials
For the Student

Question Review Table

LEARN

Activity 1: Cell-ebrity Pranksters (*Online*)

ASSESS

Unit Assessment: Cells and Cell Processes (*Offline*)

You will complete an offline assessment covering the main objectives of this unit. Your learning coach will score this assessment.

LEARN

Activity 2: Optional: Unit Assessment Review Table (*Online*)

If you earned a score of less than 80% on the Unit Assessment, complete the activity.

If you earned a score of 80% or greater, you may skip this activity.

Let's prepare to retake the Unit Assessment:

- Print the Question Review Table
- Identify the questions that you answered incorrectly.
- Complete the appropriate review activities listed in the table.

Note: This will guide you through the process of using the Unit Assessment Review Tables. You may skip this video if you've already viewed it in another unit or course. As always, check with your student's teacher if you have any questions.

Activity 3: Optional: ZlugQuest Measurement (*Online*)

Name _____   Date _____

Cells and Cell Processes: Unit Review and Assessment

Question Review Table

Before you retake the Unit Assessment, use the table to figure out which activities you should review.

Circle the numbers of the questions that you missed on the Unit Assessment. Review the activities that correspond with these questions.

Question	Lesson	Review Activity
1	3: Diffusion, Osmosis, and Active Transport	Explore: Moving Through Membranes Osmosis
2	3: Diffusion, Osmosis, and Active Transport	Explore: Moving Through Membranes
3	3: Diffusion, Osmosis, and Active Transport	Explore: Moving Through Membranes Diffusion Through a Membrane
5, 7, 9	1: The Cell Theory	Explore: What Are You Made Of? Cell Record Observer Human Cells
6	6: DNA	Explore: DNA-Instruction Manual for Life Look at Real DNA D-N-A from Y-O-U
8	4: Photosynthesis and Respiration	Explore: Energy Flows Photosynthesis and Respiration Review Gas Exchange in Plants

Question	Lesson	Review Activity
10	4: Photosynthesis and Respiration	Explore: Energy Flows Photosynthesis and Respiration Review Exhale!
4, 11, 12, 13, 14	2: Cell Organelles	Explore: Inside a Cell This is Your Life, Cell A Cell You Can Eat Visit a Virtual Cell

Student Guide
Naming and Classifying Life

Lesson Objectives

- Recognize that an organism's scientific name is made up of the genus and species the organism belongs to.
- State that Carolus Linnaeus developed a system for naming and classifying organisms that is still used today.

PREPARE

Approximate lesson time is 60 minutes.

Advance Preparation

- If you have not yet received the book The Kingdoms of Life: Classification, skip to the next unit. Return to this one when the book arrives.

Materials

For the Student

> *Come Learn with Me: The Kingdoms of Life: Classification* by Bridget Anderson
> Scientific Classification Crossword Puzzle

Keywords and Pronunciations

Aristotle (AIR-uh-stah-tl)

Carolus Linnaeus (kah-raw-LOUS lih-NEE-uhs)

genus (JEE-nuhs)

species (SPEE-sheez)

LEARN

Activity 1: Let's Read *(Online)*

There are many forms of life in the world. Some are so tiny that you can't see them without a microscope. How do we make sense of all these different organisms? To study them, scientists classify them by their characteristics. Learn how scientists do this. Read pages 6 through 11 of *The Kingdoms of Life: Classification*.

Activity 2: Scientific Classification Crossword *(Offline)*

Do you have a good understanding of scientific classification? Prove this to yourself by solving the Scientific Classification Crossword Puzzle.

ASSESS

Lesson Assessment: Naming and Classifying Life *(Online)*

You will complete an online assessment covering the main objectives of this lesson. Your assessment will be scored by the computer.

Name _____   Date _____

Naming and Classifying Life
Scientific Classification Crossword Puzzle

Use the clues on the next page to complete the puzzle.

Across

2. This genus means *catlike animals*.

5. He was an ancient Greek philospher who divided plants and animals into categories.

10. This Latin word means *appearance* or *kind*. It is the second part of the scientific name for an organism.

11. Linnaeus named species either in Latin or in this language.

13. This scientific term for *baby* can be applied both to plants and to animals.

14. First name of Linnaeus, a scientist who is famous for his system of classification.

Down

1. The process of grouping things according to the charastics they share.

3. This Swedish biologist developed a system for classifying organisms.

4. Groups of related species. The first part of a scientific name for an organism refers to this.

6. So far, scientists have identified more than _____ million kinds of organisms.

7. A place where books are classified.

8. Aristotle classified plants as herbs, shrubs, or _____.

9. Farmers classify farm animals and plants according to this.

12. Its scientific name is *Canis familarus*.

Student Guide

The Tools of Taxonomy

How does a classification system work? Learn more about Carolus Linnaeus, who led the way to the current system of classification that groups organisms according to their shared characteristics.

Lesson Objectives

- Recognize that living things are classified by shared characteristics.
- Identify the seven major levels of classification: Kingdom, Phylum, Class, Order, Family, Genus, and Species.

PREPARE

Approximate lesson time is 60 minutes.

Materials

For the Student

> *Come Learn with Me: The Kingdoms of Life: Classification* by Bridget Anderson
> Trees of the Pacific Northwest

Keywords and Pronunciations

Anton van Leeuwenhoek (AHN-tohn vahn LAY-ven-hook)

Carolus Linnaeus (kah-raw-LOUS lih-NEE-uhs)

conifer (KAH-nuh-fur)

dichotomous (diy-KAH-tuh-muhs)

genus (JEE-nuhs)

phylum (FIY-luhm)

species (SPEE-sheez)

LEARN

Activity 1: Let's Read *(Online)*

Instructions

Read pages 12 to 13 in *Come Learn with Me: The Kingdoms of Life: Classification* by Bridget Anderson to learn about the taxonomy of life on Earth.

Activity 2: Identifying Trees *(Online)*

Try your hand at identifying trees of the Pacific Northwest using a dichotomous key.

ASSESS

Lesson Assessment: The Tools of Taxonomy (Online)

You will complete an online assessment covering the main goals of this lesson. Your assessment will be scored by the computer.

LEARN

Activity 3: Optional: Dichotomous Keys (Online)

This Activity is OPTIONAL. It's provided for enrichment or extra practice, but not required for completion of this lesson. You may skip this activity.

Learn about Dichotomous Keying.

Name _____ Date _____

The Tools of Taxonomy
Trees of the Pacific Northwest

Try your hand at identifying trees of the Pacific Northwest using a dichotomous key.

 _____

The needle-like leaves are not clustered on this tree. The needles are longer than 1/2 inch. The tiny pegs on the twigs are squared with sharp needles.

 _____

This tree has leaves that are needle-like. The needles are clustered with 2 to 5 needles.

 _____

The needle-like leaves on this tree are not clustered and are no longer than 1/2 inch. There are no pegs on the twigs. The buds are small and pointed, and they are not found clustered on the twig. As you turn the pointed needle over, it is white underneath.

_____

The flattened leaves on this tree are scale-like. All of the leaves are short and sharp.

_____

The needle-like leaves, which measure longer than 1/2 inch, are not clustered. There are no pegs on the twigs. The buds are not large but are pointed. The terminal buds are not clustered. As you turn the needle over, it is green underneath.

Student Guide

Phylogenetic Trees and the Kingdoms of Life

Scientists classify all life on Earth into one of six kingdoms. Join the classification adventure and find out what the six kingdoms are!

Lesson Objectives

- Name the six kingdoms: Archaebacteria, Eubacteria, Protista, Fungi, Planta, and Animalia.

PREPARE

Approximate lesson time is 60 minutes.

Materials

For the Student

> *Come Learn with Me: The Kingdoms of Life: Classification* by Bridget Anderson
> What Would Linnaeus Say?

Keywords and Pronunciations

Animalia (A-nuh-MAY-lee-uh)

archaebacteria (AHR-kee-bak-TIHR-ee-uh)

eubacteria (YOO-bak-TIHR-ee-uh)

fungi (FUN-jiy)

genetics (juh-NEH-tihks): The study of how characteristics are passed on from parents to their offspring. Based on genetics, my daughter might have brown eyes like mine.

phylogenetic (fiy-loh-juh-NEH-tihk)

Protista (proh-TIS-tuh)

LEARN

Activity 1: Let's Read *(Online)*

The science of *genetics* explains why some organisms are more similar than others. It also explains why members of the same families tend to have similar characteristics—they may look alike, act alike, or both. Read pages 16 through 19 of *The Kingdoms of Life: Classification*.

Activity 2: What Would Linnaeus Say? *(Offline)*

Genetic relationships explain a lot about how like or unlike organisms can be. Which organisms are closely related and which are distant? What kinds of living creatures belong to each of the kingdoms? With the help of your book, *you* can give the same answers Linnaeus would give.

ASSESS

Lesson Assessment: Phylogenetic Trees and the Kingdoms of Life *(Online)*

You will complete an online assessment covering the main goals of this lesson. Your assessment will be scored by the computer.

Name _____   Date _____

Phylogenetic Trees and the Kingdoms of Life
What Would Linnaeus Say?

A. For each organism listed below, circle the organism that is more closely related genetically. (Hint: use the diagram in your book for help.)

1. human girl:

human man or female duck

2. sunflower:

worm or daisy

3. green algae:

moss or cnidarian

4. snake:

lizard or flatworm

5. crustacean:

insect or fungi

B. Use the Word Bank below to complete this paragraph.

Word Bank

genetics	different
fossils	similar
phylogenetic tree	identical

The branch of science that studies relationships between organisms is _____. Children in the same family have nearly _____ genes, while birds and insects have very _____ genes. Once genetic relationships are understood, scientists can show the relationships by drawing a _____. By studying genes from _____ and genes from animals living today, scientists gain evidence about how modern organisms are related to ancient organisms.

C. Write the letter of each kingdom in the space next to the correct description.

A. Kingdom Archaebacteria

B. Kingdom Eubacteria

C. Kingdom Protista

D. Kingdom Fungi

E. Kingdom Planta

F. Kingdom Animalia

_____ They live in wet places. Examples are algae and slime molds.

_____ Their cells use chlorophyll to help them make their own food.

_____ These single-cell organisms live in extreme environments, such as deep-sea vents.

_____ Fish, insects, and mammals belong to this kingdom.

_____ These common bacteria are found everywhere on Earth.

_____ These eukaryotic organisms absorb nutrients from dead or living plants and animals.

Student Guide
Kingdom Archaebacteria

Do you know of any organisms that live in the most extreme environments on Earth? Scientists have found bacteria from Kingdom Archaebacteria in the coldest and hottest places on Earth. Get out your microscope and take a closer look at these fascinating organisms.

Lesson Objectives

- Identify one organism in Kingdom Archaebacteria.
- Identify two characteristics common to organisms in Kingdom Archaebacteria (live without oxygen, live in extreme environments both hot and cold).

PREPARE

Approximate lesson time is 60 minutes.

Materials

For the Student

> *Come Learn with Me: The Kingdoms of Life: Classification* by Bridget Anderson
> Solving the Riddles of Bacteria

Keywords and Pronunciations

archaebacteria (AHR-kee-bak-TIHR-ee-uh)

cyanobacteria (siy-A-nuh-bak-TIHR-ee-uh)

eubacteria (YOO-bak-TIHR-ee-uh)

halophile (HA-luh-fiyl)

methanogen (muh-THAN-uh-juhn)

LEARN

Activity 1: Let's Read *(Online)*

Archaebacteria may be tiny, but they can adapt extremely well to different environments. Learn how these tiny creatures survive in some of the harshest places in the world. Read pages 20 through 21 of *The Kingdoms of Life: Classification*.

Activity 2: Bacteria Riddles *(Offline)*

Are you good at riddles? With the help of your book, you'll be able to solve the riddles of these bacteria.

ASSESS

Lesson Assessment: Kingdom Archaebacteria *(Online)*

You will complete an online assessment covering the main goals of this lesson. Your assessment will be scored by the computer.

Name_____   Date_____

Kingdom Archaebacteria
Solving the Riddles of Bacteria

Read each riddle, then solve it. (Hint: You'll find help in your text.)

1. I am shaped like a rod, and I live in the intestines of animals. What kind of bacteria am I? (Hint: my name starts with the letter S.)

   _____

2. If you've ever had a "strep throat," then I was responsible. I am the bacteria that causes throat infections. Who am I?

   _____

3. I love hot environments – even the hottest ones! I can also live without oxygen. What kind of bacteria am I?

   _____

4. All bacteria are made up of me. I am a type of cell. Who am I?

   _____

5. Because I can live in extremely salty environments, I can live in the Great Salt Lake in Utah. What kind of bacteria am I?

   _____

6. If you want to see the structure and behavior of bacteria, you need to use me. (I'm not just an ordinary microscope!)

   _____

7. I am a disease caused by the dangerous bacteria called *Borrelia burgdofferri*.

   _____

SUPER CHALLENGE: Name this term! The first one has been done for you.

1. All rod-shaped bacteria are called **bacillus**.

2. All round bacteria are called _____.

3. All spiral bacteria are called _____.

4. This term refers to things that love extreme environments. Archaeophiles are one example. _____

Student Guide
Kingdom Eubacteria

All bacteria not part of Kingdom Archaebacteria belong to Kingdom Eubacteria. This kingdom's microscopic world includes eubacteria that live near us, even within our own bodies.

Lesson Objectives

- Identify a characteristic common to organisms in Kingdom Eubacteria (live in less extreme environments).
- Identify one organism in Kingdom Eubacteria.

PREPARE

Approximate lesson time is 60 minutes.

Materials

For the Student

> *Come Learn with Me: The Kingdoms of Life: Classification* by Bridget Anderson
> Name That Eubacteria or Virus!

Keywords and Pronunciations

amoeba (uh-MEE-buh)

cyanobacteria (siy-A-nuh-bak-TIHR-ee-uh)

eubacteria (YOO-bak-TIHR-ee-uh)

paramecium (PAIR-uh-MEE-shee-uhm)

thermophile (THUR-muh-fiyl)

LEARN

Activity 1: Let's Read *(Online)*

Eubacteria may be invisible to the naked eye, but they play a very important role in our lives. Some are very helpful, while others are quite dangerous. Read pages 22 through 23 of *The Kingdoms of Life: Classification*.

Activity 2: Name That Eubacteria or Virus! *(Offline)*

Members of Kingdom Eubacteria are known as the *true bacteria*. These organisms obtain nutrients in very different—sometimes unusual—ways. Read the clues; and then name the kind of eubacteria they describe.

ASSESS

Lesson Assessment: Kingdom Eubacteria *(Online)*

You will complete an online assessment covering the main objectives of this lesson. Your assessment will be scored by the computer.

LEARN

Activity 3: Optional: Microbiologists Do! *(Online)*

This activity is OPTIONAL. It's provided for enrichment or extra practice, but not required for completion of this lesson. You may skip this activity.

Have you ever wondered what kind of scientists study bacteria and other microscopic organisms? Microbiologists do. Discover the exciting lives they lead, and solve Microbe Mysteries online.

Name _____ Date _____

Kingdom Eubacteria
Name That Eubacteria or Virus!

Read each description, then write *photo-autotroph*, *chemo-autotroph*, *heterotroph*, or *virus* in the space after each.

1. Decomposers are members of this group.

   _____

2. Some of these are considered "nitrogen – fixing machines."

   _____

3. Not all scientists think these are even alive.

   _____

4. They make their food from sunlight.

   _____

5. To reproduce, they must use the cell of another organism.

   _____

6. Sulfur, iron, and nitrogen are needed to make food for this group.

   _____

7. They contain chlorophyll.

   _____

8. They absorb nutrients from other organisms because they can't make their own food.

   _____

9. Their bodies are not made of cells, though they can use the cells of others.

   _____

10. Photosynthesis lets them make food.

    _____

11. Parasites are part of this group.

_____

12. These are not actually bacteria.

_____

13. Their name means "self-nourishment from chemicals."

_____

14. Cyanobacteria are part of this group.

_____

Student Guide
Kingdom Protista

Members of Kingdom Protista include many one-celled organisms that thrive in wet environments. Amoebas, paramecia, molds, and algae are all part of this group. Find out about some of the types of protists, and learn about these organisms that are all around you.

Lesson Objectives

- Identify two characteristics common to organisms in Kingdom Protista (thrive in wet environments, most are single celled).
- Identify two organisms in Kingdom Protista (protozoa, amoeba, paramecium, algae, seaweed, water mold, slime mold).
- State that protists are often grouped according to whether they are plant-like, fungus-like or animal-like.

PREPARE

Approximate lesson time is 60 minutes.

Advance Preparation

- You will need 10 jars and 20 cups of distilled water for the optional Soap and Algae activity.

Materials

For the Student

Come Learn with Me: The Kingdoms of Life: Classification by Bridget Anderson
Protists by Alphabet

Optional

How Does Soap Affect Algae Growth?
jar, storage (10)
measuring cup
soap - 1 1/2 cups of liquid soap
spoon - measuring
water - distilled, 20 cups
water - lake, stream, tap, or bay, 20 cups
water - tap

Keywords and Pronunciations

algae (AL-jee)

amoeba (uh-MEE-buh)

eukaryotic (yoo-KAHR-ee-AH-tihk)

fungi (FUN-jiy)

paramecium (PAIR-uh-MEE-shee-uhm)

Protista (proh-TIS-tuh)

protozoa (proh-tuh-ZOH-uh)

LEARN

Activity 1: Let's Read *(Online)*

Many members of Kingdom Protista are made of only one cell, while others are multicellular. Discover protists—the eukaryotic organisms that live in oceans, land, and lakes, as well as inside other organisms. Read pages 24 through 27 of *The Kingdoms of Life: Classification*.

Activity 2: Protists by Alphabet *(Offline)*

There are many protists. Use alphabet clues to solve the Protists by Alphabet puzzle.

ASSESS

Lesson Assessment: Kingdom Protista *(Online)*

You will complete an online assessment covering the main goals of this lesson. Your assessment will be scored by the computer.

LEARN

Activity 3: Optional: Soap and Algae *(Offline)*

This activity is OPTIONAL. It's provided for enrichment or extra practice, but not required for completion of this lesson. You may skip this activity.

You already know that algae grow in water. What do you think would happen if you added soap to the water? Find out!

Name_____   Date_____

Kingdom Protista
Protists by Alphabet

Read the clues, then fill in the answer. The first letter of each answer is given for you. Some of the answers have been completed for you.

A_____ look like jelly. To move, they have to change shape.

B_____ and pieces of dead organisms are food for slime molds.

C_____ are covered with little hairs. They move in a corkscrew fashion.

D_____ _____ have killed a lot of crops. The rotten potato in your book is infected with it.

E_____ _____ grows on a stick. There is a picture of one in your book.

F_____ move by flapping flagella. Many are parasitic.

G_____ can look furry when water molds grow on them. There is a picture of one in your book.

H_____ is one way to describe a paramecium. Its many cilia make it look this way.

I_____ _____ _____ is a famous disaster that took place in the 1840s. A downy mildew caused it to happen.

Jelly-like blobs are one way the book describes amoebas.

K_____ is a large, complex type of algae that can grow into forests underwater.

L_____ and oceans are home to the Kingdom Protista.

M_____ described in your book are slime and water.

N_____ is the Japanese name for a kind of seaweed called Porphyra nereocystis.

O_____ is produced by algae. Humans need it to breathe.

P_____ is a very complex protozoan.

Q is not the first letter of any protist in your book.

R_____, brown, and green are some of the colors algae can have.

S_____ live in the cells of other living things. They are very tiny parasites.

T_____ is how the bodies of amoebas and most protists look, which means you can see through them.

U_____ is also called sea lettuce. It is a kind of alga.

Vorticella is a ciliate. It is not mentioned in your book.

W_____ _____ look like cotton. Some grow on dead algae, and some grow on living organisms.

X is not the first letter of any of the words in this section.

Yamadaella caenomyce is a kind of algae that grows in the Red Sea, but it is not shown in your book.

Zoomastiginia is the group that flagellates belong to. (This information is not in the book.)

Name _____   Date _____

Kingdom Protista
How Does Soap Affect Algae Growth?

How do you think soap would affect the growth of algae? Could you guess? The experiment will answer the question.

Procedure

1. Fill five jars with 950mL each of distilled water. Label the jars 1, 2, 3, 4, and 5.

2. In a bowl, mix 240mL of water with 360mLof liquid soap.

3. Pour 30mL of soapy water from the bowl in jar #2, 60mL in jar #3, 90mL in jar #4, and 120mL in jar #5.

4. Fill five different jars with 950mL of lake, stream, tap or bay water. Then label the jars 6, 7, 8, 9, and 10.

5. Pour 30mL of soapy water in jar #7, 60mL in jar #8, 90mL in jar #9, and 120mL in jar #10.

6. Place all of the jars in a location with plenty of sunlight.

For the next five days, record your observations of odor and color change in the observation sheet provided. After the five days, place a 10cm strip of unlined white paper behind each jar. Look through the liquid in the jar and identify the jar that has the most algae.

Observation Sheet

Distilled Water

Sample Property	Day 1	Day 2	Day 3	Day 4	Day 5
Jar 1: Color					
Odor					
Jar 2: Color					
Odor					
Jar 3: Color					
Odor					
Jar 4: Color					
Odor					
Jar 5: Color					
Odor					

Lake, Stream, Tap, or Bay Water

Sample Property	Day 1	Day 2	Day 3	Day 4	Day 5
Jar 6: Color					
Odor					
Jar 7: Color					
Odor					
Jar 8: Color					
Odor					
Jar 9: Color					
Odor					
Jar 10: Color					
Odor					

Student Guide

Kingdom Fungi

Have you ever seen a piece of fruit with fuzz on it? Do you like mushrooms on your pizza? The fuzz and the mushrooms are both fungi! Look deeper into the diverse world of Kingdom Fungi.

Lesson Objectives

- Identify characteristics common to organisms in Kingdom Fungi (grow best in warm, moist conditions; reproduce through spores).
- Identify two organisms in Kingdom Fungi (mushroom, lichens, some molds, yeast).

PREPARE

Approximate lesson time is 60 minutes.

Advance Preparation

- If you choose to do the Rising Yeast optional activity, plan to set aside about an hour and twenty minutes for it.

Materials

For the Student

Come Learn with Me: The Kingdoms of Life: Classification by Bridget Anderson
Spreading Spores
clay
cotton ball (8)
stick
balloon - long and slender
tape

Optional

Rising Yeast
food - cup of flour (2)
food - pkg. of rapid-rise yeast
food - tsp. honey (6)
food - tsp. sugar (6)
household item - clothespins (24)
household item - drinking straws (24)
household item - medium-sized bowls (4)
measuring cup
ruler, metric
spoon
spoon - measuring
stopwatch - watch or timer

Keywords and Pronunciations

fungi (FUN-jiy)

fungus (FUNG-guhs)

LEARN

Activity 1: Let's Read *(Online)*

Toadstools, mushrooms, and molds are all part of Kingdom Fungi. Learn about the many types of fungi. Read pages 28 through 29 of *The Kingdoms of Life: Classification*.

Activity 2: Spreading Spores *(Offline)*

Create your own model of a black bread mold, which is a type of fungus. Learn how its spores spread.

ASSESS

Lesson Assessment: Kingdom Fungi *(Online)*

You will complete an online assessment covering the main goals of this lesson. Your assessment will be scored by the computer.

LEARN

Activity 3: Optional: Rising Yeast *(Offline)*

This activity is OPTIONAL. It's provided for enrichment or extra practice, but not required for completion of this lesson. You may skip this activity.

Did you ever wonder why you have to add yeast to the flour when you make bread? Have you wondered how the other ingredients affect the way yeast works? Cook up your own experiment to find out!

Name _____   Date _____

Kingdom Fungi
Spreading Spores

Do you know how spores spread? To find out, create this model.

Materials

long, slender balloon   stick

cotton balls   clay - any color

tape   permanent marker

Procedure

1. Stretch the balloon so that it will inflate easily. Don't inflate it or tie off the end yet.

2. Make 8 balls from the cotton that are no more than 1 cm in diameter. Put them in the neck of the balloon.

3. Inflate the balloon and tie it off with a knot on the end.

4. Tape the tied end of the balloon to the stick.

5. Put the bottom of the stick into the clay. Shape the clay around the end of the stick so that it stands up.

   This is a model of the spore-bearing structure of a bread mold. The balloon is the spore case, and the cotton balls are the spores.

6. Carefully poke the balloon with the pin. This is similar to how the spores of a mold get spread.

Conclusions

If these were real spores, what would happen next?

_____

_____

_____

Name _____ Date _____

Kingdom Fungi
Rising Yeast

Do you know why people use yeast to make bread? Have you ever wondered what affects the behavior of yeast? Here's your chance to find out!

Materials

2 cups of flour (plus a little extra)

24 clothespins

4 medium-sized bowls

measuring spoons

1 package of rapid-rise yeast

¼ cup measuring cup

access to warm water

spoon

6 teaspoons of sugar

metric ruler

honey

permanent marking pen

24 clear drinking straws

clock, watch, or timer

Procedure

1. Using the ruler, measure the point 3 cm from one end of each straw. Use the permanent marker to mark that point with a line.

2. Put ¼ cup of flour into each of the two bowls. Mark the first bowl as the "Control" and the second bowl as 1.

3. Pour ¼ teaspoon of yeast into each of the bowl marked 1 (do not put yeast into the bowl labeled "Control"). Using the spoon, stir together the ingredients in each bowl. Start with the Control bowl.

4. Fill a cup with warm water from your faucet. The water should be warm, not hot and steaming. Dust your hands with a little flour. Carefully add the water to the control bowl about a teaspoonful at a time and begin to knead the mixture. Your dough should eventually feel damp, not wet. Form the dough into a ball.

5. Repeat step 4 with each the remaining bowl, working as quickly as you can.

6. Working quickly, push three straws in and out of the Control dough until the dough inside the straw reaches the 3-centimeter mark. Lay these straws by the Control bowl. Repeat this step with each of the remaining bowls. Be sure to keep the straws beside the right bowls and don't mix them up.

7. Now pinch the bottoms of each of your Control dough straws, pushing the dough up from the bottom enough to clip a clothespin to the end of each straw. Mark the new height of the dough on each straw. Stand the straws upright using the clothespins as bases. Do the same with the rest of the straws. Label the batches of straws as Control and 1.

8. Mark the time on your clock or watch or set your timer for 10 minutes. Wait 10 minutes. Then mark the heights of the dough in each straw. Repeat this step 10 minutes later. Repeat after another 10 minutes has passed.

9. Throw out the straws and dough, then wash the bowls.

10. Record your results.

11. Repeat the procedure but this time you will be adding sugar and additional bowls.

Procedure

1. Using the ruler, measure the point 3 cm from one end of each straw. Use the permanent marker to mark that point with a line.

2. Put ¼ cup of flour into each of the four bowls. Mark the first bowl as the "Control." Mark the others as 1, 2, and 3.

3. Measure 1 teaspoon of sugar and add it to the flour in bowl 1. Put 2 teaspoons of sugar into bowl 2. Put 3 teaspoons of sugar into bowl 3.

4. Pour ¼ teaspoon of yeast into each of the four bowls. Using the spoon, stir together the ingredients in each bowl. Start with the Control bowl.

5. Fill a cup with warm water from your faucet. The water should be warm, not hot and steaming. Dust your hands with a little flour. Carefully add the water to the control bowl about a teaspoonful at a time and begin to knead the mixture. Your dough should eventually feel damp, not wet. Form the dough into a ball.

6. Repeat step 5 with each of the remaining bowls, working as quickly as you can.

7. Working quickly, push three straws in and out of the Control dough until the dough inside the straw reaches the 3-centimeter mark. Lay these straws by the Control bowl. Repeat this step with each of the remaining bowls. Be sure to keep the straws beside the right bowls and don't mix them up.

8. Now pinch the bottoms of each of your Control dough straws, pushing the dough up from the bottom enough to clip a clothespin to the end of each straw. Mark the new height of the dough on each straw. Stand the straws upright using the clothespins as bases. Do the same with the rest of the straws. Label the batches of straws as Control, 1, 2, and 3.

9. Mark the time on your clock or watch or set your timer for 10 minutes. Wait 10 minutes. Then mark the heights of the dough in each straw. Repeat this step 10 minutes later. Repeat after another 10 minutes has passed.

10. Throw out the straws and dough; then wash the bowls.

11. Repeat the experiment one last time: this time, substitute honey for the sugar. Do *everything else* exactly the same way.

12. After you have recorded your last observation, draw your conclusions.

Conclusions

Explain what happened when you did not put yeast into the dough.

_____

_____

How did the amount of sugar affect how the dough rose?

_____

_____

How did the amount of honey affect how the dough rose?

_____

_____

Which had a greater effect on the yeast—sugar or honey?

_____

_____

Student Guide

Kingdom Planta

Humans would not be able to survive without plants. We eat plants, such as lettuce, but so do the animals that may also become our food. Plants also supply us with the oxygen we breathe. Get ready for a journey through Kingdom Planta.

Lesson Objectives

- Compare characteristics of gymnosperms and angiosperms.
- Describe *vascular plants* as plants that have systems for transporting water, sugar, and minerals, whereas *nonvascular plants* lack these structures.
- Explain how sugar, water, and minerals are transported in vascular plants.
- Identify characteristics common to organisms in Kingdom Planta (all except mosses are vascular, all use photosynthesis to get nutrients).
- Identify two plants in Kingdom Planta.

PREPARE

Approximate lesson time is 60 minutes.

Advance Preparation

- You will need two fresh stalks of celery for the Up Goes the Water activity.

Materials

For the Student

Come Learn with Me: The Kingdoms of Life: Classification by Bridget Anderson
Compare Angiosperms and Gymnosperms
Up Goes the Water
celery - stalk (2)

Keywords and Pronunciations

angiosperm (AN-jee-uh-spuhrm)

gymnosperm (JIM-nuh-spuhrm)

Sequoia sempervirens (sih-KWOY-uh sem-puhr-VIY-ruhns)

LEARN

Activity 1: Let's Read *(Online)*

Plants come in all shapes and sizes. Some have leaves that change colors with the seasons. Some have bright flowers, and some have seeds. All belong to Kingdom Planta. Read pages 30 through 37 of *The Kingdoms of Life: Classification*.

Activity 2: Compare Angiosperms and Gymnosperms *(Offline)*

If you look carefully at the features of a tree, you can tell whether it is an angiosperm or a gymnosperm.

Activity 3: Up Goes the Water *(Online)*

Have you ever wondered exactly how—and how quickly—water can travel up the stem of a plant? A stalk of celery will give you the answer!

Safety

This activity involves working with food. Before letting your student handle the food, be certain he is not allergic to it.

ASSESS

Lesson Assessment: Kingdom Planta *(Offline)*

You will complete an offline assessment covering the main objectives of this lesson. Your learning coach will score this assessment.

Name _____   Date _____

Kingdom Planta

Compare Angiosperms and Gymnosperms

Do you remember the characteristics of angiosperms and gymnosperms? Look at each characteristic listed in the table, then write YES if it applies and NO if it does not apply.

Characteristic	Angiosperms	Gymnosperms
Do they have seeds?		
Do they have flowers?		
Do most have needle or scale-like leaves?		
Do most have woody cones?		

Now that you have reviewed the characteristics, write a paragraph that compares angiosperms with gymnosperms. How are they alike? How are they different?

_____

_____

_____

_____

_____

_____

_____

_____

_____

_____

_____

_____

_____

Name _____   Date _____

Kingdom Planta
Up Goes the Water

Celery is a *vascular plant*. These types of plants have systems for transporting water, sugar, and minerals. In this experiment, you'll be able to watch the path the water takes.

Materials

2 fresh stalks of celery	2 drinking glasses
knife	red food coloring
bowl	water
cooking syringe (baster)	cutting board

Procedure

1. Place one stalk of celery into a bowl of water.

2. With adult help, carefully cut the lowermost part of the stalk while it is under water. This keeps air bubbles from entering the stem.

3. Put a drinking glass in the bowl of water and transfer the celery stalk under water into the glass.

4. Repeat the steps with the other stalk of celery.

5. Use a kitchen syringe (baster) to remove all but 4 cm of water from both glasses.

6. Add enough food coloring to one glass to make the water very dark.

7. Observe both stalks after three hours. *What do you notice?*

_____

_____

_____

8. Remove the stalk that has been exposed to the red food coloring and lay it on a cutting board.

9. Carefully cut the stalk 3 cm above the bottom. Can you see where the food coloring moved up the stem?

10. Continue to cut the stem every 3 cm and observe the stalk. *What do you see?*

_____

_____

_____

Student Guide

Kingdom Animalia

Worms, flamingoes, and bears, oh my! It's hard to imagine that all these organisms are part of Kingdom Animalia. I wonder what else you'll find in this diverse kingdom?

Lesson Objectives

- Identify characteristics common to organisms in Kingdom Animalia (multicellular, need to get food from an outside source).
- Identify two organisms in Kingdom Animalia that are invertebrates.
- Identify two organisms in Kingdom Animalia that are vertebrates.
- Recognize that Kingdom Animalia includes organisms that are vertebrates and invertebrates.

PREPARE

Approximate lesson time is 60 minutes.

Materials

For the Student

Come Learn with Me: The Kingdoms of Life: Classification by Bridget Anderson

Keywords and Pronunciations

Animalia (A-nuh-MAY-lee-uh)

LEARN

Activity 1: Let's Read *(Online)*

Did you know that most animals do not have a backbone? Do you know how fish breathe? Discover the answers to these and many other questions. Read pages 38 through 45 of *The Kingdoms of Life: Classification.*

Activity 2: Learn More About Kingdom Animalia *(Online)*

ASSESS

Lesson Assessment: Kingdom Animalia *(Online)*

You will complete an online assessment covering the main goals of this lesson. Your assessment will be scored by the computer.

Student Guide
Taxonomy of Plants and Animals: Unit Review and Assessment

The seven levels of classification help us understand the many kinds of living things in the world. How can that knowledge be put to practical use? Find out!

Lesson Objectives

- Name the six kingdoms (Archaebacteria, Eubacteria, Protista, Fungi, Planta, and Animalia) and identify organisms from each.
- Compare the characteristics of the various groups of plants.
- Demonstrate mastery of the skills taught in this unit.
- Explain how sugar, water, and minerals are transported in vascular plants.
- Recognize that living things are classified by shared characteristics, and that there are seven major levels of classification: kingdom, phylum, class, order, family, genus, and species.

PREPARE

Approximate lesson time is 60 minutes.

Materials

For the Student

    Question Review Table

LEARN

Activity 1: The Carolus Linnaeus Zoological Garden *(Online)*

Most zoos concentrate on animals, but you've seen that there are five other kingdoms of living organisms. Help an architect plan a zoological garden that includes all the kingdoms.

ASSESS

Unit Assessment: Taxonomy of Plants and Animals *(Offline)*

You will complete an offline assessment covering the main objectives of this unit. Your learning coach will score this assessment.

LEARN

Activity 2: Optional: Unit Assessment Review Table *(Online)*

If you earned a score of **less than 80%** on the Unit Assessment, complete the activity. If you earned a score of **80% or greater**, you may skip this activity.

Let's prepare to retake the Unit Assessment:

- Print the Question Review Table.
- Identify the questions that you answered incorrectly.
- Complete the appropriate review activities listed in the table.

Note: This will guide you through the process of using the Unit Assessment Review Tables. You may skip this video if you've already viewed it in another unit or course. As always, check in with your student's teacher if you have any questions.

Activity 3: Optional: ZlugQuest Measurement *(Online)*

Name _____   Date _____

Taxonomy of Plants and Animals: Unit Review and Assessment
Question Review Table

Before you retake the Unit Assessment, use the table to figure out which activities you should review.

Circle the numbers of the questions that you missed on the Unit Assessment. Review the activities that correspond with these questions.

Question	Lesson	Review Activity
1,3	8: Kingdom Planta	Let's Read Compare Gymnosperms and Angiosperms
2,4	2: The Tools of Taxonomy	Let's Read Identifying Trees Dichotomous Keys
5	3: Phylogenetic Trees and the Kingdoms of Life	Let's Read What Would Linnaeus Say?
6	8: Kingdom Planta	Let's Read Up Goes the Water

Student Guide

The Miracle of Life

Do you ever wonder how the bodies of animals work? How are animals able to regulate their body temperatures? How do their coats change colors? These questions, and many more, are part of the area of study called *animal physiology*.

Lesson Objectives

- Recognize that all body systems play a role in maintaining a constant internal environment.
- Describe how bones and muscles interact to cause movement.

PREPARE

Approximate lesson time is 60 minutes.

Materials

For the Student

> *Come Learn with Me: How Bodies Work: Animal Physiology* by Bridget Anderson
> Cooling Effect

Keywords and Pronunciations

cell membrane: The fatty outer covering of a cell. The cell membrane allows certain substances to pass through it.

cytoplasm (SIY-tuh-pla-zuhm)**:** The jelly-like matter of a living cell that is outside the nucleus. Organelles are contained in cytoplasm.

homeostasis (HOH-mee-oh-STAY-suhs)**:** A state of balance reached through reactions within a cell or organism. Homeostatis is important for cells to function efficiently.

lysosomes (LIY-suh-sohm)**:** An organelle in animal cells that contains powerful enzymes. Lysosomes contain chemicals that process substances within the cell.

mitochondria (miy-tuh-KAHN-dree-uh)**:** The organelles that produce usable chemical energy. There can be many mitochondria in a single cell.

nutrient: Any substance that provides nourishment. Proteins are a type of nutrient for the body.

organelle (or-guh-NEL)**:** A tiny structure in the cytoplasm of the cell. Animal cells contain different types of organelles.

LEARN

Activity 1: Let's Read *(Online)*

How intelligent are animals? How do they respond to the world around them? Animal physiologists ask questions like these. Learn about the answers they find.

Activity 2: Cooling Effect *(Offline)*

How does your body cool itself when it is hot? This experiment will provide one answer.

ASSESS

Lesson Assessment: The Miracle of Life *(Offline)*

You will complete an offline assessment covering the main objectives of this lesson. Your learning coach will score this assessment.

Name _____ Date _____

The Miracle of Life
Cooling Effect

Do you know how your body cools down? This experiment will show you.

Materials

Thermometer   Graduated cylinder
Clock   Rubbing alcohol 10mL
Cotton ball

Procedure

1. Lay the thermometer on a table. Let it come to room temperature. Record the temperature on a piece of paper.

2. Moisten a cotton ball with rubbing alcohol.

3. Spread the cotton ball into thin strands. Spread a thin layer of the wet cotton across the bulb of the thermometer.

4. Blow across the wet cotton 15 times.

5. Record the temperature on the thermometer.

Conclusions

What happened to the temperature after adding the cotton ball with the rubbing alcohol?

_____

_____

How is this like the body's response when it gets too hot?

_____

_____

_____

_____

Student Guide
The Nervous and Endocrine Systems

The *nervous system* is the command center of an animal's body. This system helps maintain the homeostasis of the body. The hormones from the endocrine system also help to maintain a balance.

Lesson Objectives

- Identify some parts of the human endocrine system and their function (pituitary gland, thyroid gland, adrenal gland, and pancreas).
- Identify the parts of the human nervous system and their function (brain, spinal cord, and nerves)

PREPARE

Approximate lesson time is 60 minutes.

Materials

For the Student

> *Come Learn with Me: How Bodies Work: Animal Physiology* by Bridget Anderson
> The Endocrine System

Keywords and Pronunciations

adrenal (uh-DREE-nl)

endocrine (EN-duh-kruhn)

gland: An organ that produces special chemicals called hormones. The adrenal glands produce adrenaline when the brain instructs them to do so.

motor neurons: Nerve cells that deliver orders from the brain and spinal chord telling the body what to do. Motor neurons tell the body when it needs to move.

nerve: A thin fiber that sends messages between the brain or spinal chord and other parts of the body. The optic nerve passes messages between the brain and the eye.

nerve cord: A strand of nerve tissue that runs the length of the body and forms the main part of an animal's nervous system. The spinal cord is an example of a nerve cord.

nerve net: A simple nervous system containing nerve cells but no brain. Some invertebrates, such as jellyfish, have a nerve net.

pancreas (PAN-kree-uhs)

pituitary (puh-TOO-uh-tair-ee)

sensory neurons: Nerve cells that gather information from the body and carry it to the brain and spinal chord. Sensory neurons alert the brain when the body is damaged in some way.

LEARN

Activity 1: Let's Read *(Online)*

The nervous system involves the brain and a huge network of nerves. It carries messages between the brain and the body. Did you know that the body also has chemical messengers? Hormones of the endocrine system are chemical messengers.

Activity 2: The Endocrine System *(Offline)*

What role does the endocrine system play in your body? Use *Come Learn With Me: How Bodies Work: Animal Physiology* and this article at Kid's Health: Your Endocrine SystemKid's Health: Your Endocrine System to learn about the glands and hormones that make up your endocrine system.

ASSESS

Lesson Assessment: The Nervous and Endocrine Systems *(Online)*

You will complete an online assessment covering the main objectives of this lesson. Your assessment will be scored by the computer.

Name _____   Date _____

The Nervous and Endocrine Systems
The Endocrine System

Use the Word Bank to label the main structures of the endocrine system.

Word Bank

adrenal glands

thyroid gland

pituitary gland

pancreas

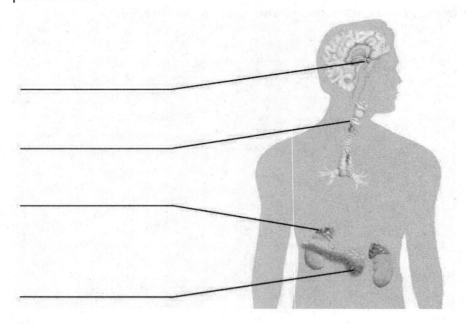

Describe the function of each gland here. Two have been completed for you.

1. Adrenal glands

_____

_____

2. Thyroid gland **produces hormones that influence the growth and development of the body.**

3. Pituitary gland **controls the growth of the human body, among other things.**

4. Pancreas

_____

_____

Student Guide
The Respiratory System

Animals cannot survive without oxygen. But how does oxygen get into animal bodies? Learn more about the respiratory systems of animals and investigate for yourself!

Lesson Objectives

- Demonstrate mastery of the skills taught in this lesson.
- Describe how the respiratory system exchanges carbon dioxide and oxygen in the lungs.
- Identify the parts of the human respiratory system (nose, mouth, trachea, lungs, diaphragm).

PREPARE

Approximate lesson time is 60 minutes.

Materials

For the Student

> *Come Learn with Me: How Bodies Work: Animal Physiology* by Bridget Anderson
> Lung Model
> bag, clear plastic - zipper-closed
> clay - small ball
> drinking straw
> rubber band (3)
> balloon
> bottle, plastic - 2 Liter
> scissors, round-end safety
> tape – masking

Keywords and Pronunciations

alveoli (al-VEE-uh-liy): Tiny air sacs in each lung through which oxygen enters and carbon dioxide leaves the blood. Alveoli are shaped like bunches of grapes.

bronchi (BRONG-kiy): The tubes in the lungs through which air passes. Humans have two bronchi—one for each lung.

carbon dioxide: A gas with no color or smell that is a mixture of carbon and oxygen. Animals breathe out carbon dioxide.

diaphragm (DIY-uh-fram): A dome-shaped muscle below the lungs that assists with breathing. When you breathe in, your diaphragm expands.

spiracle (SPIHR-uh-kuhl)

trachea (TRAY-kee-uh): A tube in animals used for drawing air into the body. Air passes from the nose and mouth into the trachea.

LEARN

Activity 1: Let's Read *(Online)*

Your respiratory system is essential to every breath you take. It helps you speak, sing, and do many other things.

Activity 2: Lung Model *(Offline)*

What structures are part of the respiratory system? How does the respiratory system work? Build a model to test out your own hypothesis.

ASSESS

Lesson Assessment: The Respiratory System *(Online)*

You will complete an offline assessment covering the main objectives of this lesson. Your learning coach will score this assessment.

Name _____   Date _____

The Respiratory System
Lung Model

What structures are part of the respiratory system? Build a model and test your own hypothesis.

Materials

2-liter plastic bottle

balloon

zipper-closed plastic bag

scissors

clay - 1 ball the size of a child's fist

1 drinking straw

3 rubber bands that can stretch across the bottom of a 2-liter bottle

masking tape

Procedure

To see how your lungs work, make a model lung.

1. Cut the bottom of a 2-liter plastic bottle at the point where the width is the same as its base. Keep the top part of the bottle for this model and discard the bottom part of the bottle.

2. Cut the zippered part off a sandwich bag. Using the top part of the bottle, place the bag around the bottom of the bottle. Hold the bag in place with a rubber band.

3. Place a straw into the neck of a balloon and use masking tape to seal it closed.

4. Remove the cap from the bottle. Hold the straw so that the balloon is inside the bottle.

5. Use clay to seal the opening of the bottle and hold the straw in place.

6. As you gently pull the plastic bag, the balloon "lung" will inflate by pulling air in through the straw (windpipe). When you gently push the bag back towards the bottle, the balloon will deflate.

The plastic bag acts like your *diaphragm*, a sheet-like muscle that separates your chest area and abdomen. Your diaphragm moves down when you inhale and back up when you exhale.

Conclusion

Use the back of this page to describe the exchange of oxygen and carbon dioxide in the lungs.

Student Guide

The Circulatory System

How do food and other materials move through the body? The transport system of the body, the *circulatory system*, is the key to it all! Hop on for a tour through the circulatory system.

Lesson Objectives

- Explain how blood flows through the human heart.
- Demonstrate mastery of the skills taught in this lesson.
- Identify the structures of the heart (atria, ventricles, valves, major veins and arteries).
- Recognize that some organisms have no circulatory system, some have an open circulatory system, and others have a closed circulatory system.
- Recognize that the circulatory system transports oxygen and nutrients to cells while carrying carbon dioxide and other wastes for removal.

PREPARE

Approximate lesson time is 60 minutes.

Materials

For the Student

> *Come Learn with Me: How Bodies Work: Animal Physiology* by Bridget Anderson
> A Circulation Model

Keywords and Pronunciations

capillary: A small blood vessel that carries blood between the arteries and the veins. Capillaries are the smallest, thinnest blood vessels.

LEARN

Activity 1: Let's Read *(Online)*

A lot of movement goes on inside bodies. Blood, oxygen, nutrients, and certain wastes move from one part to another. The *circulatory system* is what makes that happen.

Activity 2: A Circulation Model *(Offline)*

Not all organisms have a closed circulatory system. Investigate another model of circulation—the open circulatory system.

Activity 3: How Does Blood Flow Through a Human Heart? *(Online)*

The blood in the human heart follows a regular path. What changes happen to it as it follows the path of the many blood vessels and arteries? Explore a website to see a beating heart!

ASSESS

Lesson Assessment: The Circulatory System *(Offline)*

You will complete an offline assessment covering the main objectives of this lesson. Your learning coach will score this assessment.

Name _____   Date _____

The Circulatory System
A Circulation Model

Not all organisms have a closed circulatory system. Investigate another model of circulation—the open circulatory system.

Materials

1 tablespoon honey
1 drop of food coloring, any color
1 paper plate

Procedure

1. Place a spoonful of honey on a paper plate.

2. Add a drop of food coloring around one edge of the honey.

3. Gently tilt the paper plate to make the honey flow in different directions.

Conclusions

What happened to the food coloring?

_____

_____

Compare this model to the open circulatory system.

_____

_____

_____

Would this circulatory system be efficient for a human? Why or why not?

_____

_____

_____

_____

Student Guide

The Digestive System

How does food you eat get to all parts of your body? Your digestive system plays a key role in getting nutrients into your blood and wastes out of your body.

Lesson Objectives

- Demonstrate mastery of the skills taught in this lesson.
- Identify the structures involved in the digestive process and describe their function (mouth, esophagus, stomach, small intestine, large intestine, and liver).
- Sequence the digestion process.

PREPARE

Approximate lesson time is 60 minutes.

Materials

For the Student

> *Come Learn with Me: How Bodies Work: Animal Physiology* by Bridget Anderson

Optional

> Folds
> glass container, large - slender
> paper towels (5)
> tape - masking

Keywords and Pronunciations

enzymes (EN-ziym)**:** A protein in the body. Some enzymes help break food down into usable nutrients during digestion. Enzymes in your saliva break down starch, starting the process of digestion.

esophagus (ih-SAH-fuh-guhs)

peristalsis (pair-uh-STAWL-suhs)**:** Muscle contractions that move food, waste, and other contents through some digestive organs in the body. Peristalsis of the esophagus helps you swallow food.

vacuole (VA-kyuh-wohl)**:** A storage organelle of the cell. Some vacuoles help transport food molecules across a cell membrane.

LEARN

Activity 1: Let's Read (Online)

All animals need to take in food. The digestive system breaks down food and gets it into the blood for distribution to the body's cells. The same system helps the body get rid of what it doesn't need.

Activity 2: The Parts of the Digestive System (Online)

What structures are part of your digestive system? Some of them might surprise you!

ASSESS

Lesson Assessment: The Digestive System (Online)

You will complete an online assessment covering the main objectives of the lesson.

LEARN

Activity 3: Optional: Folds (Offline)

This activity is OPTIONAL. It's provided for enrichment or extra practice, but not required for completion of this lesson. You may skip this activity.

The intestines have to absorb a lot of nutrients. How do they do this efficiently? You may find the answer in some paper towels.

Name _____   Date _____

The Digestive System
Folds

In some ways, folded sheets of paper towels act just like the tissues inside the human intestines. How do you think they're similar? State your hypothesis, then test it.

Materials

5 paper towels
Slender glass jar
Masking tape

Procedure

1. Tape one piece of masking tape down the full length of the jar.
2. Fill the jar three-quarters of the way full with water.
3. With a pen, mark the level of the water on the tape.
4. Fold one sheet of paper towels in half four times.
5. Place the paper towel into the jar, making sure it is under water.
6. Remove the wet paper towel from the jar.
7. Mark the new water level on the tape.
8. Lay four sheets of paper towels on top of each other and fold them in half four times.
9. Dip the paper into the water, making sure it is under water.
10. Remove the paper towel and mark the water level.

Observations

What did you notice?

_____

_____

In which ways did the folded paper towels act like human intestines?

_____

_____

_____

_____

_____

Student Guide

The Excretory System

Your body produces wastes that are not useful and need to be removed. Your lungs get rid of the carbon dioxide that was created in your body through cellular respiration. What other wastes are in your body, and what systems remove them? Learn about the special filters and transport systems as you investigate the excretory system of the body.

Lesson Objectives

- Demonstrate mastery of the skills taught in this lesson.
- Explain how the excretory system removes cellular waste from the blood, converts it to urine, and stores it in the bladder before it leaves the body.
- Identify the organs of the excretory system and describe their function (lungs, liver, kidneys, and skin).

PREPARE

Approximate lesson time is 60 minutes.

Materials

For the Student

> *Come Learn with Me: How Bodies Work: Animal Physiology* by Bridget Anderson
> Excretory System Crossword Puzzle

Keywords and Pronunciations

bladder: The organ that stores liquid waste before it leaves the body. The bladder can stretch to hold about a pint of urine.

nephron (NEH-frahn): A tiny fiber in the kidney in which the filtering of water and waste from the blood takes place. There are approximately one million nephrons in one of your kidneys.

ureter (YUHR-uh-tuhr)

ureter tube (YUHR-uh-tuhr): A tube through which urea is transported from the kidneys to the bladder. A valve at the base of the ureter tube prevents urine from flowing back into the kidney.

LEARN

Activity 1: Let's Read *(Online)*

Everyone's body produces wastes—and everyone needs a way to get rid of those wastes. The execretory system is designed to handle some of the waste-removal problems.

Activity 2: The Excretory System Crossword Puzzle *(Offline)*

Solve a crossword puzzle based on the excretory system.

ASSESS

Lesson Assessment: The Excretory System *(Offline)*

You will complete an offline assessment covering the main objectives of this lesson. Your learning coach will score this assessment.

Name

Date

The Excretory System
Excretory System Crossword Puzzle

Use the clues on the next page to complete the puzzle.

Across

1. This expandable, sac-like organ holds urine in the body.

2. Animals with one-way digestive systems get rid of wastes through this opening.

6. This gas waste is produced by cells. It leaves the body through breathing organs and structures.

8. This liquid waste is passed through the pores of the skin. It is a part of sweat.

9. This general name is given to material that is not useful to the body and must be removed.

13. This is the tube through which urine leaves the body.

15. Cow feces, which many farmers use to fertilize fields, are given this term.

16. This is a combination of urea, water, and salt.

17. The bladder sits between these bones.

Down

1. Feces are usually a combination of old cells, _____, water, and leftover chemicals.

3. This system filters waste from the blood, stores it, and gets rid of it.

4. This organ filters blood.

5. This is the scientific name for solid waste.

7. These surround the bladder. They expand when the bladder is full, then contract to release urine down the urethra.

10. This is the number of kidneys in the human body.

11. This is the name for the tiny filter in the kidneys.

12. Animals with _____-way digestive systems get rid of their wastes through the same opening in which they eat food.

13. Urine flows through _____ tubes to the bladder.

14. This is the name for liquid waste that passes through the kidneys.

Student Guide

The Immune System and the Reproductive System

How does the human body protect itself from disease? Learn about the immune system as it "fights" to protect your body from disease and illness.

Lesson Objectives

- Describe some reproduction differences between animals.
- Identify the structures involved with the immune system and describe their function (bone marrow, white blood cells, and lymphocytes).
- Identify two ways we can work to keep our immune system healthy (get vaccines, eat healthful foods).
- Recognize that different organisms reproduce through division or fusion.

PREPARE

Approximate lesson time is 60 minutes.

Materials

For the Student

> *Come Learn with Me: How Bodies Work: Animal Physiology* by Bridget Anderson
> Immune and Reproductive System Riddles

Keywords and Pronunciations

keyword: [definition]

keyword (pronunciation)**:** [definition]

antibody: A protein that fights infection. Lymphocytes manufacture antibodies to protect the body against disease.

blood marrow: A soft, reddish substance that is inside bones and produces blood cells. Doctors sometimes examine blood marrow to check on the immune system's health.

lymphocyte (LIMP-fuh-siyt): A kind of white blood cell that produces antibodies to fight infection. Lymphocytes recognize different types of infection, and then send the correct antibodies to fight the infection.

pathogen (PA-thuh-jen): Something that can cause a disease. Bacteria is a pathogen.

vaccine (vak-SEEN): A substance containing weakened, dead, or living organisms that causes a body's immune system to fight against disease. The vaccine against polio is so effective that disease has been eliminated in many countries.

white blood cell: A colorless blood cell that is part of the body's immune system. A white blood cell protects the body against infection.

LEARN

Activity 1: Let's Read *(Online)*

The immune system is like an army. It is designed to fight anything that tries to attack the body. Learn how this army works.

Activity 2: Immune and Reproductive System Riddles *(Online)*

It's riddle time! Solve this collection of immune and reproductive system riddles.

ASSESS

Lesson Assessment: The Immune System and the Reproductive System *(Online)*

You will complete an online assessment covering the main objectives of this lesson. Your assessment will be scored by the computer.

Name _____   Date _____

The Immune System and the Reproductive System
Immune and Reproductive System Riddles

Read each riddle, then solve it. (Hint: You'll find help in your text.)

1. Animal life continues because of me. I am the system by which animals create new life. What am I?

   _____

2. I am an animal that splits up into pieces, making copies of myself in order to reproduce. What am I?

   _____

3. Some animals, such as a sea anemone, reproduce by division. But I am a different form of reproduction in which two cells from two animals of the same species join together to form a new animal. What form of reproduction am I?

   _____

4. Animals' bodies are designed to protect against things like me. I am also called a "germ." What am I?

   _____

5. When an animal gets sick, I start producing lots of white blood cells. What am I?

   _____

6. I am made of many layers and am the first line of an animal's defense against germs. What am I?

   _____

7. I am a type of medicine that teaches an animal's body to produce antibodies ahead of time. What am I?

   _____

8. I am made in an animal's bone marrow. I move around an animal's body through the bloodstream, and I am also the second line of defense against germs. What am I?

   _____

9. I am one type of white blood cell that can remember the pathogens I come in contact with. I help other white blood cells find germs by creating antibodies that attach to the germs. What am I?

   _____

10. I am made of many tissues, organs, and systems including the reproductive and immune systems. These parts and systems work together to help me function. What am I?

    _____

Student Guide
Animal Physiology: Unit Review and Assessment

A good knowledge of animal physiology is important even if you don't plan a career in medicine. Do you have a good understanding of how animals work? Here's your chance to find out!

Lesson Objectives

- Explain how blood flows through the human heart.
- Recognize that all body systems play a role in maintaining a constant internal environment.
- Describe how the respiratory system exchanges carbon dioxide and oxygen in the lungs.
- Describe the functions of the immune system.
- Describe the reproductive system of some animals.
- Explain how the excretory system removes cellular waste from the blood, converts it to urine, and stores it in the bladder before it leaves the body.
- Put the steps of digestion in the correct order and describe the function of the structures that are part of the digestive process.
- Recognize that the circulatory system transports oxygen and nutrients to cells while removing carbon dioxide and other wastes.

PREPARE

Approximate lesson time is 60 minutes.

Materials

For the Student

Come Learn with Me: How Bodies Work: Animal Physiology by Bridget Anderson
Question Review Table

LEARN

Activity 1: Animal Physiology Unit Review (Online)

Have you ever considered being a doctor or a veterinarian? To do either, you need a good understanding of physiology. You already know the basics.

Imagine that you're applying for a part-time job in a veterinarian's office. Do you think you could qualify? Find out!

ASSESS

Unit Assessment: Animal Physiology (Offline)

You will complete an offline assessment covering the main objectives of this unit. Your learning coach will score this assessment.

LEARN

Activity 2: Optional: Unit Assessment Review Table *(Online)*

If you earned a score of **less than 80%** on the Unit Assessment, complete the activity.

If you earned a score of **80% or greater**, you may skip this activity.

Let's prepare to retake the Unit Assessment:

- Print the Question Review Table.
- Identify the questions that you answered incorrectly.
- Complete the appropriate review activities listed in the table.

Note: This will guide you through the process of using the Unit Assessment Review Tables. You may skip this video if you've already viewed it in another unit or course. As always, check in with your student's teacher if you have any questions.

Name _____   Date _____

Animal Physiology: Unit Review and Assessment

Question Review Table

Before you retake the Unit Assessment, use the table to figure out which activities you should review.

Circle the numbers of the questions that you missed on the Unit Assessment. Review the activities that correspond with these questions.

Question	Lesson	Review Activity
1	1: The Miracle of Life	Let's Read Cooling Effect
2, 3	7: The Immune System and the Reproductive System	Let's Read Immune and Reproductive System Riddles
4	3: The Respiratory System	Let's Read Lung Model
5	4: The Circulatory System	Let's Read A Circulation Model
6	6: The Excretory System	Let's Read The Excretory System Crossword Puzzle
7	5: The Digestive System	Let's Read The Parts of the Digestive System Folds

Student Guide
Ecosystems and the Environment

In some way, every living thing on Earth depends on other living things, as well as on the nonliving parts of its environment. Explore the ways different organisms interact with each other and their environment, and diagram their relationships using food chains and food webs. Find out how the sun's energy drives cycles in nature.

All over our planet, living things interact with other living things and also with nonliving things. *Ecology* is the study of these interactions. Discover how both living and nonliving things make up *ecosystems*, and how all of Earth's ecosystems make up one giant ecosystem—the *biosphere*.

Lesson Objectives

- Explore concepts to be addressed during the year in Science 4.
- Define a *community* as a group of all the populations that live and interact with each other in a particular area.
- Define a *population* as a group of individuals of the same type that live in a particular area.
- Describe how organisms depend on each other for survival, such as using each other as sources for food and shelter.
- Identify both living and nonliving parts of an ecosystem.

PREPARE

Approximate lesson time is 60 minutes.

Advance Preparation

- It's important that you read the Course Introduction for Science 4 before your student begins the course. You can find the course introduction at the beginning of the Ecosystems and the Environment lesson.
- It's important that you read the course introduction for Science 4th Grade before starting this lesson.

Materials

For the Student

    binder, 3-ring
    paper, ruled
    pencil

Keywords and Pronunciation

biome (BIY-ohm)**:** A large area with a distinctive community of animals and plants and a particular climate. The tundra is a biome that covers a large area of the northern part of the continents in the northern hemisphere.

biosphere (BIY-uh-sfir)**:** The entire portion of Earth inhabited by life. The Earth´s global ecosystem is called the biosphere, and it is the sum of all the planet's ecosystems.

climate: The usual pattern of weather that has occurred in an area over a long period of time. California's climate consists of hot, dry summers and mild, rainy winters.

community: All the populations that live and interact with each other in a particular area. Frogs, ducks, insects, and fish are some of the living things that help make up a pond community.

ecology: The study of the relationship between living things and their environment. A scientist studying a deer´s diet and shelter is studying ecology.

ecosystem (EE-koh-sis-tuhm)**:** A community of organisms interacting with one another and with their environment. Ecosystems can be large cities, vast jungles and forests, small tide pools, or even a terrarium.

environment (in-VIY-ruhn-muhnt)**:** The nonliving and living factors that affect an organism or community. The wind, water, soil, and interactions with other animals are all part of a rabbit's environment.

organism (OR-guhn-ih-zuhm)**:** Any living thing that takes in food, grows, and reproduces. Organisms are alive, a characteristic that makes them different from things such as rocks and water, which are not alive.

population: A group of individuals of the same type that live in a particular area. A large population of geese lives near that pond.

LEARN

Activity 1: Welcome to Science 4 *(Online)*

Activity 2: Ecosystems and the Environment *(Online)*

Activity 3: The World Around You *(Online)*

Explore the world around you to learn about the various living and nonliving things that exist there.

1. Write your name, the date, and the lesson title on a piece of notebook paper.
2. Write the following headings on the paper, leaving plenty of space between each one: INDIVIDUAL, POPULATION, COMMUNITY, and ECOSYSTEM.
3. Write your answers to the questions below under each heading.
4. When you have finished, place the paper in your Science Notebook.

INDIVIDUAL

You are an individual in your ecosystem.

Make a list of other individuals that live with you. They can be any type of organisms, such as a cat, a mouse, grass, or a particular kind of tree.

POPULATION

You and the other humans you live with make a population.

List at least three other populations living nearby. For example, if your yard has several oak trees, or you have a tank of goldfish, they make up two different populations that live near you.

COMMUNITY

Your population and the other populations around you make up your community.

Describe how you interact with three of the populations you listed. Write two to four sentences explaining how you depend on other organisms for survival. Think about the types of food you eat, the clothes you wear, and what types of materials you use in your home every day.

ECOSYSTEM

An *ecosystem* is a community of organisms that interact and depend on each other and on other nonliving things in their environment. Nonliving parts of an environment can be such things as air, sunlight, artificial light, water, wind, soil, rocks, noise, and changes in temperature.

Think about places where you live, play, or do your schoolwork. Think of all the ways you interact with the nonliving parts of your environment. Write a list of nonliving things in your environment and then describe how you interact with them. For example, Air—I breathe air in and out to stay alive.

ASSESS

Lesson Assessment: Ecosystems and the Environment *(Offline)*

You will complete an offline assessment covering the main objectives of this lesson. Your learning coach will score this assessment.

Student Guide

Producers, Consumers, and Decomposers

From the tallest tree to the tiniest speck of bacteria, organisms called *producers, consumers,* and *decomposers* are constantly recycling nutrients that all organisms need to survive. Find out where you fit in this process. Then do an experiment and watch some common household waste decompose to become food for plants.

Lesson Objectives

- Describe how nutrients are continuously recycled through an ecosystem among producers, consumers, and decomposers.
- Describe the roles of *producers, consumers,* and *decomposers* in an ecosystem.
- Distinguish between *herbivores, carnivores,* and *omnivores* according to their diets.
- Identify examples of producers, consumers, and decomposers.
- State that all organisms need some source of energy to live.

PREPARE

Approximate lesson time is 60 minutes.

Materials

For the Student

    household item - bread
    household item - eggshells
    household item - fruit peel
    household item - lettuce leaves
    household item - newspaper
    paper, ruled
    aluminum foil
    bottle, plastic - 1 - liter, top removed
    paper, notebook - small strip
    pencil
    plastic wrap
    ruler
    scissors
    soil
    spoon
    tape, masking
    grass clippings
    household item - container with lid
    household item - large container with lid
    waste, kitchen
    shovel

Keywords and Pronunciation

carnivore (KAHR-nuh-vor)**:** An animal that feeds mainly on other animals. A tiger is considered a carnivore since its diet is mainly other animals.

consumer: An organism that depends on other organisms for food. Consumers directly or indirectly depend on producers for their energy. A robin is a consumer that eats worms.

decomposers: those organisms that break down dead organic matter

ecosystem (EE-koh-sis-tuhm)**:** A community of organisms interacting with one another and with their environment. Ecosystems can be large cities, vast jungles and forests, small tide pools, or even a terrarium.

environment (in-VIY-ruhn-muhnt)**:** The nonliving and living factors that affect an organism or community. The wind, water, soil, and interactions with other animals are all part of a rabbit's environment.

herbivore (UR-buh-vor)**:** An animal that feeds mainly on plants. A cow is considered an herbivore since its diet is mainly plants.

omnivore (AHM-nih-vor)**:** An animal that eats both plants and animals. Bears are omnivores, and eat fruits, nuts, fish, and small animals.

photosynthesis (foh-toh-SINT-thuh-suhs)

producers: Organisms, such as plants or algae, that make (or produce) their own food. Plants produce their own food through the process of photosynthesis.

scavengers: An animal that eats the bodies of dead animals. A vulture is a scavenger.

LEARN

Activity 1: Energy in an Ecosystem *(Online)*

Activity 2: Decomposition Station *(Offline)*

Watch decomposition take place in your own "decomposition station." Compare the decomposition of different objects.

Decomposers get energy from things that were once living. But not all things will decompose. What types of things might not decompose? Test different materials to find out.

Write your name, the date, and the lesson title on a piece of notebook paper, then draw a chart with three columns and eight rows.

1. Label the tops of the columns as follows: MATERIALS, PREDICTIONS, OBSERVATIONS.

2. Then write the following list of objects under the MATERIALS column: paper, fruit peel, lettuce leaves, plastic wrap, aluminum foil, bread, eggshells.

3. Predict which material will decompose or will not decompose. Write "yes" or "no" in the PREDICTIONS column next to the item.

4. Keep the chart in your Science Notebook until you are ready to make your observations.

Test your predictions by completing the following steps:

1. Place some newspaper on a flat surface and place the bottle on it. Scoop soil into the bottom of the bottle, about 5 cm high.

2. Put the piece of paper in the bottle, near the side so it is visible from the outside.

3. Cover the paper with soil.

4. Continue placing the objects in the bottle, near the side, and covering each of them with soil. Finish with a top layer of soil.

5. Moisten the soil with water.

6. Cover the bottle with plastic wrap and secure it with tape.

7. Place the bottle in a warm place, out of direct sunlight, for about 2 weeks.

8. At the end of the 2 weeks, observe the bottle and the items you placed in it. Record your observations on the chart in the OBSERVATIONS column.

ASSESS

Lesson Assessment: Producers, Consumers, and Decomposers *(Offline)*

You will complete an offline assessment covering the main objectives of this lesson. Your learning coach will score this assessment.

LEARN

Activity 3: Optional: Make Your Own Compost Pile *(Online)*

A compost pile contains items that will break down in soil and can be used to supply additional nutrients to a garden. Make your own compost pile and help recycle nutrients back into your ecosystem.

A *compost pile* speeds up the rate of decomposition of waste. Putting the *compost,* or decomposed waste, on your garden will help flowers and vegetables grow.

To make a compost pile, collect kitchen waste you would normally throw away. This waste can include eggshells, teabags, coffee grounds, fruit or potato peelings, and other uncooked vegetable waste. Do not use meat, butter, or oil, as it may attract rats or other animals looking for food. Keep the waste in a small, covered container until you have enough to start the compost pile.

Place a large, covered container outdoors in a convenient spot, but away from your house. Fill the bottom of the container with a layer of waste, 10-15 cm deep. Cover the waste with about 3 cm of soil. Soil with plenty of worms or insects works best.

As your kitchen produces more waste, keep building alternating layers of waste and soil.

Air must circulate through the compost, so do not pack it too tightly. Organisms use the oxygen in the air as they decompose and consume the remains.

Make sure the top layer is a layer of soil.

As the decomposing organisms work in your compost pile, you will notice the compost warming up. The bacteria are producing the heat. In about 2 to 3 weeks, the compost will reach its top temperature. In 3 months, you can use the compost in your garden.

You will be doing a web search to learn more. Web searches should always be done with adult supervision. K12 recommends the use of the safe search options that most web browsers come with, or one of the safe search engines produced by many major search engine providers.

Find more about this topic. Search for these key terms:

- different methods of composting

Safety

This lesson involves eating or working with food. Before beginning, check with your doctor, if necessary, to find out whether your student will have any allergic reaction to the food.

Student Guide

Food Webs: Energy Flow in an Ecosystem

Have you ever heard someone say, "You are what you eat"? Believe it or not, the food you eat provides you with energy from the sun! Find out how this happens as you use food chains, food webs, and energy pyramids to show how food and energy get passed through ecosystems.

Lesson Objectives

- Explain how a *food web* combines food chains to show the interconnected feeding relationships in an ecosystem.
- State that sunlight is the original source of energy for almost all ecosystems and therefore, all life.
- Explain how a *food chain* shows the pathway along which food is transferred from one organism to another.
- Recognize that an *energy pyramid* is a diagram that shows the amount of energy available at each level of an ecosystem.
- Recognize that energy is lost as you move up through levels of the energy pyramid.

PREPARE

Approximate lesson time is 60 minutes.

Advance Preparation

- For the Beyond the Lesson activity, set up the vivarium first, then purchase the anole and crickets from a pet store.

Materials

For the Student

    Food Chains and Webs Pattern Sheet
    household item – newspaper
    pencil
    scissors
    string – or yarn
    anole
    carrot
    cricket, live
    household item – cling film
    household item – knife
    household item – masking tape
    household item – oatmeal
    plant
    plastic bottle – 2-litre
    appel
    rocks
    soil
    water

Keywords and Pronunciation

carnivore (KAHR-nuh-vor): An animal that feeds mainly on other animals. A tiger is considered a carnivore since its diet is mainly other animals.

energy: The ability of living things to live, grow, move, and reproduce. Plants get their energy from the sun. Animals get their energy by eating plants and other animals.

energy pyramid: a diagram that shows the amount of energy available at each trophic level of a food chain; the level of a food chain that has the most energy available is the producers, the largest part of the energy pyramid; also called an energy flow or productivity pyramid

food chain: The pathway along which food is transferred from one organism to another. A worm eats a leaf, then a bird eats the worm, then an owl eats the bird. This is an example of a food chain.

food web: A diagram that combines food chains to show the interconnected feeding relationships in an ecosystem. Plants and animals can be part of more than one food chain in a food web.

herbivore (UR-buh-vor): An animal that feeds mainly on plants. A cow is considered an herbivore since its diet is mainly plants.

omnivore (AHM-nih-vor): An animal that eats both plants and animals. Bears are omnivores, and eat fruits, nuts, fish, and small animals.

vivarium (viy-VAIR-ee-uhm)

LEARN

Activity 1: Where Does the Energy Go? *(Online)*

Activity 2: Chains, Webs, and Pyramids *(Offline)*

Put organisms into various groups to show how energy flows in an ecosystem.

Use the cards from the Food Chains and Webs Pattern Sheet to make your own food chains, webs, and energy pyramid.

1. Cut the pictures from the Food Chains and Webs Pattern Sheet.
2. Read the information on each card to sort them into groups of producers, herbivores, carnivores, and omnivores.
3. Spread the cards on a table and form as many food chains as you can. You will need to reuse cards more than once.
4. Connect all the pictures using pieces of string or yarn to form a food web.
5. Tape the string in place to complete your food web.

Extension

Add a mosquito to the group of organisms. Mosquitoes feed on the blood of most mammals and birds.

ASSESS

Lesson Assessment: Food Webs: Energy Flow in an Ecosystem *(Offline)*

You will complete an offline assessment covering the main objectives of this lesson. Your learning coach will score this assessment.

LEARN

Activity 3: Optional: Make an Ecosystem! *(Online)*

This is an optional lesson extension. Please read through the activity and decide if you and your student are comfortable with the activity before you begin.

Make your own ecosystem to observe how the living and nonliving parts interact.

A <u>vivarium</u> is a small, self-contained ecosystem. The model in this activity is constructed inside a plastic bottle, but you should use a small aquarium if available. The vivarium will allow you to observe the organisms within the ecosystem and how they interact with each other.

It is important to learn more about keeping a pet lizard before beginning this activity.

You will be doing a web search to learn more. Web searches should always be done with adult supervision. K12 recommends the use of the safe search options that most web browsers come with, or one of the safe search engines produced by many major search engine providers.

Find more about this topic. Search for these key terms:

- Lizard Care
- Pet Lizard Care

Follow these steps to make a vivarium.

1. Cut the top off a 2-liter bottle. Fill the bottle about 1/3 full of soil.

2. Place the plant in the soil. Place the rocks on top of the soil. Sprinkle some drops of water over the plant and soil.

3. Put the cricket and anole in the bottle. Add a few pieces of oatmeal, and some very small slices of carrot and apple.

4. Cover the vivarium with plastic wrap and tape the plastic securely to the outside of the bottle. Poke a few holes in the plastic to allow air through, but small enough that the anole cannot escape.

5. Place the vivarium in a warm, bright, safe place. You may need to purchase a lamp. Sprinkle water on the leaves of the plant every day. The anole will lap up water from the leaves.

6. For a week, observe and record the interactions that take place in the vivarium. Identify producers, consumers, and decomposers.[1] What parts of this mini-ecosystem are living?[2] What parts are nonliving?[3] How do the parts interact?[4]

Name _____   Date _____

Food Webs: Energy Flow in an Ecosystem
Food Chains and Webs Pattern Sheet

Frog

Foods:
dragonflies and
other insects

Snail

Foods:
algae

Dragonfly

Foods:
insects

Turtle

Foods:
frogs, small fish,
duckweed, snails,
water lilies

Daphnia

Foods:
algae

Great Blue Heron

Foods:
fish, frogs, snails

Fish

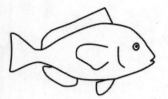

Foods:
daphnia, dragonflies,
and other insects

Mink

Foods:
frogs

Duck

Foods:
duckweed, algae

Algae

Description:
green, plant-like
organisms that float
in ponds

Water Lily

Description:
a water plant with
large, floating
leaves

Duckweed

Description:
small plants that
float at the surface
of a pond

Student Guide
Cycles in Ecosystems

Nature does not waste anything. Water and nutrients recycle through the environment to provide the food, air, and water that living things need. Study the water and carbon cycles to discover how they keep nutrient levels in balance, and how humans sometimes affect the balance by causing these cycles to change.

Lesson Objectives

- Describe how water continuously moves through the water cycle as it evaporates, condenses, and precipitates.
- Identify the ways carbon is cycled through both living (organic) and nonliving (inorganic) parts of an ecosystem.
- Recognize that cycles in nature provide organisms with the food, air, and water they need to live, grow, and reproduce.
- Use the greenhouse effect to explain how humans have caused a change in the carbon cycle.

PREPARE

Approximate lesson time is 60 minutes.

Materials

For the Student

> The Water Cycle/Carbon Cycle Connection
> crayons, 64 colors or more
> paper, notebook
> pencil
> The Greenhouse Effect
> jar - with lid
> soil
> thermometer (2)

Keywords and Pronunciation

inorganic: Matter that does not come from an animal or plant. Rocks and minerals are inorganic.

organic: Matter that comes from an animal or plant and contains carbon. Leaves, whether alive or dead, are organic.

LEARN

Activity 1: The Earth's Natural Cycles *(Online)*

Activity 2: The Water Cycle-Carbon Cycle Connection *(Offline)*

Review how water and carbon constantly cycle through the Earth. Explain the importance of the water and carbon cycles to living things. Describe how the greenhouse effect is linked to the carbon cycle and how human activity has affected this cycle.

ASSESS

Lesson Assessment: Cycles in Ecosystems *(Offline)*

You will complete an offline assessment covering the main objectives of this lesson. Your learning coach will score this assessment.

LEARN

Activity 3: Optional: The Greenhouse Effect *(Offline)*

Make a model to demonstrate how the greenhouse effect warms the Earth's atmosphere.

Name _____   Date _____

Cycles in Ecosystems
The Water Cycle / Carbon Cycle Connection

Carbon Cycle

Write the number next to the part of the picture that is described below. Then draw arrows in RED connecting each number to show the path of carbon in the carbon cycle.

1. During photosynthesis, plants use carbon dioxide from the air to make food.

2. Animals consume carbon when they eat plants.

3. Living organisms return carbon dioxide to the air when they breathe out.

4. Organisms die and decomposers release carbon into the soil, air, or water.

5. Some carbon is trapped for millions of years, forming coal and oil.

6. Factories burning coal and oil release carbon dioxide back into the air to be used by plants to make food.

Water Cycle

Write the letter next to the part of the picture that is described below. Then draw arrows in BLUE connecting each number to show the path of water in the water cycle.

A. Light energy from the sun evaporates water from oceans, rivers, ponds, and, lakes. The water becomes water vapor.

B. Water vapor in the atmosphere condenses to form clouds and precipitation.

C. Precipitation falls back to the Earth's surface.

D. Water seeps into the ground.

E. Water that cannot seep into the ground runs off the surface forming streams and rivers and filling up ponds and lakes to be evaporated again by the sun.

Think About It

1. How does carbon dioxide on Earth act like the glass panes in a greenhouse?

   _____

   _____

   _____

   _____

2. In what ways does carbon dioxide become part of the Earth's atmosphere?

   _____

   _____

   _____

   _____

3. Tell how humans have changed the balance of carbon dioxide in the Earth's atmosphere.

   _____

   _____

   _____

   _____

Name _____   Date _____

Cycles in Ecosystems
The Greenhouse Effect

Follow the steps to demonstrate the greenhouse effect. Then answer the questions below.

1. Place 5 cm of soil in the bottom of a jar.
2. Place one thermometer in the jar and cover it with the lid.
3. Place the jar near a window in direct sunlight.
4. Place the second thermometer next to the jar.
5. Observe the temperature on both thermometers after 30 minutes.

Which thermometer do you think will have a higher temperature reading after 30 minutes, the one in the jar or the one next to the jar?

_____

_____

After 30 minutes, which temperature reading was higher? Why?

_____

_____

_____

_____

Student Guide
Changing Environmental Conditions

Is there anything you can't live without? You might have a book or a bike you like very much, but if you didn't have them you would still be able to survive. Something in the environment that a living thing must have in order to survive—such as temperature, water, or air—is called a *limiting factor*. Think about your limiting factors as you learn about those of other organisms.

Lesson Objectives

- Identify a *limiting factor* as any environmental condition that can reduce an organism's ability to survive (for example, changes in temperature and abundance of food, water, sunlight, and nutrients).
- Recognize that conditions within an ecosystem are constantly changing, causing plants and animals to adapt, move, or die.
- Recognize that limiting factors can change from ecosystem to ecosystem and from organism to organism.
- State that organisms can live within a certain range of environmental conditions.

PREPARE

Approximate lesson time is 60 minutes.

Advance Preparation

- Print the Temperature Control Lab sheet. Assist your student with beginning the investigation. Note: the seeds will need one week to grow before measuring to complete the experiment. Stop just before the section labeled "Scientists' Notes." Review the procedure with your student when you teach the entire lesson.
- If you are using a pre-moistened sponge, 10 mL of water should be enough to moisten it for the experiment. If you are using a dry sponge, be sure to use the same amount of water to moisten each of the nine sponges.
- The lamp must provide sufficient heat for the experiment. If you can, find the type of bulb, of any wattage, that will provide the heat. If you cannot find one bulb that will heat efficiently, try arranging a number of bulbs until the experiment works. Be creative in finding a heat source that does the job.

Materials

For the Student

    Temperature Control
    birdseed - 1 cup
    light bulb, 60 watt
    sponge, kitchen (9)
    bags, zipper-close (9)
    lamp
    markers - permanent

---

paper, construction, 9" x 12" - black (3)
pencil
ruler
scissors
water
Too Hot!
shovel
thermometer - outdoor (2)
towel - white

Keywords and Pronunciation

limiting factor: An environmental condition that affects or limits the ability of an organism to survive. A limiting factor for an earthworm is the amount of water present in the ground.

photosynthesis (foh-toh-SINT-thuh-suhs)

LEARN

Activity 1: Environmental Changes *(Online)*

Activity 2: Temperature Control *(Offline)*

Limiting factors are conditions that affect an organism's chance of survival. Is temperature a limiting factor to the rate of seed germination?

Use caution if you are allergic to mold. It is likely that as your seeds grow, some mold will develop with them.

Safety

The seeds and seedlings in the Temperature Control experiment may become mouldy. Use caution handling them if your student is allergic to mold.

ASSESS

Lesson Assessment: Changing Environmental Conditions *(Online)*

You will complete an online assessment covering the main objectives of the lesson.

LEARN

Activity 3: Optional: Too Hot! *(Online)*

Learn why many desert animals stay underground during the day.

Name _____   Date _____

Changing Environmental Conditions
Temperature Control

Something in the environment that limits an organism's ability to survive is called a *limiting factor*. Temperature is an important limiting factor. In this activity, you will investigate whether seeds will germinate or sprout in different temperatures. You will answer the question: Is temperature a limiting factor for seed germination?

Safety

Use caution if you are allergic to mold. It is likely as your seeds grow, some mold will develop with them.

Hypothesis

Write a sentence that tells whether temperature is or is not a limiting factor for seed germination.

_____

_____

Materials

sponges, 9	scissors	construction paper, black 8.5" x 11", 3 pieces
bird seed, 1 cup	ruler	
plastic bags, zipper-closed, 9	lamp	
	water	
pencil	incandescent light bulb, 60 watt	
permanent marker		

Procedure

1. Soak each sponge, then squeeze out excess water.

2. Place a sponge in each of the nine plastic bags. Then divide the bags into three groups: counter, freezer, and lamp.

3. Use a permanent marker to label the bags in each group as counter, freezer, or lamp. Then within each group, label the bags 1, 2, and 3.

Procedure

1. Soak each sponge, then squeeze out excess water.

2. Place a sponge in each of the nine plastic bags. Then divide the bags into three groups: counter, freezer, and lamp.

3. Use a permanent marker to label the bags in each group as counter, freezer, or lamp. Then within each group, label the bags 1, 2, and 3.

4. Cut the construction paper into nine pieces big enough to completely cover a sponge.

5. Sprinkle a tablespoon of birdseed evenly across the surface of each sponge. Do not seal the bags.

Carefully place three of the sponges in the freezer, three on the counter, and three under the lamp. Cover each bag with a piece of black construction paper. You must keep the lamp turned on during the entire experiment. All seeds should be completely shielded from light. Wait one week before checking your seeds for growth.

Scientist Notes

In an investigation, scientists test how one thing affects another. This one thing is called a *variable*. The word variable comes from the word *vary*, meaning *change*. To test a variable, you change it in some way to see if there are any effects. A variable may or may not have an effect on something in your experiment. You can test only one variable at a time.

Read the procedure carefully and observe your experiment. You are testing the effect of one variable on seed germination. Which variable are you testing? Circle it below.

    A. sponge color

    B. water amount

    C. temperature

In this experiment, no matter how careful you were, some sponges might have been a little wetter or had more seeds than the others. Maybe a sponge on the counter got warm from a nearby stove. Maybe you held the ruler a little differently each time you measured the length of your sprouts.

In experiments, you can't avoid small differences like these. They happen by chance. That's why you tested three sponges in each location instead of one. To make sure that small differences like these don't affect your tests too much, you repeated the experiment three times in each location, in the freezer, on the counter, and under the lamp. This repetition is *replication*.

Observations

Observations are descriptions of things such as color, cloudiness, or height. In this investigation, you are observing height. Recording observations is sometimes called *collecting data*.

Collecting data is often best done during an experiment – not after.

On each sponge, find the seed that grew the longest sprout. Measure its length in centimeters and write your data in the chart.

Length of Longest Germinated Seed

Sponge number	Counter	Freezer	Lamp
Sponge 1			
Sponge 2			
Sponge 3			

Make a Graph

For this type of experiment, a bar graph is the best way to record your data. For each location, draw a bar to show how long in centimeters each sprout is.

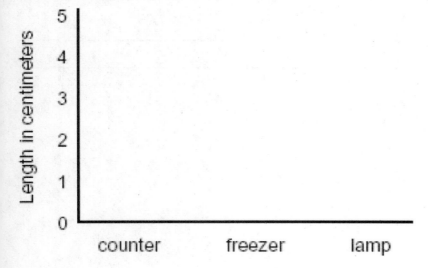

Conclusions

Look carefully at your data and your graph before you answer the questions.

1. You tested this question: Is temperature a limiting factor for seed germination? What is the answer, based on your experiment?

   _____

   _____

2. Did your results match what you thought would happen? Check the hypothesis section.

   _____

   _____

3. What other limiting factors would you like to test on seed germination?

   _____

   _____

4. Let's say that in your next experiment, you test if seeds will germinate in the dark or in the light. What would be your variable?

   _____

   _____

Name _____   Date _____

Changing Environmental Conditions
Too Hot!

What do you think the climate of the desert is like? During the day, the desert is very hot. Temperature is a limiting factor for animals in the desert, and some may not survive in such hot daytime conditions. Instead, certain desert animals dig holes in the ground and stay there until the temperature cools down.

On a sunny, warm day, compare the temperature above ground to the temperature underground.

1. Dig a hole about 10 cm deep that is large enough to insert one thermometer.
2. Cover the hole with a white towel.
3. Touch the second thermometer to the top of the ground.
4. After 5 minutes, read each thermometer. Read the underground thermometer as soon as it is removed from the ground.

Is the temperature cooler underground or on top? The soil on top of the ground will warm up because it is exposed to the direct sun. The soil in the hole is cooler because it does not receive direct heat.

Student Guide

Ecosystems: Interdependence of Life: Unit Review and Assessment

Complete this unit of study by visiting a desert ecosystem. Use all you know about organisms in ecosystems to describe food chains, food webs, limiting factors, and how organisms survive in an ecosystem that is constantly changing.

Lesson Objectives

- Describe some ways in which organisms are dependent on each other for survival, including the need for food, pollination, and seed dispersal.
- Explain how producers and consumers (herbivores, carnivores, omnivores, and decomposers) are related in food chains and food webs in an ecosystem.
- Explain that an environment is the living and nonliving parts of an ecosystem.
- Explain that certain organisms, such as insects, fungi, and bacteria, depend on dead plants and animals for food.
- Explain that ecosystems are characterized by both their living and nonliving parts.
- Explain that, in all environments, organisms are constantly growing, reproducing, dying, and decaying.
- Recognize examples of populations, communities, and ecosystems.
- Recognize that all organisms need some source of energy to stay alive.
- Recognize that conditions within an ecosystem are constantly changing, causing plants and animals to adapt, move, or die.
- Recognize that cycles in nature provide organisms with the food, air, and water they need to live, grow, and reproduce.
- State that sunlight is the major source of energy for ecosystems, and describe how its energy is passed from organism to organism in food webs.
- Recognize that conditions within an ecosystem are constantly changing. Further recognize that some plants and animals survive because they either adapt to such changes or move to another locations, while others die.
- Recognize that objects with the same electrical charges repel and objects with different electrical charges attract.

PREPARE

Approximate lesson time is 60 minutes.

Materials

For the Student

> Ecosystems Vocabulary Review
> pencil
> Desert Ecosystem

Keywords and Pronunciation

carnivore (KAHR-nuh-vor): An animal that feeds mainly on other animals. A tiger is considered a carnivore since its diet is mainly other animals.

community: All the populations that live and interact with each other in a particular area. Frogs, ducks, insects, and fish are some of the living things that help make up a pond community.

consumer: An organism that depends on other organisms for food. Consumers directly or indirectly depend on producers for their energy. A robin is a consumer that eats worms.

decomposer: An organism that gets its energy by breaking down and consuming things that were once living, such as dead leaves, fallen branches, animal droppings, and the remains of animals and plants. Mold growing on a rotting tomato is a decomposer.

ecology: The study of the relationship between living things and their environment. A scientist studying a deer´s diet and shelter is studying ecology.

ecosystem (EE-koh-sis-tuhm): A community of organisms interacting with one another and with their environment. Ecosystems can be large cities, vast jungles and forests, small tide pools, or even a terrarium.

food web: A diagram that combines food chains to show the interconnected feeding relationships in an ecosystem. Plants and animals can be part of more than one food chain in a food web.

herbivore (UR-buh-vor): An animal that feeds mainly on plants. A cow is considered an herbivore since its diet is mainly plants.

limiting factor: An environmental condition that affects or limits the ability of an organism to survive. A limiting factor for an earthworm is the amount of water present in the ground.

omnivore (AHM-nih-vor): An animal that eats both plants and animals. Bears are omnivores, and eat fruits, nuts, fish, and small animals.

photosynthesis (foh-toh-SINT-thuh-suhs)

population: A group of individuals of the same type that live in a certain area at a certain time. The population of deer grew larger every year after the wolves left the area.

producers: Organisms, such as plants or algae, that make (or produce) their own food. Plants produce their own food through the process of photosynthesis.

LEARN

Activity 1: Ecosystems: Interdependence of Life Unit Review (Online)

Activity 2: Ecosystems Vocabulary Review (Offline)

There is a lot to learn about the world of ecosystems. How organisms interact with each other and the environment around them can be complicated. Review some of the keywords and concepts from the unit to help tie it all together.

Activity 3: Ecosystem Challenge (Offline)

LEARN

Activity 1: Ecosystems: Interdependence of Life Unit Review *(Online)*

Activity 2: Ecosystems Vocabulary Review *(Offline)*

There is a lot to learn about the world of ecosystems. How organisms interact with each other and the environment around them can be complicated. Review some of the keywords and concepts from the unit to help tie it all together.

Activity 3: Ecosystem Challenge *(Offline)*

If you visit a desert ecosystem, you'll find more than just cacti and sand. See if you can identify producers, consumers, and decomposers, make food chains and food webs, and determine limiting factors for the communities you find there.

ASSESS

Unit Assessment: Ecosystems: Interdependence of Life *(Offline)*

You will complete an offline assessment covering the main objectives of this unit. Your learning coach will score this assessment.

Name _____   Date _____

Ecosystems: Interdependence of Life: Unit Review and Assessment

Ecosystems Vocabulary Review

Use the words in the Word Bank to fill in the blanks below.

Word Bank

herbivore	climate	organic
carnivore	energy pyramid	inorganic
omnivores	ecology	environment

1. An _____ is a diagram that shows the amount of energy present at each level of a food chain.

2. The study of living things in their environment is called _____.

3. Matter that comes from an animal or plant and contains carbon is _____. Matter that does not come from an animal or plant such as rocks and water is _____.

4. A _____ eats only meat, while an _____ eats only plants. _____ eat both meat and plants.

5. The usual pattern of weather an area has over a long period of time is its _____

6. The nonliving and living things that affect an organism are part of its _____.

Write the name of each level on the line next to the illustration.

Word Bank

population   biosphere   community

ecosystem   biome   individual

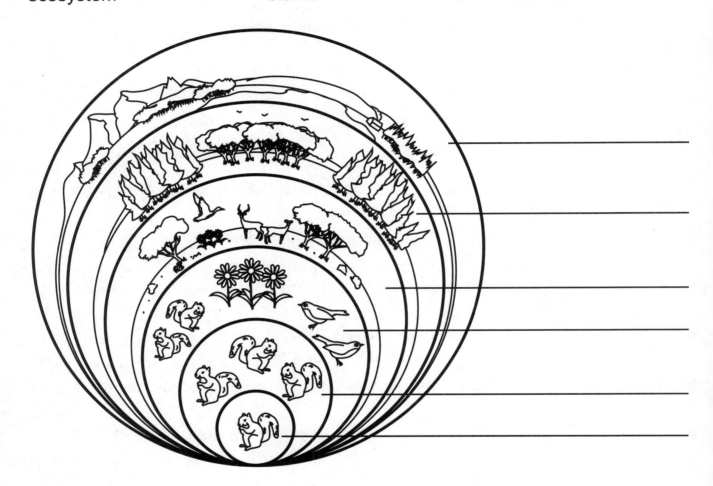

Write the letter of the matching definition on the line next to each word.

_____ food chain   _____ decomposers

_____ food web   _____ energy

_____ producers   _____ limiting factor

_____ organism   _____ scavengers

_____ consumers

A. Organisms, such as plants or algae, that make their own food.

B. Organisms that depend on other organisms for food.

C. Organisms, such as bacteria or fungi, that get their energy by breaking down things that were once living, such as fallen leaves, dead wood, animal droppings, and dead plants and animals, causing them to decay and rot.

D. Animals that eat dead animal bodies.

E. Any living thing—that is any life form that takes in food, grows, and reproduces.

F. The pathway along which food is transferred from one organism to another.

G. A diagram that combines food chains to show the interconnected feeding relationships in an ecosystem.

H. The power plants need for growth, and animals need for growth, movement, and more. Plants get this from the sun.

I. An environmental condition that affects—or limits—the ability of an organism to survive.

Name _____ Date _____

Ecosystems: Interdependence of Life: Unit Review and Assessment

Desert Ecosystem

Ecologist's Notebook

- Hummingbirds stop in mid-air to sip nectar from desert flowers.
- As bees sip nectar from flowers, they collect pollen. They fly from flower to flower, pollinating plants so that new plants may grow.
- Tortoises lay eggs in the sand and nibble on wildflowers.
- Wood rats, also called pack rats, use sticks, rocks, leaves, cactus spines, and even bones to make large nests. These nests protect them from predators such as foxes and hawks. Rats eat leaves.
- Grasshoppers hop from plant to plant, nibbling leaves and grass and jumping to escape predators.
- The horned lizard has spiny scales that protect it from predators. It rests on rocks and eats insects.
- Roadrunners can fly, but prefer to run after the lizards they eat. Their feet are adapted for gripping the ground. Roadrunners also eat berries and seeds.
- Jackrabbits are faster than roadrunners and can even outrun a coyote! Jackrabbits eat leaves and grass. Their long ears help them stay cool.
- Coyotes prey on jackrabbits, but they eat birds, lizards, and berries, too. Coyotes can live almost anywhere!
- Mushrooms growing in the desert get nutrients from dead plants and animals.

An ecologist studies living things in their environment. Study the animals in the Desert Ecosystem picture and read over the notes from the Ecologist's Notebook. Let's see what kind of information you can learn from studying this environment.

1. Name an herbivore and omnivore you observe in this part of the desert. Use the Ecologist's Notebook to help you.

_____

_____

2. Create a food chain with one producer, two consumers, and a decomposer.

Food chain:

3. Draw an energy pyramid with four levels. Write the names of four desert organisms in the levels to show how energy flows through this ecosystem. The top level should be a consumer.

Energy pyramid:

4. Describe how one organism is adapted to the environment of the desert.

_____

_____

_____

_____

5. Do you notice a food, water, or shelter resource for which many organisms might compete? Describe the resource and the competition.

_____

_____

_____

_____

6. Describe how the wood rat interacts with the non-living parts of the desert.

_____

_____

_____

_____

7. Draw arrows on the desert illustration to show how carbon could cycle through the desert. You may need to look back at the work you have done with nutrient cycles in this unit.